No Bloodless Myth

No Bloodless Myth

A Guide Through Balthasar's Dramatics

Aidan Nichols OP

T&T CLARK
EDINBURGH

T&T CLARK LTD
59 GEORGE STREET
EDINBURGH EH2 2LQ
SCOTLAND
www.tandtclark.co.uk

The lines from *Genesis* by Geoffrey Hill are reprinted by permission from
Collected Poems (Penguin 1985) and *New and Collected Poems 1952–1992*
(Houghton Mifflin Co, Boston and New York 1994).

First published 2000

ISBN 0 567 08702 6

British Library Cataloguing-in-Publication Data
A catalogue record for this book is available from the British Library

Typeset by Waverley Typesetters, Galashiels
Printed and bound in Great Britain by MPG Books, Bodmin

By blood we live, the hot, the cold,
To ravage and redeem the world:
There is no bloodless myth will hold.

Geoffrey Hill, *Genesis*

Contents

THE LAST ACT

Preface

In *No Bloodless Myth* (I am once again indebted for a title to Geoffrey Hill),
I continue the exploration of Balthasar's great trilogy by considering his
sustained (five volume) meditation on the relation between Christianity
and the theatre – seen not for its own sake, fascinating though the subject
is, but *as a parable for the drama of redemption itself.*[1] Other writers this
century had spotted the theological suggestiveness of drama as an art
form. But no one has exploited the rich veins of ore to be found there on
this colossal – industrial! – scale.

Theo-Drama is a wonderfully rich and rewarding work. And once
again, my aim is to render it more productive for the Church by providing the reader with a guide which will let them see the wood in the
trees.

A word on translation. The Anglophone public is fortunate to have
Theodramatik in a translation which is, frankly, a masterpiece.[2] Graham
Harrison's English version of the final volume only became available
when I had finished this work. I have substituted his translations for my
own in the great majority of cases. Where, occasionally, I have preferred
my version, the page references to the Ignatius Press edition are given
also.

AIDAN NICHOLS, OP
Blackfriars, Cambridge
Memorial day of Blessed Dominic
of the Mother of God, 1998

1 H. U. von Balthasar, *Theodramatik* (Einsiedeln 1973–1983).
2 Idem., *Theo-Drama: Theological Dramatic Theory* (San Francisco 1988–1998).

INTRODUCTION

1

Transition from Aesthetics

When Balthasar's theological aesthetics was published his critics commented that this was a quietist work, which treated the Christian disciple as a passive contemplator of a Christ reduced to an icon. They were quite correct in saying that Balthasar regarded many of his modern co-religionists as insufficiently penetrating in their grasp of what had appeared in Jesus Christ. They were right too in reporting how in Balthasar's judgment the first thing to be said about Christ's appearance is that it is an epiphany of the glory of God, holding spellbound those who glimpse it.[1] But only a very superficial reading of the aesthetics could have led to the criticism that this work has nothing to say about Christian responsiveness in life and action, nor about the narrative content of the Jesus story with its implicit claim to challenge all those other life-stories in which people have expressed their sense of what human living is about.

Meeting the critics

In the first place, Balthasar had made it clear that, in all authentic perception of the divine glory in Jesus Christ, seeing goes hand in hand with transformation. Taking his cue from the Leonine Nativity Preface, he sees that here perceiving is impossible without a being caught up in love. A theory of perception cannot be had in this context without a doctrine of conversion, and so ultimately of sanctification. Not for nothing does Balthasar count the existence of the Christian saints with the evidence for the objective revelatory form. As in traditional apologetics, the lives of the saints are signs of the authenticity of divine revelation in Christ. That hagiology should thus be subsumed under Christology tells us in and of itself that the theological aesthetics are at the antipodes from any consciously anti-activist, merely spectatorial account of Christianity.

And similarly, the second count – the criticism that the Christ of the aesthetics is reduced to an icon, that Balthasar has de-potentiated the power of Christ's words and deeds which are meant precisely to challenge human self-understanding and to elicit the self-commitment of human

---

1 See my *The Word Has Been Abroad: A Guide through Balthasar's Aesthetics* (Edinburgh 1998).

freedom to the cause of the Kingdom in the world – is also off-target. The art of God in Jesus Christ, in *Herrlichkeit*, is explicitly a *narrative* art. It is the unfolding form of the Redeemer, relayed in the sequential order of the various crucial scenes of his life, which constitutes the true centre or mid-point of divine revelation. The dialectic of disclosure and con-cealment in the appearing of the divine Glory was resolved in favour of its positive pole only with the Cross and Descent into Hell, as became clear in the Resurrection. The self-emptying divine Love, which is what the Glory of the Trinity turns out to be, thus manifests itself as judgment on human lovelessness and the re-orientation of human nature, at least in principle, to its true transcendent end. What the icon of Christ contains is, in Balthasar's words, a 'synthesis of saving history'; it shows the Father's saving will as at once justice and mercy, the rejection of mankind and its redemption.[2]

However, Balthasar would be the first to admit that the aesthetics cannot lay out all the themes of Christian theology, or at any rate not lay them out with equal cogency and liveliness. From the outset he made it plain that, just as among the transcendentals, the beautiful and the good as also the true are co-constituting, for no one of these is a manifestation of being without reference to the others, so also in the ambit of revelation the aesthetics cannot be separated from a dramatics, still to be written, if it is to have its maximum force. Moreover, he shows that a theological aesthetics opens us of its own nature to a theological dramatics. So far from being merely parallel theological raids on the divine treasures of revelation, aesthetics and dramatics are inter-related essentially, not accidentally – not contingently but of their very nature.

Aesthetics needs Dramatics

How does Balthasar justify this assertion? In the opening pages of the second volume of *Theo-Drama* (the first, as we shall see, is given over to *Prolegomena*), he will do so in three ways.[3] First, he points out how, even among 'intramundane phenomena' – things which have their being and significance entirely within this world – the graceful quality of being in its self-manifestation calls forth a grateful response from the perceiver. A word of being which is eloquent of being's gloriousness calls for an answering word, a response. Expressive form inaugurates a dialogue. It requires from man an adjudication, which must necessarily take place in language. Such dialogue, or linguistic confrontation, is highly germane to drama.

Secondly, to appreciate a form aright, to receive aright its message, depends in some way or other on our having appropriate dispositions. Without a basic readiness to receive what the form has to offer, a willingness to entertain its message, the dialogue between the eloquent appearing of being and human language is more than likely to be at cross-

---

2 Cf. *The Glory of the Lord: A Theological Aesthetics*. VII. *Theology: The New Covenant* (ET, Edinburgh and San Francisco 1989), p. 324.

3 Idem., *Theo-Drama: Theological Dramatic Theory*. II. *Dramatis Personae: Man in God* (ET, San Francisco 1990), pp. 23–33. Cited below as *TD* II.

purposes. And for such willingness or readiness to be in place, some engagement on the part of human freedom is required. But what else is this beauty-inspired confrontation in language where human freedom is set in motion, for good or evil, than the dramatic itself – that quality of existence which the theatre brings out, with its many voices, its plots and *dénouements*, its dramatisation of choice and freedom, whether against the grain of reality or in harmony with it, all for the sake of enabling us the better to understand our lives and the world in which those lives are set? The beauty of visual art opens up, in this sense, a dramatic dimension. As Balthasar writes:

> We need to make it clear that *'l'art pour l'art'* is a totally derivative and depraved form of the encounter with beauty: the blissful, *gratis,* shining-in-itself of the thing of beauty is not meant for individualistic enjoyment in the experimental retorts of aesthetic seclusion: on the contrary, it is meant to be the communication of a meaning with a view to meaning's totality; it is an invitation to universal communication and also, preeminently, to a shared humanity.[4]

Applying this analogically to Jesus Christ who as the mid-point of revelation's objective form is the chief locus of Christian theology, Balthasar affirms that when the divine Word becomes flesh and steps forth among the multitude of figures that surround us – the forms, both cosmic and human, of the world, there comes inevitably a *decision* which, because it embraces all other decisions that human beings could ever make, is *the* theme *par excellence* of theological dramatics. And this is the question as to whether, in the vocabulary of the Johannine Prologue, the Word's 'own' will 'receive' him or not. This can also be put in more Balthasarian language, which the man himself now proceeds to do, when he asks, Will the 'code-words' of a cosmos and a human history whose own sense and bearings are unclear 'resolve into the Word, the Logos, ultimate meaning' or, by contrast, will they 'shut tight, undecipherable, once and for all'.[5] The divine Theophany, the appearing of the triune Glory in Jesus Christ, is the way into what is truly central for dogmatics, the inter-action, within both creation and history, of man's finite and God's infinite freedom.

And so finally we come to a *third* sense in which aesthetics not only prompts but even requires a 'transition to dramatics': the one who has

---

4 *TD* II, pp. 29–30.
5 *TD* II, p. 26. As the Irish Balthasar scholar Gerard O'Hanlon has remarked: 'Already within the aesthetics there was implicit in the enrapturement that accompanied the perception of the form an opening to the truth shown in Jesus that the deed of love in freedom is what is at the centre of reality, divine and human. We are asked not simply to contemplate Jesus but with Christian *eros* to follow him, be disciples, giving witness even to the point of death to what we have seen in him. Jesus reveals to us that God is love, and by his Cross in particular he shows us that the human response to God's love has to take account of the reality of evil. If God is love, and if, in particular, this love is in dialogue with our freedom and with evil, are we not in the midst of a drama which involves both God and ourselves?' G. O'Hanlon, SJ, 'Theological Dramatics', in B. McGregor, OP, and T. Norris (eds), *The Beauty of Christ: An Introduction to the Theology of Hans Urs von Balthasar* (Edinburgh 1994), p. 94.

been encountered by beauty is not only challenged in his freedom, he is also branded for life, and thus becomes conscious of election. The elect person feels obliged to proclaim the Logos. Having a glimpse of the divinely beautiful *sends* the one thus privileged not only in the idiomatic sense of rendering him ecstatic (a coining for which we are indebted to the culture of Pop) but also in the theological sense of mandating him to go forth on a mission. The wonder of Being, communicating itself in the beautiful, tends of its nature to produce dramatic heroes – however ordinary (or extraordinary) their missions may be. Each is at once unique and universal. Indeed the more unique, the more universal – for the stronger the lens, the greater its capacity to focus the light universal. And this is what Jesus Christ is, as Light from Light in human flesh:

> The Beautiful, graciously manifesting itself, becomes the incarnated Word, electing those to whom it can communicate itself.[6]

Mysteriously, while pouring itself forth in the raging waters of dramatic missions co-defined by the hard rocks of a fallen world, this river remains, at its Source, what it ever serenely was. That is, for Balthasar, the message of St John's Apocalypse: existence is at once a Liturgy and (to change the metaphor from geological to military) a battlefield.

Aesthetics must, then, as Balthasar remarks at the outset of the first volume of *Theo-Drama*, the *Prolegomena*, 'surrender itself and go in search of new categories'.[7] Thus, although the theological aesthetics was, from one point of view, written with an eye to the theological logic, since it aimed to show that the logic of a theology whose departure point is glory can hardly be rationalist, it would be premature of such an aesthetics to attempt the rewriting of theological logic by its own light alone. A missing stage must be filled in first. Within the revelatory form we must identify the saving event which is that form's active content, and show how the power of the divine action in the Word made flesh encompasses all existence and brings its tensions and conflicts to triumphant resolution. Only so can we assert in theological logic the universal validity of the Christian gospel.

That is clearly vital if, in the words of First Peter, we are to 'give a reason for the hope that is in us' (3.15). Yet a logic crucially dependent on dramatics will not obscure the fact (this at any rate is Balthasar's hope) that total reality – the full range of that to which the concepts of a theological logic apply – *includes*, and so cannot prescind from, the existential character of life. Contrary to what superficial estimates of Balthasar's theology pretend, his writing is filled with positively eschatological urgency where the need for action is concerned. Should contemplation

---

6 *TD* II, p. 33.
7 *Theo-Drama: Theological Dramatic Theory*. I. *Prolegomena* (ET, San Francisco 1988), p. 16. Cited below as *TD* I. Yet this in no way implies the annulment of the theological aesthetics. Balthasar can express the 'transition' involved by writing: 'All we need to do is to take what is implicit in our aesthetics and make it explicit in dramatic theory; thus we shall set forth the *problems associated with the various freedoms* in order to arrive at the dimensions of theo-drama.' *TD* II, pp. 35–36 (italics original).

fail to come to grips with the secular 'now' within the horizon of what has been achieved definitively, it will slip into unreality. We can say, 'Lord, Lord!' in the depths of spirituality and mysticism, we can 'eat and drink with him' sacramentally, but it is all in vain if we do not carry out the will of our heavenly Father. Furthermore, the mere proclamation of the word of salvation – which is incumbent upon us – will not elicit faith if the herald himself does not fashion his life into a dramatic word of testimony. Neither faith, contemplation nor kerygma can dispense us from *action*. And the libretto of God's saving drama which we call Holy Scripture is worthless in itself unless, in the Holy Spirit, it is constantly mediating between the drama beyond and the drama here. It is not a self-sufficient armchair drama; its very form shows it to be a multifarious testimony pointing to an action at its core that goes beyond all words.[8]

8 *TD* I, p. 22.

PROLEGOMENA

2

Rationale for Dramatics

Balthasar's task, then, on completion of the theological aesthetics and looking ahead to the construction of the theological logic whose first humble
building-blocks were put in place by the general ontology of his theological logic, is to identify what he calls a 'network of concepts and images'
in which to express the unique divine action which is revelation's content.
The *Prolegomena* will take that as their task.

Life as drama

And this is where dramatics comes in. For insofar as existence is com-
posed of actions, of events where one or more agents by their collaboration, competition or conflict conspire to change the course of affairs, life
is naturally dramatic. It is the function of theatrical drama to exhibit
the dramatic quality of existence itself and so to hold up a mirror to the
drama of life that we may not only better understand it but also re-
orient ourselves within it according to whatever light the dramatic
author, as interpreted by his cast, and their director, can throw. Balthasar
writes:

> As human beings, we already have a preliminary grasp of what
> drama is; we are acquainted with it from the complications, tensions,
> catastrophes and reconciliations which characterize our lives as
> individuals and in interaction with others, and we also know it in a
> different way from the phenomenon of the stage (which is both
> related to life and yet at a remove from it).

And as to the stage itself he comments:

> The task of the stage is to make the drama of existence explicit so
> that we may view it. For the stage drama is the missing link:
> it transforms the event into a picture that can be seen and thus
> expands aesthetics into something new (and yet continuous with
> itself), while at the same time it is already translating this picture
> into speech.[1]

1 *TD* I, p. 17.

Theatrical drama is therefore the linguistic portrayal in graspable form of the drama of existence itself. Where better to look, then, not only for a speculative grasp of the divine irruption into existence which is the dramatic event of the Word of God, but also for encouragement to us personally to enter into relations with the theo-drama and play out our own rôles by way of response to that singular divine action which spans the successive covenants of creation and Old and New Testaments, and leads up to their prospective consummation at the *eschaton*, the end of time?

Balthasar emphasises the inherent difficulty of the task a *theological* dramatics sets us. In the first place, if God is to 'play' through human beings and, ultimately, at the plot's turning-point (the Incarnation), *as* a human being, then he must, to a greater or lesser extent, go incognito, and this means in its turn that:

> by entering into contact with the world theatre, the good which takes place in God's action really is affected by the world's ambiguity and remains a hidden good.[2]

And in the second place, despite – or is it because of? – that very ambiguity, such a dramatics stringently requires a self-involving response of engaged action from ourselves.

> The *good* which God does to us can only be experienced as the *truth* if we share in *performing* it (John 7.17; 8.31f.); we must 'do the truth in love' (Ephesians 4.15) not only in order to perceive the truth of the good but, equally, in order to embody it increasingly in the world, thus leading the ambiguities of world theatre beyond themselves to a singleness of meaning that can only come from God.[3]

And so, commensurate with the difficulty of the project is the scope – if successfully attained – of its reward. A final integration of the scattered and partial meanings which existence offers can hardly be called a bagatelle.

Unifying the theologies

And if the content of such a theology could hardly be more important, the same is no less true of its form. A theodramatic theory, Balthasar suggests, is ideally suited to the task of unifying all those partial approaches to theological method which, in their own far from satisfactory fragmentariness, are all too typical of the dislocated condition of modern theology. Writing in the early 1970s, what exactly does Balthasar have in mind? He lists nine motifs of theological methodology. Each one has got hold of something and yet, if it is to deal theological weal rather than woe, needs not only all the rest but also a comprehensive structure of theological method in which to articulate its relations with them.

2 *TD* I, p. 19.
3 *TD* I, p. 20.

The nine ideas, each of which attempts to provide Christian reflection with a philosophical or theological principle of order, are in turn: 'event' – namely, the 'actualism', or vertical divine 'eruptionism' of those two influential Protestant biblical theologians Rudolf Bultmann and, with whatever significant differences, Karl Barth; secondly, the salvation-historical approach; thirdly, a concern with 'orthopraxy', right action, as against orthodoxy, right thinking or, perhaps, worship – since the term *doxa* can mean both; fourthly, a theology based on the notion of 'dialogue' both in inter-subjectivity between God and man and in the general openness of the human being to a wider truth; fifthly, political theology, the European parent of the later liberation theology; sixthly, the theology of the future, also called the 'theology of hope'; seventhly, a theology of 'function' by which Balthasar means the theological appropriation of structuralism, then the latest news from Paris (we must remember that the *Theodramatik* was started in that bygone era when those who wished to be considered *à la mode* called themselves merely modern, not *post-modern*); eighthly, and connected with the previous point, a theology employing the psychological and sociological key concept of 'rôle'; and, lastly, a theology which takes as its axis the problematic of freedom, and freedom's inseparable co-theme, the meaning and destiny of good and evil. All of these *Tendenzen*, in Balthasar's opinion, converge upon one centre, where alone they can meet, integrate and bear fruit for theological thought. That centre is theological dramatics.

Let us pass the nine in succinct review.

1. Event. Yes, with Bultmann and Barth, God does judge and save the world by breaking vertically into time, at once in act and in word, both as himself, in the kerygmatic proclamation of the gospel, as with Bultmann, and in his Word-made-man, reconciling the world to himself, as with Barth. But no, this is not a timeless and context-less happening, for the vertical event of salvation unfolds into a series of times of salvation comparable to the acts of a play, and without this serial unfolding it cannot be rightly assessed.

2. History. Yes, with the historically minded, revelation is always to be contextually evaluated, and each ecclesial generation with its particular human requirements and distinct historical viewpoint must determine how the salvific event is to be lived and expressed. But no, the horizontal must not absorb the vertical; rather, full justice must be done to the eschatological dimension, already inaugurated in Incarnation and Atonement, which changes the significance of historical time. When God in Christ appears on the stage of world history, one is called to get involved with the unique time of his appearing, to live at the 'turn of the ages' evoked by St Paul. Shorn of this dramatic context, the historicisation of revelation threatens dogmatics with dissolution into cultural history, while the desperate solution to that problem offered by such Transcendental Idealists as Karl Rahner, who find beneath the flux the unitary salvific will of God, the same in all ages but climactically portrayed in the event of Jesus Christ, reduces theology, in the spirit of Hegel, to a glorified philosophy.

3. Orthopraxy. Yes, its henchmen are right to wish to drag Christianity, as Balthasar puts it, 'out of the scholar's study' and to 'set it on the world stage where it is to act and prove itself'. But no, they are wrong to abbreviate it to a guide to practical behaviour. Orthopractic theology, in Balthasar's judgment, fails to preserve a necessary distance between 'God's praxis which operates on man and man's praxis which takes its direction from God's'. And to know of that divine praxis, in all its superlative priority over human effort, there is required a doctrine of faith, and a right doctrine at that. By a merely apparent paradox, orthopraxy actually *under*estimates the size of the field laid out for Christian action, and does so by insufficient advertence to its dramatic quality. As Balthasar writes:

> For what God's primal act in reality was, what implication it had for the world, is ... something that can only be accepted and pondered in a faith that precedes all personal initiative ... Following Christ, which has become possible through his self-surrender, will not consist in doing *some right thing* but in fundamentally surrendering everything, and surrendering it to the God who has totally emptied himself, so that he can use [that right thing] for the world, according to his own purposes.[4]

4. Dialogue. Yes, the I–thou theologians are right to say that at the heart of the events of Scripture lies the covenant gift to man, in both creation and salvation, of an 'area of independent being where he can freely hear and answer' God's Word, and so, ultimately, collaborate responsibly with the covenant Lord. Indeed, without dialogue, drama is unthinkable. But no, dialogue is not Christianity's only category; the action is not reducible to dialogue. As with all human existence – and this much its theatrical reflection shows, not every plot is unravelled in speech and counter-speech. The key to the protagonists' relations can be some event of which, for instance, only an audience is fully aware. Balthasar points out that, of the many dialogues in which St John composes his life of Jesus hardly one is 'genuine': the more the Word reveals itself the less people wish to hear it. And as for dialogues with non-Christians, when ultimate frameworks have no common boundaries the Christian's last word must be no word at all, but the testimony, the *martyria*, of his existence or, if need be, of his literal martyrdom, his blood. (Here one may find the source of Pope John Paul II's introduction of the martyrdom theme into his encyclical on fundamental ethics, *Veritatis Splendor*, whose chief aim is precisely to show that, for a Christian ethics, open dialogue with other ethical views is not enough.)

5. Political theology. Yes, political theology is right to oppose the privatisation of the gospel, its withdrawal from the public space of society and abandonment of the claim to shape public doctrine in

4 *TD* I, pp. 33–34.

civil affairs. The main scenes of, for instance, the Acts of the Apostles, take place in the public arena, just as in the Hellenic world drama had been directed to the *polis*. And in the Gospels a king who is not of this world but acts with complete seriousness on the public world stage is bound to be involved in the political drama. But no, the existence of the Christian cannot be classified in secular terms; he belongs to a Kingdom which comes from God through Jesus' dying in expiation of the world's sin and being raised as 'first-fruits of the dead'. To attempt a static copy of the Kingdom by recreating traditional theocratic Christendom would be to betray that eager awaiting of the Kingdom of which the gospel speaks; to attempt its progressive if asymptotic realisation through such basic elements as justice and peace would be to fall back behind Christ into the Old Testament. The dramatic situation of the world, as the Christian knows that to be, goes far beyond the category of politics, and if the political has anything to say about ultimate meaning it must now consent to be taken beyond itself, and be set in relation to this further dimension.

6. Futurism. Yes, the theologians of hope are right to recover the future orientation which was characteristic of primitive Christianity, but no, they are wrong to eliminate the realised eschatology brought about, as the Fourth Gospel witnesses, in the event of Jesus Christ. Futurism, even when bolstered by appeals to utopian vision and calls for revolutionary transformation, does not in any case succeed in reproducing the full extent of the biblical drama, which, as apocalyptic shows, enfolds both the world and God, and all of heaven, earth and hell.

7. Function or structure. In structuralism, a functional or structural 'grid' is laid over the contingencies of history in order to render them rationally accessible. Yes, such a notion can have some Christian serviceableness in that, thanks to the divine initiative in salvation, we are entrusted with a mission and hence a function, a function, moreover, which operates within a structure, the Church, which is above the subject, in part constitutes him or her and certainly demands service of them. But no, in and of itself structuralism's would-be total absorption of the free historical subject into a universal code where persons are reduced to the 'speaking of the structures' could never be reconciled with Christian anthropology. Such a privileging of impersonal rules of reciprocity and exchange is, Balthasar comments, a strikingly anti-dramatic undertaking, as well as being otherwise questionable. For if the 'whole' from which the 'function' takes its meaning is a purely finite entity, why should it be deemed to possess a normative character? So only some further factor implanted among the functioning subjects, such as (to orthodox faith) the infinite presence of the incarnate Logos, can both justify the claims made for the structure and rescue the inalienable uniqueness of the persons who carry out its functions. Structuralism, in other words, must submit to theo-drama, or perish.

8. Rôle, understood both psychologically and socio-logically. Rôle-playing as a way of understanding ecclesial and especially ministerial existence, and the frequently concomitant definition of persons as simply 'bundles' of rôles, are recurring features of a sociologically or psychologically informed theology. Yes, to a degree I can find my identity by slipping into the rôle in which society has cast its dramatis personae; this is, after all, one version of being in relation, serving the other in serving the whole, which we found to be, within certain limits, a valid aspect of structuralist thinking. But no, performers cannot be treated as sheerly interchangeable without shipwrecking all human dignity, which depends in part on the uniqueness of persons. Only in a theodramatic setting, so Balthasar predicts, will this tension between rôle and identity achieve satisfactory resolution.

9. And lastly, there is the little matter of freedom, and its choice of good and evil. So deep-rooted are the world's evils, and, to twentieth-century perception, systemic, that God can be deemed, as by Carl Gustav Jung, to express his freedom in both good and evil, just at the same time as, with the percolating down of the refined philosophical insights of Kant and Schelling, an essential autonomy is ascribed to man, an element of absoluteness found in human freedom. Here Balthasar does not adjudicate between the positive and negative charges of a variety of existentialist theologies and attempted theodicies. Rather does he confine himself to recording the extreme importance of the question, How are divine and human freedom inter-related? As he writes

> What is the relationship between divine and human freedom? Should we suppose that God accepted some limit on his freedom when he created man, by whom his world could be brought either to perfection or to destruction? Is he powerless in the face of autonomous man's 'No'? And how is this divine powerlessness related to the Godforsakenness of his Son on the Cross?[5]

Balthasar does not answer these questions at this juncture because these are the very questions that theodramatic reflection, treating in turn the dramatis personae of the world-plot, its development, *dénouement* in Jesus Christ and last act, the eschaton, will set itself to consider.

Planning the work

But if, in these nine ways, theological dramatics could turn out to be the overarching form of an apt and all-inclusive soteriology which, in a fragmented theological culture, theological methodologists have so far sought in vain, how will Balthasar approach the construction of this architectonic scheme? How will *Theodramatik* itself unfold?

5 *TD* I, p. 50.

Its construction is markedly different from that of *Herrlichkeit*. The latter plunges more or less directly *in medias res*. Only a comparatively few pages, giving the background to the loss of the dimension of beauty from Christian theology, both Protestant and Catholic, and its slow recovery in a handful of authors, together with some brief remarks on the beautiful as the marriage of *species* and *lumen*, form and splendour, separate the preface from Balthasar's exposition of the main lines of a Christocentric, aesthetically conceived theology of revelation. But with *Theodramatik*, Balthasar finds it necessary to devote well over six hundred pages to prolegomena before we can launch out on an account of the basic dramatis personae of the theodramatic action, the infinitely free God and finitely free man. The reason (aside from sheer fascination with the theatre, expressed in sometimes prolix synopses of plots, analyses of plays) is that the theological aesthetics, by contrast with dramatics, could to a degree take for granted a variety of relevant concepts – many of the key philosophical notions to be deployed theologically in the aesthetics had already been laid out in *Wahrheit der Welt*, later to become the opening volume of the theological logic.[6] Take ideas like: the plenitude of being; the dialectic of being and appearance; truth as solid evidence and openness to a wider whole; knowledge as both receptive and spontaneous, and as made possible by a light which is a participation in a Light unending; images as the invitation to read off from them form, which is itself the sign and sacrament of the depth of being: for all of these notions, directly pertinent to theological aesthetics as they are, Balthasar could refer the reader back to his earlier work. But with *Theodramatik* the situation is different. True, there are themes in the general ontology, such as Balthasar's reflections on language and on freedom, which can scarcely be called irrelevant to the theological dramatics. But whereas the notions of beauty in nature and art are already actively entertained in *Wahrheit* as key ideas in the exploration of the truth of being, the model of theatre, as crucial to a portrayal of human existence, is at best subjacent there. Thus the first requirement in writing *Theo-Drama* was to establish a repertoire of theatrical concepts which would play an analogous part in the composition of a theological dramatics to that of the fund of ontological concepts in the making of the theological aesthetics. It is for this reason that the prolegomena to the dramatics required a book of their own.

And just as the ontological notions in *Wahrheit der Welt*, if scanned with one eye on the theological aesthetics that will follow them, offer a first preliminary sketch of what a disclosure of transcendental beauty might do for us, so to read the prolegomena to the theological dramatics is not only to encounter some fascinating reflections about the theatre and the light it casts on human life but also to gain an initial glimpse of how Balthasar could perhaps apply the key concepts of dramatic theory to salvation in Jesus Christ.

---

6 *Wahrheit*. I. *Wahrheit der Welt* (Einsiedeln 1947); reissued with modifications as *Theologik*. I (Einsiedeln 1985).

Answering objections

First, however, Balthasar must clear away some objections to the whole theodramatic idea. For while the Church has patronised artists, musicians and poets, her relation with the stage has been more stormy – and there are philosophers, so Balthasar points out, who would find that no mere accident. If for the dramatologist and (somewhat unreliable) lay theologian Rudolf Kassner there can *simply be no analogy* between Christianity and the theatre since the Incarnation entailed no disguise, and Christ, consequently, played no part (to which Balthasar counterposes the objection that one who never took a *rôle* could hardly have a *mission*), the great Idealist thinker Hegel, in his much more elaborate theory, concurs, treating drama as essentially a pre-Christian phenomenon which, once the divine is (with Christ) subsumed under the universally human, dissolves into ordinary reality, into the prosaic. Balthasar thinks that Hegel came to his conclusion that drama – at any rate as the potent experience it was for the Greeks – is dead, only because he has thrown out of the window the genuinely dramatic – indeed, super-dramatic – elements in Christianity itself. A desiccated orthodoxy and a flaccid liberalism alike may have obscured to Hegel two things which this religion

> possessed in the New Testament and . . . retains in Catholic dogmatics, namely, the real, active power of the life, suffering and Resurrection of Jesus on behalf of all men, which in turn grounds the active, real power of the exalted Christ to give men an inner participation in his universal mission.[7]

But the notion that the risen Christ remains particular would in any case have been anathema to Hegel: all that ultimately counts in his eyes is the total process. What we learn from Christ's Passion, for the German philosopher, is that the Absolute eternally plays out a tragedy, expressing itself in the world of objectivity, and in that form 'dying' there – yet also rising phoenix-like as the finite is reintegrated in the 'world spirit'. But in this case (once again) the tragic *ceases to be an analogy* for the Passion. Rather does the Passion embody what all tragedy was attempting to say. 'Analogy, which is essential to a theory of theo-drama, is absorbed in identity'.[8]

In pointing out where Hegel went wrong, Balthasar is able to give us a tempting foretaste of the main dishes he will be serving, and especially of the crucial inter-relation of Christology and ecclesiology in theo-drama. Essentially, Hegel misconstrued the relation of the universal to the particular. Every personal mission – and it is the happening of such 'missions' which makes the life of the Church drama-filled and provides the materials for a Christian theatre – contains something of the universally relevant mission of Christ. Just as in the Old Testament there were prefigurations of Christ, so in the plays of Shakespeare, for example,

7 *TD* I, p. 65.
8 *TD* I, p. 67.

characters can 'post-figure' him.[9] But those missions do not for all that lose their particularity. From their criss-crossings, indeed, there arises:

> a genuine and unlimited richness of dramatic tensions, conflicts and collisions, both inside and outside the Church.[10]

Yet Balthasar's criticisms of Hegel, however fundamental these may be, hardly diminish the force of the latter's claim that, compared with the age of the Attic tragedians, drama is depotentiated in the modern world. The reasons for that loss of power lie not – as Hegel surmised[11] – with Incarnation and Atonement which (as we shall see) have, on the contrary, tightened the dramatic tension of history. Rather do they concern the loss of a framework of ultimate meaning.

> If meaninglessness, considered as a mode of action, has the last word, it annihilates itself and ends in Beckett's garbage cans. The alleged absolute freedom which can play the part of both God and the devil (Sartre) dissolves in pure *ennui*. The attitude of revolt (Camus) is absurd if it is absolutized, since, in order to survive, it must always presuppose whatever it is negating … Be the content of 'given' absolute meaning never so hidden and ineffable … it must be *presupposed*, to form the framework within which drama can take place.[12]

Actually, Balthasar was not a pessimist about the future of theatre. The plays of Thornton Wilder and Bertold Brecht, with their internally competing 'horizons', show how twentieth-century drama falsifies Hegel's prediction that all tension is being smoothed away in an increasingly 'one dimensional' reality. Despite the ambiguous attitude of both philosophers and churchmen to the theatre (Plato expelling the actors from the *polis*, Marcel a dramatist himself; Molière refused the last sacraments, Calderon himself a priest), the theatre, Balthasar predicts, will always survive, because, as he puts it, 'life manifests a fundamental urge to observe itself as an action exhibiting both meaning and mystery'.[13] Existence has a need to see itself mirrored, and this makes the theatre a 'legitimate instrument' in the elucidation of being. At the same time, Balthasar underscores the ambiguity of this image of a mirror to life. As a mirror, theatre enables existence to attain understanding of itself, but equally, like a mirror, theatre must eventually take second place, to make room for a truth which it reflects only indirectly. What that divinely dramatic truth is, the dogmatic volumes of *Theo-Drama* will rehearse.

---

9 M. Roston, *Biblical Drama in England* (London 1968).
10 *TD* I, p. 68.
11 For Hegel, Christ's life, death and Resurrection made available a general law, of which his own destiny was simply the highest symbolic representation: thus Balthasar's 'Basic Questions in Christology', in idem., *You Crown the Year with Your Goodness: Sermons through the Liturgical Year* (ET, San Francisco 1989), p. 307.
12 *TD* I, p. 75.
13 *TD* I, pp. 78–79.

3

The Theatre of the World

The Church has sometimes used drama to express the action-filled content of revelation, but her theologians have not in any all-embracing way (till Balthasar!) presented revelation as itself divine theatre. (Just so, the Church has blessed iconographers in their work of portraying the visibility of the divine epiphany in revelation, but her divines have rarely seen revelation in formally aesthetic terms, as the artwork of God. Balthasar's twelve mini-monographs in *The Glory of the Lord* on earlier theological aestheticians do not claim as much as *that*.) And these are not merely trams running (hitherto) on parallel lines. The theme of 'what the actress said to the bishop' is a regular *topos* in popular comic writing in modern Anglo-Saxonry, and it testifies to a long-standing sense of incongruity between theatre and Church.

Actors and churchmen

As the last chapter briefly noted, the wranglings of churchmen and actors were never resolved in any way so decisive as a dogmatic definition – as happened with the *Bilderstreit*, the 'war against the images', in the Iconoclast crisis of the eighth and ninth centuries. Now Balthasar is quite aware of the layered complexities of the denunciation of the stage by Fathers and councils – frenzy and riot were never far from the anxious minds of the pagan ethicists, both Greek and Roman, whose fears these Christian voices in part uncritically echoed. The early patristic writers might have been more willing to ask whether the Church could not learn from drama as well as from philosophy if they had lived in the era of the Attic tragedians and not at a time when the pagan poet Ovid had solicited the emperor Augustus to 'close these haunts of degeneracy'.[1] And if Balthasar can point to the 'overflow' of the Liturgy in the mystery plays of the Western Middle Ages,[2] the deployment of mythological themes as pointers to the drama of Christ in the Spanish theatre of the sixteenth and seventeenth centuries, and the 'martyr plays' of the classical French stage, he also recognises a wellfoundedness in the continuing disquiet about

---

1 *TD* I, p. 90.
2 See, e.g., H. Craig, *English Religious Drama of the Middle Ages* (Oxford 1955).

the acting profession. Does not the actor embody the dangerous possibility that we may not 'be ourselves', may possess 'more than one "I"'? He does not raise that question, however, in some mere moralising spirit, as if actors (and actresses) were inevitably unserious people. Rather, the interest of the question is that its answer may lie only in theology, and in the deepest dramatic theology at that.

On the whole, Balthasar considers it a mercy that the early Church drew a sharp line under the history of the pagan stage. On very different presuppositions from her own, Plato anticipated the Church's reaction in proposing to expel the playwrights and poets from the *polis*.

> What Plato criticized in Homer and his dramatic derivatives was above all the ambiguity of the gods, which did not correspond to the 'basic norms of theology'.[3]

Moreover,

> The biblical and Christian history of salvation was such a totally new beginning over against the mythical theatre that it was simply impossible to effect a transposition and assimilation, at least in the early stages. The mystery of God's stepping into the world had to be clearly distinguished from everything mythological. Only at a later stage of reflection, if at all, could this mystery be understood ... as the true drama.[4]

We are not to tear up, then, the texts of Tertullian and Novatian, Cyprian and Augustine, Gregory Nazianzen and other Greek Fathers which fulminate against the ancient stage,[5] nor unchurch the fourth-century synods which excommunicated those who earned their living from the pagan theatre. What we are to do, however, is to note the way patristic apologetic urges Christians to attend to the 'much more magnificent world theatre of creation and salvation history', the 'much more exciting dramas of our martyrs'.[6]

These (few) references are of course literary tropes, not proposals to open Christian amphitheatres. Only falteringly, and over long protracted time, did the Church admit the actual drama (and the acting profession) as a proper exhibition of her own life. In the thirteenth century St Thomas Aquinas with his customary good sense defended as 'not impermissible in itself' the office of *jongleurs* whose aim is 'to bring cheerfulness, *solatium*, to man'.[7] If the Council of Basle, in 1415, allowed them (on certain conditions) the Easter sacraments this was at least in part because actors had reorganised themselves into troupes in the would-be service of the Church. It helped that in the Renaissance a learned theatre arose – the *commedia dell' arte* – in Italy, followed by a Jesuit-sponsored theatre in the

---

3 *TD* I, p. 90, with an internal citation of *Republic* 379c.
4 *TD* I, pp. 91–92.
5 Balthasar found numerous texts conveniently gathered with Teutonic thoroughness in the first volume of Hermann Reich's *Der Mimus* (Berlin 1903).
6 *TD* I, pp. 95 (with reference to Novatian's *De spectaculis*, 10) and 97 (with reference to Augustine's *Sermons*, 14, 3 and 17, 7).
7 Thomas Aquinas, *Summa Theologiae*, IIa. IIae., q. 168, a. 3.

countries of the Counter-Reformation. But though continuing hostility to the stage is mainly associated with Calvinism (no play was shown in London after Charles I's flight from the city in 1642 until the restoration of his son, Charles II, after England's Puritan interlude in 1660), few Puritan tracts were fiercer than Bishop Bossuet's *Maximes et refléctions sur la comédie* (1694), while the popes were only intermittently tolerant of the theatre well into the eighteenth century.

And yet, so Balthasar holds, rightly understood the gospel provides the theatre with an incomparable backdrop.

> The Church, both in her content and in her form, continues to repre-sent the absoluteness of the eternal, divine plan; and this absolute-ness, even where it is resisted and vehemently combated, remains the indispensable foil and counterpoint against which genuine drama can arise and catch fire.[8]

The mystery plays of the Middle Ages contain questionable – crude, caustic – elements; in Habsburg Spain, the priest, penitent and adventurer Lope de Vega could write not only wondrously spiritual *autos sacra-mentales* but also comedies of 'wanton worldliness',[9] the 'generalized, ethical wisdom' of Shakespeare, Calderon, Racine, Goethe, Grillparzer and Hofmannsthal has sometimes a Christian face and sometimes not. What matters to Balthasar is not this tangled history *per se*, but the evidence it suggests for the possibility of theological dramatics.

> If there *is* such a thing as theo-drama ... and if it is fundamentally the event of God becoming man and his action on the world's behalf, there must be dramatic ways (legitimately so) of presenting it, be they ever so indirect, risky, precarious and ambiguous. And such forms of presentation ... must yield conclusions with regard to the nature of this same theo-drama.[10]

The aim of *Theodramatik* is not, after all, to revive a Christian theatre – any more than that of *Herrlichkeit* was to reinvigorate a Christian art. These may – or may not – be side effects; they do not form part of the author's goal. Balthasar's purpose is, rather, to succeed where Hegel failed, by bringing into centre stage the *drama intrinsic to divine salvation*.

How can we *not* think up the concept of theo-drama when we consider: the mediaeval Passion-and-Resurrection plays that made salvation visible in a drama (and the plays of the Antichrist and Judgment that showed forth its eschatological dimension); the centring of drama on the Mass in the endings of the plays for Corpus Christi and (in dependence on these?) Calderon's *Great Theatre of the World*; the 'postfiguration' of Christ's struggle in the martyrs in, say, Corneille's *Polyeucte* – notably as seen through the eyes of Péguy; the way that Schiller (and more radically de-Christianised playwrights like Sartre and George Bernard Shaw) need the 'laws of bronze' of the Church's teaching on faith and morals as the 'absolute' against whose 'necessity' their heroes can try their strength.

---

8 *TD* I, p. 119.
9 *TD* I, p. 108.
10 *TD* I, p. 112.

Indeed, the choice that confronts everyone is to play the script of existence either as, ultimately, a 'graceless tragedy' or as 'tragedy under grace'. Meaninglessness can only be ungracious. And so:

> If revelation is the ultimate precondition on the basis of which existence (and its reflected image, drama) can experience genuine tragedy – and not a tragedy which dissolves in meaninglessness – the path is clear for us to get a view of the dramatic elements inherent in revelation itself.[11]

The world stage

Since, on the Catholic view of the creation–redemption relationship, grace always presupposes nature just as nature yields (or should do) to trans-formation by grace, we can expect to find, within the experience of the naturally dramatic, a repertoire of concepts – an 'instrumentarium', Balthasar calls it – fit, if not yet honed, for use in programme notes for the supernatural drama.

The first of these is, of course, that comparison between the world and the stage which furnishes Balthasar with his 'model' in this work. London's Globe Theatre, erected in 1599, had over its entrance a citation from the twelfth-century Christian humanist John of Salisbury, *Totus mundus agit histrionem*, 'All the world acts a play'.[12] The poet Thomas Heywood in his *Apology for Actors*, a work of James VI's reign, found the shape of the Globe Theatre highly convenient in summarising (in lightly Judaeo-Christianised form) the 'all the world's a stage' tradition.

> If then the world a Theatre present,
> As by the roundness it appears to fit,
> Built with star-galleries of high ascent,
> In which Jehove doth as spectator sit,
> And chief determiner t'applaud the best,
> And their endeavours crown with more than merit,
> But by their evil actions dooms the rest
> To end disgrac'd, while others life inherit.[13]

That 'tradition' began in the ancient world – 'on the Trojan strand',[14] remarks Balthasar – with the dramatic play of Homer's men and women under the gaze of the gods; Paul the apostle feels himself a 'spectacle', *theatron*, to the world, to angels and to men (I Corinthians 4.9), and Balthasar can say, beautifully, of Sophocles' *Oedipus at Colonus*

---

11 *TD* I, p. 123. The vocabulary is drawn from the contemporary dramatist Balthasar most admired, Reinhold Schneider, and notably from a study published by the Johannesverlag, Balthasar's own publishing house: thus *Rechenschaft* (Einsiedeln 1951), pp. 23–26. For what he learned from Schneider, see H. U. von Balthasar, *Tragedy under Grace: Reinhold Schneider on the Experience of the West* (ET, San Francisco 1997).
12 Cited in E. R. Curtius, *European Literature and the Latin Middle Ages* (ET, London 1979), p. 140.
13 Quoted from M. C. Bradbrook, *The Rise of the Common Player* (London 1962), p. 92.
14 *TD* I, p. 135.

> In the tragedies the suffering man is lifted up like a monstrance and shown to the gods who, though invisible, are watching.[15]

Even the anti-histrionic philosopher does not scruple to use the 'theatre of the world' idea. For Plato's late work *The Laws*:

> Life is a play in the presence of God insofar as it is an education according to the Muses and enters into the divine life-rhythm; but at the same time this rhythm is a gift from God: God is the real mover. Thus man moves in the proper order when he allows himself to be moved as a 'divine marionette' by God.[16]

In Epictetus, it is the Poet behind the universe who gives each actor his part. In Marcus Aurelius the same comparison expresses a paradox: play and gravity, distance and commitment coincide in our walk-on part in life. In the concluding myth of Plato's *Republic* pre-existent souls choose their parts: soul and rôle, though not identical, belong together. For Plotinus the world can be a dramatic unity even if it contains many conflicts; but just as an actor can acquit himself well or badly in his part, so a soul can harmonise poorly with the destiny the Creator–Poet assigns it.

In Job, the trials of the just man are watched by the All-seeing One; in the Septuagint (and Vulgate) of the ending of the book of Isaiah those who rebelled against God become a spectacle in Gehenna, outside the City of the End. For the Writer to the Hebrews, the church of the Hebrew Christians is in the course of being *theatrizomenoi*, 'publicly exposed', to abuse and affliction (10.33); for Clement of Alexandria, the man who is really wise

> faultlessly plays the role God has given him in the drama of life; for he knows what he has to do and to suffer.[17]

And just as the Globe Theatre's inscription, and the poem it inspired, sum up an antecedent tradition, so also do they look ahead to one that reaches from themselves to our time. The phrase 'All the world's a stage' is Shakespeare's in *As You like It* (Act II, Scene 7), but Shakespeare's continental contemporaries and successors had similar ideas. For Cervantes in *Don Quixote* (II, 12) it is a commonplace; Quevedo, drawing on Epictetus, gives it new depth; but it is Calderon who exploits it in a structuring fashion in his plays. Balthasar strikes a chord that will be heard over and again in the theological dramatics when he writes of Calderon's conception in the *autos*:

> it is the individual's mission that personalizes him for his life in the world, and this comes directly from the Lord of the play, God.[18]

The image of life as theatre is, however, omnipresent in the Baroque age. For cultural historians it is one of the Baroque's defining characteristics

15 *TD* I, p. 137.
16 *TD* I, p. 138.
17 Clement, *Stromateis* VII, 11, 65; cited *TD* I, p. 156.
18 *TD* I, p. 167.

and even its supreme sign. On great occasions, the princely court cele-
brates itself as representative world theatre – though here the metaphor
of the play can convey a variety of world-views, from deeply Christian
to areligious. For the Baroque drama, the rôles allotted on the world
stage were typical rôles. But as Romanticism succeeds via Idealism to
Enlightenment the 'I' of dramatic agency becomes poet, actor and
spectator all at once, and the unity of the world play is preserved, if at all,
only by postulating, after the fashion of Idealism's transcendental
reflection, some pre-established harmony of 'Absolute Spirit'. That is
powerfully articulated by Schelling in the 1800 *System des transzendentalen
Idealismus*:

> If we think of history as a play in which each participant plays his
> part completely extempore and as seems best to him, we can only
> envisage this confused performance proceeding meaningfully if
> there is One Spirit giving utterance in all the parts, and if the Poet, of
> whom the individual actors are merely fragments ... has from the
> outset harmonized the objective result of the whole action with the
> extempore acting of all the individuals so that, in the end, something
> intelligible must emerge. However, if the Poet were purely *external*
> to his play, we would be merely actors performing what he had
> written. Whereas if he is *not* independent of us but unveils and
> manifests himself only successively, through the play of our freedom
> – such that, if this freedom did not exist, he would not exist either –
> we are co-writers of the whole script, ourselves inventing the
> particular role we play.[19]

Consequently, in the Romantic theatre, consciousness begins to 'vacillate
between libertinage or self-identification with the Absolute', on the one
hand, and, on the other, 'the sense of being subject to alien destiny'.[20] The
world-stage metaphor takes on distorted and even demonic forms, as
dramatists pick up on artistic antennae the anxieties of an age – whether
Hegelian, where an unknown *Weltgeist* pulls the strings of my existence,
or mechanistic, where I may feel myself less a puppet, more an automaton.
Individuals (Balthasar singles out Joseph von Eichendorff) may rise
above these errors (not for nothing was Eichendorff also the translator
into German of Calderon), but late Romanticism could not give their
perceptions programmatic form. The Christian idea of rôle as mission –
which alone could unite finite personal destiny with the infinitude of
divine commission – was no longer available in Romanticism's theatre of
the world, except – in the entire nineteenth century – for Hugo von
Hoffmansthal who, significantly,

> sees himself as the heir and representative of a Europe that had its
> center in the Catholic monarchy of the Danube (in its organic
> relationship with Spain) ...[21]

19 Cited *TD* I, p. 182.
20 *TD* I, p. 185.
21 *TD* I, p. 215.

and so could reach back, not least via the Austrian popular theatre, to Calderon's Catholic Baroque. That just account of the dramatic inter-relation of the I, the world, and God cannot be suitably replaced by Goethe's intimations of totality (in *Faust*), Franz Grillparzer's surmisings about fate, or Friedrich Hebbel's larger-than-life heroes bursting the bounds of the human 'not because of a mission they have received, but in virtue of their inner wealth and unfathomable depths'.[22] No more can Balthasar accept as an adequate substitute Henrik Ibsen's anthropological postulates of a 'freedom and truth' for which the playwright offers no criteria; Ibsen's drama opens a road all right, but into a 'sociologico-psychological jungle'.[23] Under Nietzsche's influence, the postidealist drama of Shaw shows how

> the theatre of the world can no longer produce a meaningful play, for what apportions the roles, the blind life force, does not know what it is doing. And the playwright, situated on a level above the dramatic action, pulling the strings and imparting a meaning to the play, can only do this insofar as he denies any meaning to the immanent action itself.[24]

The outcome is Luigi Pirandello's tell-tale *Six Characters in Search of an Author* (1921) where, for lack of a metaphysic that can undergird the world theatre, the distinction between reality and illusion becomes impossibly blurred. Pirandello would call the complete edition of his plays (1958) *Maschere nude*: what looks out at us in the spectacle is 'bare masks' and nothing more.

Hofmannsthal, then, *is* an exception: he alone, especially in the cycle that opens in 1911 with *Die Frau ohne Schatten* and *Jedermann*, recovers on stage a world theatre which is cosmocentric only because in the last analysis it is theocentric. ('Anthropocentrism', in a noted axiom of Hofmannsthal's, 'is chauvinism'.)[25] Given the unrepresentative character of Hofmannsthal's writing, where modern theatre is concerned, we cannot rely on the persistence of the 'theatre of the world' tradition in the playhouse itself. The kind of plays that give theo-drama its cue (because they themselves *reflect* theo-drama in the first place) require the simultaneous operation of too many presuppositions to be common compositions in the contemporary world. They imply, first, a distinction between the finitude of the play as performed and its non-finite meaning, such that a temporal play can offer a glimpse of an eternal meaning. They require, secondly, a distinction between the 'I' and its allotted rôle, for it is in the rôle that the 'I' acquires or fails to acquire its own shape – unlike modern ego-philosophy the ancients knew how in speaking of the relation between the free person and destiny we are close to 'a mystery that can only be penetrated by a word that comes from the source of being'.[26] Then, thirdly, that 'theatre of the world' entails a distinction

22 *TD* I, p. 201.
23 *TD* I, p. 208.
24 *TD* I, p. 244.
25 Cited *TD* I, p. 216.
26 *TD* I, p. 253.

between two kinds of responsibility on the part of the actor – *for* his performance and *to* his director. 'What kind of presence can the "Master" have in the events of the world play that will not threaten the actors' free responsibility within the performance?'.[27] To answer that question post-Pirandello will need a good deal of *theological* elucidation.

These three distinctions are, to Balthasar's mind, not merely useful. They are indispensable in creating that kind of dramatic tension which a theatre that is reality-oriented requires. For the world and the stage are neither altogether different nor are they simply identical. Balthasar expresses what he considers their true relation when he remarks:

> It is not a case of arbitrarily contrasting the stage and life, for the aesthetic illusion always *refers* to concrete reality and, by means of the performance, participates in it. But neither is it some kind of imperfect identity between [world and stage], for, if man, being the image of God ... is a creator, the world he creates ... is always only an ideal world that knows itself to be related to the real world, for the man who creates it is a 'riddle' to himself, a riddle that God alone can solve.[28]

And if the God who alone can untie the knot of existence himself appears on the world stage, this does not invalidate the basic comparison of existence to the drama but gives that drama of lived existence new, transcendent dimensions.

This Hofmannsthal knew. But we cannot count on a crop of Hofmannsthals to come who will save us, by the sheer illuminating power of their own dramatic genius, from the hard work of identifying the theological components and categories Christian theatre – and the Christian use of the metaphor of theatre – take for granted. So the suitably sensitivised theologian must help us out when the inspiration of contemporary theatre fails. Yet the revelation of Old and New Testaments is indeed itself dramatic. Biblical revelation is

> the history of an initiative on God's part for his world, the history of a struggle between God and the creature over the latter's meaning and salvation.[29]

Moreover, just as grace implies nature and redemption creation, so there is always, in existence, some form of divine–human dramatic tension. The Creator God, in his gift of freedom to the creature, does not withdraw deistically from the play he has begun but is always involved with his world. But the script of creation is not, however, the transcript of the *entire* drama; this is what the concept of supernatural revelation tells us. The event of God's becoming man and the redemptive action of this humanised God on the world's behalf is where the theodramatic plot really thickens. And despite the disclosure, to theologically aesthetic perception, of the divine Glory in the Incarnation, Cross and Descent into Hell, let no one say, Balthasar writes, that 'everything has basically been said and shown, that drama is exhausted'. For:

27 *TD* I, p. 255.
28 *TD* I, pp. 267–268.
29 *TD* I, p. 125.

no one knows all the implications of God's action which took place in Christ; the history of the Church and the world is there in order to bring them to light, not systematically, but dramatically.[30]

Author, actor, director

That primary idea of the world as stage does not exhaust the repertoire of theatrical ideas serviceable for the replaying of the saving plot. In the second place, Balthasar finds considerable theological utility for – in particular – a *Trinitarian* understanding of soteriology in that fundamental theatrical trio, the author, the actor, and the director. As many dramatists and indeed novelists have testified, the characters they create are both their own yet independent of them. It is the mystery of authorial inspiration, in all great drama, that the characters in the play are allowed to develop in their own fashion, and yet their interplay is guided from a position of ultimate superiority. Authorial creativity from within the figures is matched by their author's encounter with them from outside. This freedom means that, just as the author does not necessarily approve of all his characters' actions and intentions, so at the same time they do not always grasp the author's ultimate purpose. That purpose, for Balthasar, always entails a desire by means of the play to cast light on existence at large, in a perspective or against a 'horizon', the backdrop of an ultimate framework, of the author's own. Even when, in the theatre of realism, the dramatist's aim is to show life simply 'as it is' , this always entails some version of showing why life appears in such a way, or why things are not as they seem. The 'standpoint of the author', as Balthasar puts it, is 'entirely filled up by the creative activity of a unificatory endeavor that sheds light on existence'.[31] How the author does just that is explained by Balthasar through drawing into this new context that key word of the aesthetics, borrowed in the first instance from Goethe but with multiple associations in realms ranging from ancient philosophy to the spiritual interpretation of Scripture, *Gestalt*.

> The constellation into which [the author] draws the individual figures (*Gestalten*) of his play in order to make them into a whole (*Gesamtgestalt*) signifies the whole of reality in microcosm, and it is to this reality that the author wishes to direct his audience's attention.[32]

The author gives the actor, therefore, not only his or her rôle, but also the higher task of entering into that wider framework of meaning which embraces the rôle and which the rôle serves.

Adapting a text of the twentieth-century French novelist and diarist Julien Green, the dramatic author is 'God the Father as far as his characters are concerned'.[33] Or, as Balthasar glosses that remark:

30 *TD* I, p. 118.
31 *TD* I, p. 262.
32 *TD* I, p. 279.
33 J. Green, *Journal*, I (Paris 1938), p. 27.

He [the author] stands at the point where the drama (which is to unfold between the individuals and their freedoms) comes into being as a unity, so that, via an arbitrariness that seems incapable of being co-ordinated, it may attain unity once more.[34]

Not that the author *epitomises* the drama – yet he 'brings it forth and causes it to be performed'. Experimental theatre may for a while prefer the notion of creative corporate extemporisation, but, so Balthasar predicts, the need will soon re-assert itself for

some antecedent context of meaning within which the individual actor's imagination can develop, unhindered.[35]

The author enjoys 'ontological primacy' *vis-à-vis* the actor (just as, so Balthasar will later argue, the actor does *vis-à-vis* the director of the play).

Balthasar strings together a catena of texts from dramatists and philosophers interested in the stage – Gabriel Marcel and Maurice Blondel, Schopenhauer and Hegel, A. W. Schlegel and G. B. Shaw, Claudel and Pirandello, to make the point that the alternation of 'creativity from within', as the author guides his characters' interplay, and 'encounter from without', as he lets them develop a life of their own, positively demands the 'theological model' invoked by Green.[36] And the author, finally, does not bequeath to actor and director a *mere* script. It is the author's responsibility to see to it that his play is performable – he must have the intention to 'guide and accompany' the actor's and director's work 'in its freedom and spontaneity'.[37]

Yet in and of itself, the work of the playwright is only potentially drama. It needs the *actor's* contribution before it can become actual. The actor, for Balthasar, is the 'centre' of the encounter between two spheres of existence and truth: first, the sphere of reality, embodied in the audience, to which the actor belongs by virtue of his humanity, and, secondly, the sphere of what Balthasar terms 'an "identity" that is not directly accessible to this reality', an identity presented by the play itself in its performance. And that is the drama considered as a work of art behind which there stands its originator, the author. The actor, therefore, *synthesises* the reality of life with aesthetic reality. In a German pun not easily capturable in English, the disguise (*Verstellung*) of the actor's rôle ministers to the presentation (*Vorstellung*) of a reality that can enter the realm of empirical existence only through disguise. For in Balthasar's understanding of theatre, the pleasure we gain from the performance is always based on a marriage of two factors: the enjoyment of the projection of what we already tacitly know about human living, on the one hand, and, on the other, an excited anticipation of something further to be discovered, a possible solution of life's enigma, which the play will implicitly disclose.

34 *TD* I, pp. 268–269.
35 *TD* I, p. 269.
36 *TD* I, pp. 276–277.
37 *TD* I, p. 279.

Balthasar insists that the author–actor relationship is not to be compared with that of master and servant. Rather, 'their mutual interdependence points to the unity of the work it brings about'.[38] Citing the author and actor Georg Simmel's essay 'On the Philosophy of the Actor', 'the actor plunges into the ground of being from which the poet has created his character', manifesting his

> *wanting* to do what, on the basis of the role, he *ought* to do; not as when, in the ethical realm, we obey a command that comes to us ready-made, as it were, from outside, but as when we spontaneously impose the imperative upon ourselves.[39]

And to cap it all, how can we avoid calling the actor a mediator? He is the go-between who embodies the mind of the author for the sake of the audience.

So just as the mystery of authorial inspiration effortlessly calls to mind 'paterology' – the theology of the first Trinitarian Person, the Father, so too the mystery of dramatic agency calls out for illumination from Christology – the theology of the second Trinitarian Person, the incarnate Son. It is characteristic of the actor, in the theatrical context, that he places his existence selflessly at the disposal of the character he plays, just as, in an allusion to an essay by Gabriel Marcel, Christ's life was essentially a 'humble, facilitating representation of the divine'.[40] As the theological aesthetics has already pointed out, everything Jesus is was invested in his divine commission. So for the Russian actor and theoretician of acting K. S. Stanislavsky, acting requires a total *disponibilité* of soul, mind and body, from relaxation exercises for every part of the body so that it is prepared for every gesture right up to the complete activisation of imagination in the service of the rôle.

Of course the stage actor (and actress) needs a certain vanity in order to mount an exhibition of themselves (whether this be a 'first person actor' who wants to portray himself in all his rôles or, like Eleanora Duse, a 'third person actress' – for Duse appeared to her audiences to be a quite different woman in each). Yet the humility required for professional objectivity is at least as striking a reality. This oscillation explains the ambivalence of society's response to the acting profession (and not just in the West – the cultures of China and India tell the same story). If the actor has the 'power to mediate a higher truth of existence', he can also undergo the temptation to obstruct that truth by self-affirmation of an intrusive kind.

The actor or actors do not suffice, however, in and of themselves to carry out the author's intention in its fullness. As Balthasar puts it:

> Neither the individual actor nor the sum of individual actors will suffice to embody the indivisible unity of the play's ideal content.

---

38 *TD* I, pp. 283–284.
39 G. Simmel, 'Zur Philosophie des Schauspielers', *Logos: Internationale Zeitschrift für Philosophie der Kultur* IX (1920–1921), p. 360.
40 *TD* I, p. 294; cf. G. Marcel, 'Réflexions sur les exigences d'un théâtre chrétien', *La Vie intellectuelle* (25.3.1937), pp. 461–462.

For this we need a new authority, creative in a different and unique way, to translate the ideal unity into real, concrete unity.[41]

This is of course to say that we need a *director*. All dramatic performance requires a director who can in effect bring together the author, with his originating creative contribution, and the art of the actors, with their differing creative abilities. Balthasar arranges the sequence of author, actor, director in a Trinitarian *taxis* (order) where the order of naming is significant. The author has a priority to the director, for the latter must follow the text, albeit in a living, not wooden fashion. However, because the actor has responsibility for bringing his rôle to life, he has a certain priority to the director as well. The director's task, in conjunction with the author, is to keep before the actors their common creative goal, with which their own imagination and creativity must freely integrate. Typically, the director is easily overlooked, precisely because he succeeds when he effaces himself, and becomes present in performance rather as the atmosphere or medium of the production than as a distinct force. When Eugène Ionesco writes of the director that he

> must let himself be led; he should not want anything of the play. He should annihilate himself, be a perfectly receptive vessel[42]

we can hear, in and beyond the deliberately exaggerated language, the accents of the Christian doctrine of the Spirit, who places himself, in the concealment of his hypostasis, at the behest of Father and Son. The mystery of a play's perfect direction cannot be disassociated from pneumatology, the theology of the third Trinitarian Person, the Holy Ghost.

So far Balthasar has spoken of the three chief figures who must interrelate to each other if true theatrical creativity is ever to be achieved. But the perfect rehearsal is still not the play in performance. So now he must consider a second trio involved not so much in creativity as in what he terms 'realization'. And these are 'presentation', audience, and 'horizon'.

Audience, against the play's 'horizon'

What Balthasar has to say about a play's presentation merges imperceptibly into his account of its audience. For, evidently, the presence of the audience is what makes a rehearsal into the real thing. The presenters of a play, if they are fortunate, can look forward to the fashioning of a 'substantial closeness and relationship' between themselves and the public – generally speaking, this will be when they can hope for a particular public possessed of expectations cognate with the presenters' own.[43]

Audience, after all, is as crucial to drama as is the body of humanity at large to the divine redemptive action. For Balthasar, the audience can never be described as purely spectatorial.

41 *TD* I, p. 262.
42 E. Ionesco, *Notes et contre-notes* (Paris 1966), p. 262.
43 *TD* I, p. 305.

Throughout the theatre's history people have tried to establish communication between the actors and the audience in new ways. There is the 'path of flowers' in the Far East, in which the actors move from among the audience and proceed to the area which is cultically set apart; there is the chorus of the Greek theatre, in which (according to both Hegel and Nietzsche) the spectators see themselves represented, with their reactions and reflections, on the acting area (a technique frequently used in modern times); and there is the medieval mystery play [where the whole town becomes a stage] and the tradition of stage managers communicating with the audience (quite apart from the abuse current in the French baroque and rococo theatre, where privileged members of the audience were allowed to sit on the stage itself).[44]

But whatever the set-up, an underlying willingness to respond to whatever will come about in the unfolding of the action must count as the specific contribution of those in the auditorium to the dramatic tension. As Balthasar writes, with a reference to Jesus' prediction of the turning-point (*peripateia*) of the drama of St Peter:

If the performance is to win our unreserved involvement – for it excludes any neutral 'observation' – it presupposes that we are unreservedly ready to be carried wherever it takes us, even 'where you do not wish to go', into areas that are painful, disturbing and possibly unbearable.[45]

As in Aristotle's analysis of drama, the spectator is struck by a strange fear, the object of which is the whole human condition. In tragedy he is frightened out of the spectatorial attitude; in comedy, by laughing at human ridiculousness he also allows his life to be called in question. In each case he stumbles against the ultimate 'horizon' or all-surrounding framework of meaning which the author through the actors coordinated by the director has enacted in his play.

The 'horizon' to which the dramatist would point, through his script in its performance, is the next of Balthasar's 'elements of the dramatic' to figure prominently in his conceptual repertoire in the prolegomena to *Theodramatik*. Through drama people have always searched for an insight that cannot simply be read off from the immanent course of the world, but radiates rather from a background which can suddenly, in Balthasar's metaphor, 'explode' in the beautiful and gripping play on the stage. Suddenly, by a 'bombshell', the play becomes inwardly relevant to the audience-member, and relates him to something that transcends it.

And here the Christian horizon is unique.

In Greek tragedy it was possible for a god to step out of the invisible background of watching deities and appear on stage; he could proclaim divine thoughts and intentions, but only as an individual, not on behalf of the entire divine world. Christ, the Son of God, is

44 *TD* I, p. 311.
45 *TD* I, p. 309.

not just *any* incarnation: he is the sole incarnation, revealing God's whole mind. God the Father, who sends him, remains in the background as the real 'spectator' before whom 'the great theatre of the world' is performed; but since Father and Son are one, this role of spectator on God's part cannot be separated from his entering into the action on the stage. And when the Spirit proceeds from the Father and the Son and is breathed into the Church of Christ, something of God himself speaks in the mouths of the actors.[46]

Insofar as late antiquity grasped the notion of Providence, its representatives understood that 'the horizon within which the play is acted out is by no means an uninvolved background that relativizes the entire foreground play to the level of shadowy futility'. But now, in Christianity

> with a dramatic dimension that bursts forth from the Absolute itself, it comes to meet the human play and imparts to it an ultimate destination, acting alongside man, from within.[47]

Balthasar agrees with Hegel (to this extent at least) that the horizon of the theo-drama of the New Testament cannot be fully expressed in a stage play, since in the Incarnation God has become his own medium to mankind, and hence the horizon of this drama is God's own.

> We can surmise in advance ... that a dramatic dimension that comes from God's horizon and is implanted in the world, comprehending and judging everything within the world and leading it towards its redemptive meaning, is so unique and exuberant that it can only be reflected in a fragmentary and broken way on the stage.[48]

Fragments of dramatic meaning

Indeed, post-Christian theatre for Balthasar operates in terms of three thematic fragments which have their unity only when seen against the Christian horizon: the themes of death, of the struggle for the Good, and of judgment – not the worst example of how the history of drama and the exploration of dramatic theory can help us to identify more fully (and here Balthasar parts company with Hegel) the structure of the divine drama itself.

Where would post-Christian theatre be without these 'fragments' from a Christian culture: *death* as drama's

> absolute cardinal point, in whichever of its mysterious meanings (liberation, atonement, substitution, the ultimate act, the door into a transformed future, and so forth)

and drama's enactment before

---

46 *TD* I, p. 319.
47 *TD* I, pp. 319–320.
48 *TD* I, p. 320.

an ultimate, supra-individual authority that *judges between good and evil* and is represented in man by the voice of conscience, even if the subject matter that exhibits this distinction is purely secular, entirely unreligious, and even if the horizon is cloaked in anonymity.[49]

Balthasar goes so far as to suggest that the modern theatre is an exercise in ecumenism: just as in good ecumenism partial versions of Christian truth are propelled towards Catholic fullness (this seems to be his thought) so, even in a self-consciously secular theatre, well-posed questions are nudged towards the most 'open' of all horizons. Plays with an ideological programme that would close off this horizon (he has in mind the more rigorously Marxist–Leninist of Brecht's theatre, notably, *Die Massnahme* of 1930) are inhabited, if they are any good, by characters who schizophrenically call into question the 'horizontal' horizon that is supposedly the play's own. Thus the 'true, transcendent, vertical horizon' re-appears after all.[50] At the other extreme, an anti-ideological dramatist like Ionesco, who regards all existence as contradictory and gestures towards a pure transcendence, a Buddhistic 'ultimate singleness of meaning',[51] shows that sheer verticality is in the end as 'untheatrely' as naked horizontalism.

Neither Brecht's theatre nor Ionesco's, for Balthasar, grasps the finite aright – and hence there is a dislocation in the positioning of our three crucial 'fragments' of drama-after-the-gospel, death, struggle for the good, and judgment.

> Drama, with its horizontal-temporal restriction that calls for the action to be meaningfully brought to a conclusion within it, provides a metaphor of the dimension of meaning in all human finitude, and hence it also allows us to discern a (vertical) aspect of infinity.[52]

Chronological time may continue after the drama's finish, as in *Hamlet*, *Macbeth* and Shakespeare's history plays; yet the dramatic action itself is a concentrated form of an overall meaning, and with its ending the world too comes to a kind of end. Dramatic action is possible and meaningful, however, only 'within a given situation or constellation' – the number of which students of the theatre from the eighteenth century onwards have tried to estimate, not very usefully to Balthasar's judgment. It suffices to say that any dramatic situation will include two constitutive dimensions: one in which human beings with their free decisions both clash and co-operate in the 'dialogue of words and the diapraxis of deeds', and another, opened by the first, which locates the characters within the framework of humanity as a whole. But this second dimension raises the question not only of 'the individual's meaning within this totality' but also of 'the

49 *TD* I, p. 321. Italics added.
50 *TD* I, p. 331.
51 *TD* I, p. 342.
52 *TD* I, pp. 344–345.

totality's meaning within Being (and hence the meaning of Being as such)'.[53] That is why, incidentally,

> if a time should come when all divine visibility in the world should cease, when all questioning of God – even in the form of revolt or despair – should fall absolutely silent, drama would have lost its most essential dimension.[54]

Drama without fate, freedom and providence – a threesome superlatively matched, Balthasar thinks, in Calderon[55] is barely thinkable.

Now the finitude of the dramatic action is determined in significant part by the first of the three separated fragments of Christian drama – *death*. It is not just a biological given, of course, for from it – as the martyrs showed most plainly – the life that preceded it can take its imprint. Balthasar considers a vast array of themes in 'thanatology', all copiously illustrated from the plays of world literature. Thus we find: 'death as destiny', whether imposed by gods – Sophocles' *Ajax*, or men, as in Peter Weiss' Auschwitz Oratorio, *Die Ermittlung* (1965); 'death as the interpreter of life', lighting up all that went before – either meditatively, as in Jeanne d'Arc's nocturnal conversations with the king in Shaw's *Saint Joan* (1923) or in a single moment as with the Swedish playwright Pär Lagerkvist's *Den svara stunden* (1918); and 'the immanence of death' when, as Balthasar explains this phrase, 'those who flee from death as something alien, in fact carry death within them',[56] a theme particularly associated with the *fin-de-siècle* drama of Maurice Maeterlinck. Again, there is the motif of death as a 'borderline', crossed, it may be, by gods, ghosts, or the Angels, or enabling an anticipation of death in life – hellishly, in Sartre's *Huit-Clos* (1945), but by proleptic realisation of an absolute justice foreign to this world in Camus' *Les Justes* (1949). (And in Shakespeare's late comedies, resurrection is anticipated too, in the reappearance of those believed dead.) Then there is the theme of 'death as atonement', not necessarily in some metaphysically founded expiatory sense, for in Arthur Miller's *Death of a Salesman* (1949) it is by suicide in a *petit bourgeois* setting that Willy Loman can give his family a new (financial) start, and of 'death and love – especially dear to Marcel – but countless dramas deal with lovers who die together since their 'we' 'cannot fall apart into a separate "I" and "thou"'.[57] 'Death as atonement' and 'death and love' naturally suggest the further motif of 'death on behalf of someone else' – which strikes Balthasar as especially important since the most 'exalted' way to make death, otherwise passive, something active is to die for another. Such death can be bodily (Georg Kaiser's *Die Bürger von Calais*, 1914) or spiritual (Paul Claudel's *L'Annonce faite à Marie*, 1912), but the paradoxes of the exchange of deaths in Georges Bernanos' *Dialogues des Carmélites* (1948–1949) are hardly attainable without the help of the Church's dogma. Finally, there is death as the 'unmaking of kings' – significant, because

---

53 *TD* I, p. 354.
54 *TD* I, p. 359.
55 See *TD* I, pp. 361–369, for an encomium of the Spanish dramatist in these terms.
56 *TD* I, p. 377.
57 *TD* I, p. 389.

the king represents the divine order and authority in the world. Here Shakespeare is unsurpassed – and in this motif, most passiologically presented in *Richard II*, we are invited to view also the consequences of such deaths for later generations.

But the death theme, though pervasive, is not to be separated from that of the *struggle for the good*. It is axiomatic for a classically minded philosopher that the proper goal of decision-making is the good. However, as Balthasar laconically remarks, 'as long as we are in the flesh ... the Good exhibits gradations'.[58] The dramatic spectrum runs from a particular kind of tragedy, the martyr play, where the best possible course of action in the circumstances coincides with *union* with the Absolute Good (point maximum), to the comedy genre, which by exhibiting a relative sort of happiness within limits can '*symbolize* the absolute Good and testify to a belief in it' (point minimum).[59] In any case, there is always a need to establish a hierarchy of goods, and to take all necessary action against evils: sufficient matter, these, for a hundred playwrights. It is characteristic of the movement of world history that a step ahead in one direction, such as justice, may require two steps back in another, say freedom. Still, the theatre presupposes that clarity of objectively grounded conscience is possible – if only for one character on stage. The Absolute

> announces itself only in the relative goods and values, but eventually it does this so clearly that no further hesitation is legitimate.[60]

Passions, however, and what would nowadays be called 'ideology' becloud this: Shakespeare's *Troilus and Cressida* expresses at one and the same time 'the hierarchy of values and its practical unfeasability'.[61] It seems to be the task of the drama in life to imply that there is 'an ultimate light by which human action will be judged' and *also* that 'it is no man's place to make such judgment'.[62]

The third dramatic 'fragment' – judgment – is thus in place. Balthasar considers that the well-known problem of *genre* in drama – What is tragedy? What is comedy? What is tragi-comedy? – can be approached in just those terms he has been putting forward. For judgment of human decision-making as ordered to the good (in the light of the finitude that death brings before us) is nothing other than the *question of meaning*. And to that question – What sort of meaning can be found on earth? – tragedy, comedy and tragi-comedy are precisely would-be answers. Between the genres lies overlap, but that is not to say the distinctions are pointless.

> There can be tragedies depicting the fall of the hero within a horizon of meaning or meaninglessness, just as there can be comedies in which the partial reconciliation takes place either as a symbol of a belief in total reconciliation or, on the contrary, as an element of

58 *TD* I, p. 414.
59 Ibid., italics added.
60 *TD* I, p. 418.
61 *TD* I, p. 421.
62 *TD* I, p. 424.

lightheartedness against a background of horror. Finally there can
be tragi-comedies that observe the events (which have a simultaneously tragic and comic effect) either with conciliatory humor or
with grimness.[63]

A closed tragic world view – 'pantragicism' – denying all overarching
meaning to the tragic action is ruled out for Christians, but Balthasar sides
with Dietrich Mack against George Steiner by affirming that the tragic
situation is perfectly well know to them.[64] The 'Christian realm' includes
the possibility of doubt, failure, suffering, conflict, unbelief, bafflement at
pre-death existence and apparent meaninglessness. And while the words
'doubt' and 'unbelief' cannot be applied to the Man of Calvary, his abandonment (because, on Balthasar's theology of the Paschal Mystery, it is
ultimately 'God on the Cross abandoned by God')

> is more profound than anything we can imagine and ... underpins
> everything in the world that can be termed 'tragic'.[65]

For the 'closed tragic world view', by contrast, the structure of reality is
'one of antagonistic and mutually annihilating forces and values', while a
mediating sort of tragic design suggested by the critic Albin Lesky[66] where
the hero necessarily perishes but we sense a reconciliation at a higher
level is inherently unstable, and must eventually be resolved into either
the tragedy of situation, open in Paschal fashion to a gracious transcendence, or the tragedy of tragicism with its denials. In this sense tragedy,
'shorn of transcendence, shorn of "faith", annihilates itself'.[67] Moreover,
the nature of the 'transcendence' involved is key: the 'wounds' of the
tragic hero in his self-destruction are not healed if they are merely
subsumed into a stoic passionlessness. Christian theology alone, maintains
Balthasar with breathtaking confidence, can prevent the nullification of
the tragic dimension because it combines an account of God's redemptive
initiative in his free creation's favour with an affirmation of the unmerited
quality of his self-gift.

But laughter is as much a part of life as weeping. So comedy too cannot
be denied its sense for 'the quality of life as a whole'.[68] What lies beyond
human competence, however, is to cause the two – tragedy and comedy –
to coincide. We cannot see where their lines intersect. Balthasar's analysis
of comedy parallels what he had to say about tragedy. An acknowledge-
ment of comic situations as enabling us to hear a 'fundamental resonance
of existence' is fine (and comedy's proper office). Post-Idealist, Romantic
comedy, however, tends to present human finitude as systematically
grotesque – and here, as with tragicism, comedy cancels itself out.

---

63 Ibid.
64 D. Mack, *Ansichten zum Tragischen und zur Tragödie* (Munich 1970); G. Steiner, *The
   Death of Tragedy* (London 1961).
65 *TD* I, p. 429.
66 A. Lesky, 'Zum Problem des Tragischen' in *Die griechische Tragödie* (Stuttgart–
   Leipzig 1958), pp. 11–45.
67 *TD* I, p. 430.
68 *TD* I, p. 437.

What then of tragi-comedy which mixes or alternates tears and humour? Since A. W. Schlegel it has been seen as the quintessentially modern type of drama, while Victor Hugo, in his preface to *Cromwell* (1827) thought it the most naturally Christian one: man as a soul is tragic, as a body is comic. What we more commonly find, however, is that the loss of the metaphysical dimension in modernity (and postmodernity) leads to an obliteration of the distinction between the ridiculous and the sublime. Hence the frequent reference of modern imaginative literature to the 'contradictions of existence'.

But the question of meaning will not go away, and so Balthasar returns in his conclusion on the surviving dramatic fragments to the topic of judgment. How many plays are assimilated by their playwrights (Aeschylus, Sophocles and Euripides; Aristophanes and Menander; Shakespeare, Corneille and Calderon; Goethe and Kleist; Gogol and Brecht) to the form of a court process, at least allusively. The dramatic public wants to know whether the right thing has been done – or the right criterion of justice applied. With the gospel, personal responsibility so comes to the fore and ethical norms acquire so clear a profile that the drama can present its judgments as (provisional) anticipations of the ultimate – the 'Last' – Judgment. It is important that such theatre acknowledges the fallibility of all human justice, however – which it can do by judging a corrupt judge, as in Kleist's *Der zerbrochene Krug* (1811) or Gogol's *The Inspector General* (1836). Furthermore

> in the world A.D., in what we have called the 'postfiguration' of the gospel, the possibility of allowing mercy to take the place of justice (a universally human possibility, already found in the ancient world in the concept of 'sanctuary') can become a major dramatic theme that also brings ancient motifs into the brighter light of Christianity.[69]

For Balthasar it is above all a Shakespearian theme. In a dozen pages of interpretative writing on the themes of pardon and grace in Shakespeare, Balthasar comes to the conclusion that just as

> he takes up a position beyond tragedy and comedy, because the world he portrays is a mixture of both elements, so he also rises above justice and mercy by allowing both of them to persist, partly in each other and partly in opposition to each other. But all the time he is utterly certain that the highest good is to be found in forgiveness.[70]

Rôle and personality

On the stage, as in Christian existence, identity is invested in rôle. Considered as an exploration of rôles, then, theological dramatics, like theological aesthetics, can change our life. As always, Balthasarian

---

69 *TD* I, p. 465.
70 *TD* I, p. 478.

theology is *betende Theologie*, theology that 'prays', energetically related to God just because it is ever self-involved. And as previously the model of aesthetic form in *Herrlichkeit* enabled us to gain a better hold on the epiphany of the divine Glory in revelation understood as the provision of a unique Object for contemplation of a transforming kind, so now in *Theodramatik* the model of dramatic form is to give us greater insight into the manifestation of the divine Goodness in revelation performed as a unique saving action responded to by mission. The dramatis personae of that action – those who, in the play, become characters by virtue of their rôles – will, evidently, be key once we embark on a theodramatic reading of the saving revelation. All the more reason that Balthasar should make his final item in the conceptual inventory of theologically useful dramatic ideas that very notion of *rôle*, not least in its relation to *identity* and *mission*.

What does rôle have to do with self-identity? 'Almost everything' was the answer of Erving Goffman in his influential *The Presentation of Self in Everyday Life*.[71] We do not need to go all the way with the father of 'rôle-play' to recognise that between what I represent and what I internally am there is a mysteriously combined symbiosis and disjunction. And this raises the question, '*who* in reality plays the dramatic play of existence'?[72]

Every attempt at a philosophy of the (human) subject soon discovers that the 'I' is elusive. As a striking metaphor of Balthasar's would have it, 'We can never get it within our sights, for it itself holds the rifle'.[73] Naturally I am the product of a 'chance' event (the sexual congress of two individuals) yet my ability to raise the question 'Who am I?' nonetheless so distances me from the world as to make me touch on the divine. Balthasar illustrates the seemingly irresoluble nature of the question, inner-worldly yet other-worldly as it is, from a variety of sources. Thus for the French personalist philosopher René Le Senne, the acting 'I' cannot become itself except through the medium in which it plays, its *character*, which in turn cannot be isolated from the environment in which it lives. In different terminology his near contemporary the philosopher of action Maurice Blondel expressed the same seeming paradox: through the drama of action I find myself by finding the whole.

It is when we try to spell out what such claims imply that we run into trouble, or rather encounter that *aporia* which the Greek schools left their Western successors to deal with as best they might. If we emphasise the way the 'I' relates to the totality precisely via its rôle, we shall suppose with the Stoics that I belong to that whole only in the rational performance of the limited rôle I am allotted in life. If, however, with the Neo-Platonists, we stress the way that what comes to itself in that rôle really is an 'I' that can relate to the whole, and so look back to its own origin in God, then empirical activation of the rôle sinks finally to an 'almost insubstantial play of shadows'.

We should expect to find the matter difficult. It is after all the puzzle set by the most enigmatic imperative of all time: the Delphic Oracle's *Gnôthi sauton*, 'Know yourself!'. Balthasar shows how in the Greco-Roman

---

71 E. Goffman, *The Presentation of Self in Everyday Life* (New York 1959).
72 *TD* I, p. 482.
73 *TD* I, p. 484.

classics, the accent of interpretation shifts – from 'Consider God and be aware of your limitations' to 'Recognise your nobility, your kinship with the everlasting gods', and thus could give rise to the two broad currents of thought he has labelled (not without historical justification) the 'Stoic' and the 'Neo-Platonist' respectively.

Balthasar's aim in this closing section of his Prolegomena is to persuade us that, while 'Stoic' and Neo-Platonist' accounts of the rôle-identity relation – extending themselves, clothed in a dozen dissimilar carapaces, into the modern world – have something to tell us about dramatis personae, they leave the issue ultimately unresolved. It may be helpful to state his own solution to the conundrum – put most lapidarily in the last few paragraphs of the book – in advance. Though it was drama that led him to rediscover the crucial nature of rôle, the realisation that a character is rooted in personal identity *through mission* was one that could only have come to him through perusal of the Scriptures.

> We needed to get away from the arbitrariness of a 'role' that was simply thrown over a colorless 'I' like some coat that happened to be to hand and could at any time be exchanged for another and to arrive at an 'I' that was irreplaceable as such and thus could be enabled to take on a genuinely dramatic role in the realm, not of the theatre, but of life.

If, by missing the key significance of the idea of mission

> we had not discovered this unique 'name' ... of the individual addressed by God and endowed with his personal name, the irreplaceable human being, the 'absolute, unique instance' ... we would not have been justified in attempting a theory of theo-drama, for the unique God would have lacked a partner. The fact that this partner came to light in the field of biblical theology, transcending all the approaches made by mysticism, philosophy, psychology and sociology, is no surprise, since from the outset he himself is a product and an element of that dramatic tension that unfolds exclusively, in our view, in the realm of the Bible.[74]

Only mission binds rôle and 'I' together and gives God a fellow-agent.

To reach this conclusion Balthasar travels a weary and circuitous course, reproducing in various respects his youthful investigations into the anthropology of philosophers both ancient and modern, as well as the founding fathers of depth psychology Freud, Jung and Adler – to which he adds for good measure a consideration of the sociologists and notably that most genial member of the sociological fraternity, the American religious humanist Peter Berger. The young Balthasar was steadied, in his Viennese sojourn while a doctoral student, by the Christianised psychology of the Catholic convert Rudolf Allers who persuaded him that, while rôles are vital to the self, identity is not simply the summation of rôles.[75] Now that lesson returned to him, for the upshot

---

74 *TD* I, p. 645.
75 Nichols, *Word Has Been Abroad*, p. x. For Allers' critique of Freud, see R. Allers, *The Successful Error: A Critical Study of Freudian Psychoanalysis* (ET, London 1942).

of his survey is that rôle's positive significance as the due acceptance of our limitedness (in our particular situation, with its opportunities, and our own peculiar inheritance and gifts) is always in danger of passing over into its dark opposite, which Balthasar terms 'role as alienation'.

Into the 'Stoic' camp Balthasar corrals not only historic Stoics of antiquity like Epictetus but also such late eighteenth-century Romantics as Herder and the turn of the twentieth-century fathers of psychoanalysis. In each case the goal of wisdom or of therapy is to integrate the human being into an all-embracing totality. For Epictetus, 'the divine spark in man must accept a limited role in the great play of the world' and 'know when it is time for him to leave' although 'return to God' here happens 'only in the sense of man's constitutive elements being returned to the cosmic economy'.[76]

For Herder's essay 'Die Bestimmung des Menschen':

> immortal is that through which we have emerged from the confines of our 'I' and poured what is our own into the nameless treasury of humanity ...[77]

What Freudian analysis offers the ego is simply, as the master wrote to Roman Rolland, the chance of

> mediating successfully between the demands of the instinctual life (the 'id') and those of the external world, that is, between inner and outer reality.[78]

For Jung, while the 'ego' exists initially only as a variety of the human collective, the aim of therapy is to assist in the formation of a unique self. And yet the latter's 'uniqueness' (Balthasar explains) is for Jung simply the 'mode in which the elements are integrated into the totality'.[79] For Alfred Adler, third of the trio of psychologists, each individual finds his or her truth chiefly in 'cultivating his sense of community, in fitting into the play of human society'[80] so that, despite the metaphysical ambitions of Adler in his last period, his much vaunted 'individual psychology' dissolves into a sociology of rôles.

Must sociologists – by virtue of the methodology of their discipline – inevitably coarsen further the 'Stoic' approach? Actually, 'rôle-sociologists' are a distinct breed – Balthasar makes Talcott Parsons and (especially) Rolf Dahrendorf the primates among them. In recent decades Catholic theologians of a 'progressive' hue have sometimes given the impression that sociology might replace philosophy as theology's chosen handmaid. But Balthasar shows how drenched in the elixirs of metaphysics sociologists are. For Dahrendorf, the human actor can learn a multiplicity of social rôles and is, *au fond*, unaffected by them[81] – a

---

76 *TD* I, p. 499.
77 *TD* I, p. 503, commenting on a passage of the essay in J. G. Herder, *Sämtliche Werke* (Cotta 1852–1854), 13, p. 55.
78 E. Freud and L. Freud (eds), *Sigmund Freud, Briefe, 1873–1879* (Zurich 1960²), pp. 410f.
79 *TD* I, p. 517.
80 *TD* I, p. 529.
81 R. Dahrendorf, *Ein Versuch zur Geschichte, Bedeutung und Kritik der Kategorie der sozialen Rolle* (Obladen 1973), pp. 21–23.

Kantian insistence on a noumenal freedom untroubled by the empirical world. By contrast, those critics of Dahrendorf who, by a more thoroughgoing reception of rôle-theory, held that man exists *in* his rôles such that self-identity is not in tension merely with social processes but is in outright dependence upon them (here one might mention George H. Mead)[82] were accepting without always realising the fact the Hegelian postulate that spirit's hiddenness from itself coincides with its openness to the world. Actually, Balthasar thinks it a transgression of the intellectual division of labour for sociologists to attempt a resolution of the question: they do not have the tools to finish the job. Far better, with Peter Berger and Thomas Luckmann, to acknowledge the boundaries of their discipline and advert to the way symbolisms beyond sociology's competence to adjudicate can and do legitimise personal identity. In the words of the authors of *The Social Construction of Reality*:

> Mythologically speaking, the individual's 'real' name is the one given to him by his god. The individual may thus 'know who he is' by anchoring his identity in a cosmic reality protected from both the contingencies of socialization and the malevolent self-transformations of marginal experience.[83]

And in his *Invitation to Sociology* (Balthasar says it should really have been entitled 'Invitation to Sociology to See Itself in the Context of an All-embracing Anthropology'!) Berger goes further. The puppet theatre of socially allotted rôles is *not* all there is. 'Society as drama' is only available to us when we admit the free choosing of life-rôles and the deliberate transformation of their meaning.

> Now, social reality suddenly becomes relatively dependent on 'the cooperation of many individual actors ... Stage, theatre, circus and even carnival – here we have the imagery of our dramatic model, with a conception of society as precarious, uncertain, often unpredictable.' 'In this way, the dramatic model opens up a passage out of the rigid determinism into which sociological thought originally led us.'[84]

We are not, then, simply 'emanations from a whole'. But if – and this is the direction in which Berger's thought, especially with *A Rumour of Angels* (1969), presses – we take our stand on man's relation with the eternal as the proper corrective to concern with rôles, shall we not come to see those rôles as in the last analysis modes of alienation of man from his true essence? Here the 'Neo-Platonist' stream of commentary begins to flow.

That means, to Balthasar, in this context, not chiefly the historic Neo-Platonists so much as Meister Eckhart and Idealism. All being, as it exists outside the One, can be considered in a 'land of unlikeness' – the metaphor

82 G. H. Mead, *Mind, Self and Society* (Chicago 1963).
83 P. L. Berger and T. Luckmann, *The Social Construction of Reality* (Garden City, New York 1966), p. 118.
84 *TD* I, pp. 543–544, citing P. Berger, *Invitation to Sociology* (Garden City, New York 1963), pp. 159–160.

begins with Plato and migrates through Plotinus and Augustine to
Bernard of Clairvaux at the heart of the mediaeval West.

> To the extent that creatures are, were or will be in God, they
> participate more in being and are more true there than in them-
> selves.[85]

From this tradition of thought – mediated in his case mainly by Dionysius
the Areopagite – St Thomas draws the conclusion that the perfections of
things exist 'in a more eminent mode' in God.[86] But at the same time he
also strenuously maintained – for instance in his discussion of Providence
– the significance and dignity of the embodied individual. That effort is
relaxed and even abandoned in Thomas's fellow-Dominican Eckhart
whom Balthasar sees in *Theodramatik* (as earlier in *Herrlichkeit*) as a
precursor of Idealism.[87] As in the theological aesthetics, this criticism is
not meant to bear on Eckhart's *intentions*.

> There can be no doubt that this whole metaphysical theology is
> conceived as a theology of grace, a theology of the unimaginable
> intimacy between man 'born of God' and the Divinity; yet it uses
> intellectual components that come from the Platonist realm (in part
> fashioned by Arab philosophers) and cause nature, and hence man's
> personal freedom, to dissolve in the supernatural.[88]

The bridges modern students have sought to build from Eckhart to Indian
(Vedantic) and Japanese (Zen Buddhist) mystical metaphysics – where
personal rôle appears yet more clearly still as alienation – are by no means
without foundation.

For Eckhart what is vital is that the 'I' should die, so as to enter
the depths of the Godhead. Salvation history shrinks accordingly to
that one point of human-divine union where the soul is ever and again
reborn anew. So too in the Idealists the empirical personal 'I' is dissolved
in the essential or ideal spirit, as the titanic attempt to master reality
loses sight of the individual almost (suggests Balthasar) by inadvertence.
But no scheme of thought where the personal is so relegated by virtue
of an 'ecstatic vision of impersonality in the divine'[89] can serve our
turn. Here once again is the alienated 'I', and Balthasar finds its extra-
biblical fate summed up most explicitly in that philosopher by whom
he was at one and the same time most fascinated and most repelled –
Hegel.

Hegel's predecessors in the apostolic succession of transcendental
Idealism, Fichte and Schelling, were not able to focus the question so
clearly. Fichte, for whom the particularities of empirical individuals must
be sacrificed to 'pure I-ness', *blosse Ichheit*, so that one's consciousness can
coincide with humanity itself, conceded to his 'aesthetic' (Romantic) critics
that the idea of humanity at any rate needs specific persons to make

---

85 *TD* I, p. 546.
86 Thomas Aquinas, *Summa Theologiae*, Ia, q. 4, a. 2, corpus and ad i.
87 Nichols, *Word Has Been Abroad*, pp. 149–150.
88 *TD* I, p. 556.
89 *TD* I, p. 575.

historic breakthroughs – and after reworking his system in pantheistic terms could say the same of God-in-us, a God not distinct from us, however, by any act of creation. Schelling begins in Fichtean fashion, by understanding individuality in extremely negative terms, qualified only by a grudging recognition of the occasional instrumental usefulness of individuals to spirit; but, after the death of his wife in 1809, he tries to make room for persons and their immortality – though without abandoning the (false) assumption that 'man, as a particular being distinct from God, is self-ish'.[90]

As a response to the Delphic command, 'Know yourself', Hegel's writings offer 'the most rigorous course of self-transcendence ... in the entire literature of asceticism'. For self-knowledge is only possible, as Hegel sees things, if we are willing to undertake a 'ruthless process whereby all that is particular is stripped of its illusion of being able to reach truth in and for itself'.[91] Only 'spirit', the total transparence of reality to itself is 'self-subsistent, absolute, concrete being. All previous configurations of consciousness are abstractions of it'.[92] That in the 'generalized individual' of Hegel's civil community, philosophical version of the Church though it be, the individuality of the person is shattered tells us that Hegel grasped neither the Resurrection nor the Parousia and so misconceived the nature of the ecclesial communion which those events of cosmic import found. As the Spirit of the 'risen and pneumatically universalized Jesus Christ', the ecclesial Spirit – the Holy Spirit in his proper truth, not his secularised version as Hegelian *Geist* – imparts his gifts in a way that is not only universalising but *personalising too.*

The only place where the connexion between the 'I' in all its particularity and 'some all-embracing life or essence' is really exhibited is the Bible. The concrete character of the freedom the Creator and Redeemer God bestows on human beings is visible from that vantage point alone. There may be here and there some defective foreshadowings: the mission of the king as divine representative in the royal ideology of the ancient Near East (including Israel); the *genius* or *daimôn* of the outstanding individual, as in Goethe's notion of the 'genial creative artist'; and the idea of the 'individual law' in the turn-of-the-century social (and more than social) philosopher Georg Simmel who aimed to show how the singularity of highly differentiated individuals 'shines through what is communicable and to that extent universal'.[93] What is missing in these 'hollow moulds', however, is the 'I'–'thou' dimension of identity and action. And here Balthasar cannot help noticing that the 'I'–'thou' thinkers of the 'dialogical' school, emerging independently in Germany and France after the Great War, were biblically inspired philosophers (and chiefly Jews). Among those thinkers it is Franz Rosenzweig and his *summa* of cosmic personalism, *The Star of Redemption*, that stands out: here the category of man's being *addressed, summoned and sent by God* received at

90 F. W. T. Schelling, *Sämtliche Werke* (Stuttgart–Augsburg 1856–1861), 7, p. 364.
91 *TD* I, p. 579.
92 G. F. W. Hegel, *Werke* (Berlin 1832–1840), 2, p. 329.
93 *TD* I, p. 616.

long last the anthropological recognition it was due.[94] For the naming of
the individual human being by the biblical God is simultaneously their
commissioning for communion – of perhaps a dramatically *mouvementé*
kind – with others also so named.

> Only insofar as he is addressed by God can this 'I' recognize 'his
> brother', recognize 'that he is *not a "he-she-it", but an "I"*, an "I" like
> me, not a coinhabitant of the same, directionless and centerless place,
> not a fellowtraveller on a journey through time without beginning
> or end, but my brother, the companion of my destiny'.[95]

Rôle need not alienate from identity if identity is given in mission.
Appeal to a Christian counterpart of Rosenzweig, Ferdinand Ebner,
enables Balthasar to take one final step. Crossing the threshold into the
New Testament is to enter a world of theo-drama in visible action, since
individuals in Christ, the Word incarnate, share in the divine unicity by
becoming absolutely unique themselves yet cannot come before God to
receive this 'quality of divinity' without a humble 'praying in fellowship
with all human beings'.[96]

In the incarnate Son, person and rôle are identical – his *missio* is, St
Thomas teaches, but the prolongation of his eternal *processio* as the Father's
dialogue partner *par excellence*. And thanks to the saving economy of the
Son, and of the Spirit which completes it, the rupture between rôle and
identity in *our* case is closed over in mission.

> The Spirit is two things: he is most interior to the 'I', making the
> person a son and causing him to cry 'Abba, Father'; and he is the
> socializing 'between', rooting human fellowship in a (trinitarian)
> personal depth that cannot be realized by purely earthly means. Both
> dimensions, the aloneness of the 'I' with God and its subsequent
> opening-up to the world in its entirety, are inseparable in the biblical
> event of mission.[97]

Since, according to the witness of Scripture, we are called not in the
same way, certainly, yet together, the words 'Know yourself', addressed
to one who is in Christ, cannot produce fruitful reflection without
reference to the individual's fellowship with others in the Church. Just as
in *Herrlichkeit*, the mediation of the divine form in Christ was impossible
without the Church, so here too, in dramatics:

> The stage erected before the world's eyes, to which [the Christian] is
> sent as an actor, is always occupied by an ensemble of fellow actors;
> he is inserted into the ensemble.[98]

Just how that works out, Balthasar's theodramatic theology aims to tell.

---

94 F. Rosenzweig, *Der Stern der Erlösung* (Frankfurt 1954).
95 *TD* I, p. 638, citing F. Rosenzweig, *Kleinere Schriften* (Berlin 1937), p. 364.
96 *TD* I, p. 642, citing F. Ebner, *Das Wort und die geistigen Realitäten: Pneumatologische
    Fragmenten* (Regensburg 1921), pp. 184–185.
97 *TD* I, pp. 646–647.
98 *TD* I, p. 647.

PERSONS IN THE DRAMA:
MAN IN GOD

4

A Spectacular Development?

Balthasar is aware that his self-set task – of producing a theological dramatic theory – is a *novum*. It is an innovation in Catholic dogmatics, though, like any well-founded development in the act of faith's reflection on itself, by no means a wholly unheralded one. In *The Glory of the Lord* Balthasar felt constrained by what would strike others, accustomed to a more conventional theology, as the 'funny-peculiar' nature of his project, and he sought to justify the ways the basic sources of Catholic theology – Scripture and Tradition – entered there into theological rationality in its specifically aesthetic mode. Here too, in *Theo-Drama*, he must look at how these inexhaustible sources of theology (inexhaustible because they are the 'founts' of revelation itself) are going to be drawn on by a theological rationality of a specifically dramatic kind.

Balthasar is keen to stress, in the second volume of *Theo-Drama*, *Man in God*, that his voluminous survey of the playwright's presentation of the drama of existence in the *Prolegomena* should not be misconstrued as an attempt to create a theological dramatic theory 'from below'. If there *is* a theo-drama, then its distinctively dramatic quality will derive from God, in his own revelation and action as director of the play. Enlightenment will issue, accordingly, more 'from above'. And so:

> If the infrastructures prove useful, it is because the created world is oriented toward the world of redeeming grace, and the fragmentary nature of the former receives its unity and wholeness in the latter.[1]

Of course everything Balthasar has had to say in his *Prolegomena* to a study of the divine dramatic action either presumes or affirms that there is a drama of life, awaiting expression on the stage, and that the human drama and its theatrical manifestation furnish a repertory of questions to which the saving revelation, if it really conveys to us the true beauty that is our ultimate good, must answer. There really *is* a human question to which the revelation of the divine philanthropy is the response. The human person is unthinkable without freedom, the stuff of which drama is made, and a freedom moreover that comes in two mutually related versions – one which 'moves toward making a definite Yes or No decision'

1 *TD* II, p. 53.

and another that 'forms a kind of vast, inexhaustible space within which these definite decisions fall'.[2] What bewilders us about the human situation is the way these two varieties of human freedom though always related never coincide. Finite as Everyman's existence is, and curtailed by death, the infinite space of freedom which is his can never be filled. And *that* is the stuff of which not just drama in general but tragedy in particular is made. Human culture, human thinking, human imagining know many ploys for circumventing or avoiding such tragedy. Unfortunately (or otherwise) none of them actually work. It will not do to reduce human freedom, materialistically, to biological laws, or make its human carrier and his or her tragic situation just the expression of conditions that are 'not as they should be' – the strategy of various philosophies of thought and action, from Idealism to Socialism.

There is a deeper question of meaning which necessarily places us before the Absolute – since what is at stake in the tragedy of the human person is the issue as to whether finite spirit's infinite capacity can ever be fulfilled. And in biblical terms, that 'Absolute' can only be the living God, the personal divine One who alone in the last analysis gives human existence meaning.

Yet the way we choose to approach the biblical God in this context makes all the difference in the world. If, for instance, we approach the biblical revelation after the fashion of an *epic storyteller* – a Christianised Homer, Turgenev or Poet of the *Nibelungenlied* – what we shall do is to see persons and events against the background of the Absolute as Providence or Destiny. Typically, the epic narrative emphasises the preciousness of the transitory, and its mood is elegiac, a melancholy beyond comedy and tragedy alike. What the epic mode typically misses is how for the Judaeo-Christian revelation the Absolute comes to 'meet the transitory world on its pilgrim path'.[3] The epic reporter is usually too 'distanced' from the events to be helpful as an exclusive guide, though the objectivity of his reportage gives him an affinity, Balthasar thinks, with the classical theologians who produced the conciliar doctrine of the Church.[4] A tell-tale sign, however, of the drawback of the epic approach (at the end of the twentieth century chiefly found as 'narrative theology') is the way it gravitates towards the (Lutheran) *sola scriptura* principle.

> Where the ultimate norm is no longer the revealed action but its mirroring in Scripture (which is of course inseparable from the former), epic-narrative theology – accredited by the distanced attitude of the reporter – will quite logically assume the role of judge over the events and their actualization.[5]

So perhaps we may prefer to draw closer to the biblical God by reproducing the style of the *lyric poet*: an exuberance which would represent, as vividly as possible, the Scriptural event. Practised by the

2 *TD* II, p. 38.
3 *TD* II, p. 44.
4 *TD* II, pp. 55–56.
5 *TD* II, p. 56.

Fathers and the mediaeval monks and early Schoolmen, Balthasar the former Jesuit finds its acme in the Ignatian school of meditation. There,

> once the past event has been awakened by the 'memory', the person must proceed to make its content present through 'reflection, insight' and bring it alive to such a degree that the 'will' can draw consequences from it for today, just as if the event itself were here and now.[6]

In their own – very different – ways, both lyric and epic are, to Balthasar's mind, excessively external in their standpoint, and the fact that the first addresses God, the second one's fellow men (for religious lyric God is a 'Thou', for religious epic a 'He') also suggests their partiality or incompleteness. Can we find a mode of approach to the living Absolute of Scripture as the true Giver of meaning to human freedom which will escape the weaknesses of these alternatives and yet capitalise on their strengths? Certainly we can. It is none other than the dramatic, where God's action challenges the believer, appropriates him and makes him a witness in such a manner that, as the Pauline Letters demonstrate, epic and lyric are held together yet transcended in something far more co-involving.

> Here it is irrelevant whether [Paul] is speaking more 'lyrically' or more in 'epic' terms, for in both respects, above all, he is speaking dramatically: he shows how the drama comes from God, via Christ, to him, and how he hands it on to the community, which is already involved in the action and must bring it into reality.[7]

And what this amounts to is that Christian revelation, because it is theo-drama, can re-create the sense of ancient tragedy that the divine has a real part in the fate of mortals – and revelation can do so, thanks to the union of the two natures of the Word, united as these are in his single person, in no fictitious mode but in very truth.

> God has become man without ceasing to be God ... a precise answer to the dreamy babblings of the myths.[8]

> The drama of Christ is the recapitulation and the end of Greek tragedy, just as it recapitulates and bids farewell to the individual tragic figures of the Old Testament.[9]

The many myths of paganism and the ritual dramas from which they were born give way, like the varied figures of Jewish revelation, to a new unity that is still dramatic (unlike the abstractions of philosophy) and yet is even more comprehensive than the most ambitious ideological scheme. As Balthasar explains:

> Within the drama of Christ, every human fate is deprivatized so that its personal range may extend to the whole universe, depending

6 *TD* II, p. 55.
7 *TD* II, p. 57.
8 *TD* II, pp. 45–46.
9 *TD* II, pp. 49–50.

on how far it is prepared to cooperate in being inserted into the normative drama of Christ's life, death and Resurrection. Not only does this gather the unimaginable plurality of human destinies into a concrete, universal point of unity: it actually maintains their plurality within the unity, but as a function of this unity.

And that is indeed

> the aim of an organic integration of all individual destinies in Christ (Eph. 1:3–10 [the Father's plan for uniting all things in Christ]), which is simultaneously the commissioning of the organic fullness of vocations and tasks by the organizing center (Eph. 4:7–16 [all the *charismata* bestowed through the ascended Lord]).[10]

For this is a play where 'all the spectators must eventually become fellow actors, whether they wish it or not'.[11] The drama that came to its climax in Jesus Christ overarches everything – which is why the New Testament interprets both creation, protology, and the consummation of the creation, eschatology, in its light. There is 'no standpoint from which we could observe and portray events as if we were uninvolved narrators of an epic', for this drama has 'already drawn all truth and all objectivity into itself'.[12] Thus does Balthasar read the message of the Johannine Apocalypse – a work to which he will return in volume IV, *The Action*, on a massive scale. For St John, God is at once *above* the world's struggle, in his absolute transcendence, and also *in* it, in his gracious (meaning, ultimately, *hypostatic*) self-involvement, as the slain yet glorified Lamb. Just why Balthasar reckons this closing book of the biblical canon so highly for theological dramatics emerges when we hear him decant its significance for our subject.

> With this image, which concludes Holy Scripture, we return to the point at which, according to our expectation, Christian revelation must fulfill the inchoate yearnings of *mythos* and, at the same time, banish its uncertainties. While God is not involved in the drama of destiny in a way that would render the outcome of the struggle un-certain, he does not sit in splendid isolation either, remote from the world's destinies.[13]

The Balthasarian challenge to theology

What all this means for Balthasar is that we must recognise the *priority of theo-drama over theology*. Unless theo-drama is accorded primacy, the varieties of contemporary theology Balthasar analysed in his *Prolegomena* simply cannot find that central point of convergence which they need. The centre is not to be defined conceptually, however, as in a theological super-system where the different competing systematic theologies might

10 *TD* II, p. 50.
11 *TD* II, p. 58.
12 Ibid.
13 *TD* II, p. 62.

be integrated at the level of ideas. The theo-drama is not, says Balthasar, to be articulated as an *idea* at all: as the 'all-embracing context', it cannot 'fall under any general concept'. What one can do, however, is to state its presuppositions – first, the play of freedoms, human and divine, that will be taken up into its course and, secondly, the central meaning God has given this 'play of freedoms' in his Son, Jesus Christ. (Here Balthasar outlines the course he will follow in the rest of Volume II of *Theodramatik* – on God's freedom and man's, and volumes III and IV – on Christ and his counterparts, and the climactic act of Christ's drama, the Atonement.) The divine–human play reaches its *dénouement* in the incarnate Son and the multifarious rôles he confers in the missions of Christians: it is on this dramatic reality that the ninefold of modern theological *Tendenzen* must for their own sakes' converge if they are not simply to cancel each other out. When, by contrast, they recognise the authentic hegemony of theo-drama, each comes into its own. The divine drama enacted upon earth with the concurrence of human freedom can do justice to a theology of (1) eschatological event and (2) saving history, because while 'essentially governed by the vertical' it also 'comprehends an historical, horizontal breadth'.[14] It can make sense of (3) a theology couched in terms of 'ortho-praxy', since it regards faith as 'an attitude of homage and receptivity [cf. the 'doxy' of 'orthodoxy'] vis-à-vis the preeminent divine activity in the drama of Jesus Christ', the divine 'praxis' that gives us the cue for human practice.[15] Theo-drama can also show how theology is (4) dialogue, for no drama can be simply monologue. Indeed, God's willingness to allow himself to be affected by his dialogue with man goes so far as the 'wonderful exchange' of 'standpoints and situations' when the Incarnate Lord ascends the Cross. (And actually, the dialogue of the One with the Other begins in eternity, when the Source generates the Word.) Moreover, theo-drama can legitimise (5) a political theology for, while to begin with it places the emphasis on the individual disciple's call to follow his Master, it also envisages disciples in the plural as engaged for warfare with evil powers.[16] Then again, theological dramatics makes sense too of (6) a theology of the future or of hope. This drama is a still unfinished (though far from indecisive) one, where the

> once-for-all, temporal history of Christ is ... constantly transposed into the ever-new present, ... yet remains wholly operative, actual and open to development in all its parts.[17]

'Simultaneous' through faith with the Christ-drama (here Balthasar looks to the Danish Existentialist Kierkegaard) and above all in the Mass (here he invokes the German Benedictine Odo Casel), the Church's members do not simply repeat what was done then, for the insights and actions prompted by the Spirit in continuance of the Son's work are ordered to the plenitude of the Parousia which is God's future for the world.

What of (7) a theology sensitive to the aspect of 'structure' or 'function'? The event of Jesus Christ imprints a structure upon the history it enters.

14 *TD* II, p. 66.
15 *TD* II, p. 69.
16 *TD* II, p. 72.
17 *TD* II, p. 74.

It gives a new configuration to the Old Testament history fulfilled in Christ, and by the personal determination of Jesus himself leaves behind in succeeding history an ecclesial structure through which the Saviour will be present in ever-renewed ways. But only theo-drama – the affirmation of the theodramatic character of that structuring event – can prevent people treating what preceded and followed Jesus as instantiations of general laws (laws of religious development, or the institutionalisation of inspiration, one presumes) and thus abandoning them to a '"structuralism" that has no events'.[18]

The theodramatic centre

In terms of Balthasar's theological taxonomy, the nine varieties of modern theology discussed under the heading 'Unifying the theologies' in Chapter 2,[19] he should still consider two: a theology couched in terms of (8) rôles (and hence missions) or of (9) freedom (and hence of what to do with freedom, for good or evil). In fact, the bulk of the second volume of *Theo-Drama* is devoted, as we shall shortly see, to that topic of freedom, human and divine, while all of Volume III concerns rôles. Balthasar assumes the benign willingness of the reader to admit the likely congruence of theodramatics with those two master-ideas in other people's theologies. He can thus proceed serenely to a fuller delineation of the true centre-point of the nine theologies ('The Single Drama'), a mid-point which is simultaneously the hermeneutical departure point of theological dramatics, the eyrie from which the terrains of Scripture and Tradition are scanned.

Scripture testifies that the unique form (*Gestalt*) to which the theological aesthetics drew our attention is in fact the unique drama played out by God with his creation. It is not required that we obtain a total overview of that drama's shape (such a God's-eye-view would be impossible for us – even from 'the gods' – the most eminent seats – of Balthasar's theatre!). What is required is that we be given evidence of the divine guidance (through Son and Spirit) of the play's action – and thus of its ultimate unity. And in a *tour de force* of exposition of the beginning of the Letter to the Ephesians Balthasar argues that this is – despite all internal biblical pluralism – the overall claim of the New Testament:

> Jesus Christ, in his dramatic role, which encompasses all dimensions of the world and of history, becomes the norm of every real and possible drama in the personal and public domains.[20]

To be the 'norm' for all dramas, corporate and individual, the tragedy of Christ must be deeper than all others – and it could only be known to be so if it were also known to be divine. At the same time, this tragedy must be filled (though Balthasar does not put it quite like this) with the atmosphere of comedy – in that it must bespeak a *gracious* destiny whose reach does not fall short of the abyss. 'No other foundation can one lay'

18 *TD* II, p. 67.
19 See above, pp. 14–16.
20 *TD* II, p. 83.

(I Corinthians 3.11) than his Paschal Mystery, the saving drama into which our own 'plays' must be incorporated as ever fresh aspects. In a theodramatic reworking, then, of the doctrine of justification:

> As the perfect man with his peerless drama, he is the living frame-work within which every human destiny is acted out; every human destiny is judged by his perfection and saved by his redeeming meaning.[21]

And though the 'theodramatic form' of Christ (here, at the centre of biblical revelation, the vocabularies of aesthetics and dramatics fuse) cannot be fully penetrated until all its aspects are known (and this must mean when world history and the history of persons is completed, at the end of the ages), still, the truths found in Scripture and Tradition give us access to those aspects that are indispensable – the Word's Incarnation, preaching of the Kingdom, preparing of the Church, Passion, solidarity with the dead, reunion with the Father and Parousia at the close of time as well as the creation of the world through the Logos and the Spirit and so the mystery of the divine Trinity in which the origin, history and destiny of the cosmos take their rise.

A new hermeneutic

Like any overall interpretation of the Christian revelation, theodramatics will cast its own light on fundamental theology: it will have a particular way of establishing its own ground, the legitimacy of its appeal to Scripture, to Tradition with its various monuments, and to the magis-terium of the Church. As is well known, in Catholic teaching the truth of revelation cannot be demonstrated through verification in the court of appeal of some higher or more comprehensive truth – for the simple reason that *no* truth can be higher or more comprehensive than revelation's. Indeed, the contrary is the case: revelation enables us to recognise distortions or narrownesses in all the other truth-claims we encounter. At the same time, however, certain rational indices, arising from outwith revelation, can point to the credibility of its unique truth-claim – and ensure in this way that the act of faith is not misconceived as the denial or inversion of truth's extra-revelatory sources. Translating that into theodramatic terms, Balthasar argues that, on the one hand, the dramatic action which unfolds in its totality in the 'theatre' of Judaeo-Christianity is self-interpreting, and, on the other hand, that what – for those who have not yet heard the gospel – already 'seems ultimate within the human horizon, and is experienced as such' is taken with full seriousness by theo-drama, indeed with more seriousness than anywhere else.[22] In the divine action, God uses the 'hieroglyphs of human destiny' to 'write his own, definitive word', such that the drama – enacted in Jesus' death, descent, and Resurrection – which 'unravels man's fate' is in one sense witnessed (the incarnation of the Logos as Jesus, and the vindication in the Resurrection of the crucified Messiah has, for the New Testament

---

21 *TD* II, p. 87.
22 *TD* II, pp. 94–95.

writers, its 'eyewitnesses'), and yet in another sense it can only be 'believed'. That here God has drawn to a transcendent resolution all the puzzles proposed by the myriad dramas of man cannot be demonstratively – which means, in the context of a stage play, *ostensively* – shown.[23]

Balthasar's emphasis on the 'self-attestation' of the divine drama is intended to express its sovereign reality, *vis-à-vis* human interpretative activity in general, and more especially its continuing identity, *vis-à-vis* successive human cultures and mindsets across time. However, he does not deny that there will be *some* 'transposition' of how we see the drama, according to the context of life-situation of those who are doing the seeing. Not surprisingly, for a theologian who wants passionately to be regarded as fully Catholic, Balthasar emphasises, though, that

> if transpositions are to succeed . . . they must not be bought at the cost of losing any of revelation's substance or weight. The light that streams forth in the self-illumination of the dramatic action must be neither obscured nor trivialized, that is, robbed of its divine uniqueness.[24]

What is desirable is not a quantitative maximalisation of propositions to be believed (which is how the 'development of doctrine' has sometimes been regarded), but the utmost respect for the plenary sense of revelation 'handed on in the Church in all its vitality'.[25] For the sense of the divine drama to be preserved over time, it is not astonishing that there should be such a thing as the magisterium – an organ that embodies the rule of faith within the Church as a whole, and so can act as (in Newman's phrase, echoed here by Balthasar) a 'regulatory principle' for the drama criticism practised on God's play by theologians.[26]

It is obvious that the drama displayed in revelation cannot be adequately captured by the propositional statements of doctrine (vital though these may be to its understanding). But Balthasar is also at pains to stress how the drama exceeds the biblical text likewise.

> It is clear that Scripture is by no means the finished stage text governing the enacting of real history; evidently, the scriptural text becomes fixed at the end of events rather than at the beginning.[27]

And if that is true of the production of the inspired texts and their collating in a canon of Scripture, it is also the case that the understanding of the 'fixed' Scripture cannot be complete till the divine play reaches, with the Parousia, its finale. And this is a shattering thought, which alerts us to the eloquent silence made audible by the biblical word.

---

23 *TD* II, p. 95.
24 *TD* II, p. 98.
25 *TD* II, p. 100.
26 For the twists Balthasar gave Newman's work, see A. Nichols, OP, 'Littlemore from Lucerne: Newman's *Essay on Development* in Balthasarian Perspective', in I. Ker (ed.), *Newman and Conversion* (Edinburgh 1997), pp. 100–116.
27 *TD* II, p. 103.

God's last word has not been said until the 'word' 'resurrection' has been developed and formulated in such a way that its whole range is made visible. God's final word is so vast, however, that it makes room for us to hear his silence too, just as the stars reveal the night sky.[28]

Yet the biblical word and text are not for all that simply external to the events they attest. At times, the scriptural word *is* the Word of God moving history; in other cases, it is the *reflection* of that word. Playing on the German verbs *bezeugen*, 'to attest', and *(ein)zeugen*, 'to generate', Balthasar has it that the Bible is not merely attestation, since it shares in the office of the divine Word that never goes forth without result (cf. Isaiah 51.11).

What seems on the surface to be a book is inwardly 'spirit and life'; it is always ready to be used and interpreted by the living God according to his design, to be disclosed to the individual who loves him, or the group or the epoch, as a word that is new and ever-new beyond all imagining.[29]

So Scripture is 'part of the drama itself, moving along with it'.[30] Note, however, the exigent conditions – indicative of a patristically-minded and Catholic rather than biblicist and Protestant approach – which Balthasar names as always to be borne in mind if the Scriptures are to fulfil their appointed rôle. The 'only really Christian interpretation of Scripture' is one that reads the Old Testament with a view to the Incarnation of the Logos, and the New Testament in the light of that event, and both together by Christ's Spirit. Moreover, Scripture can be called a manifestation of the Logos only if we hold open that 'body' of biblical texts not just to the historical and physical body of the Saviour but also to his eucharistic and ecclesial one. (Here Balthasar has learned from the investigation of the 'triform body' in ancient and mediaeval exegesis by his erstwhile confrère and lifelong friend, Henri de Lubac.)[31] And finally, Scripture is at its most dramatic when God uses it in our lives to provoke our own 'Amens' to its message. Then above all it becomes 'a dramatic instrument in the hand of the saving and judging Word'.[32]

Balthasar cannot set out here a total account of what constitutes, in the light of aesthetics and dramatics, the structure of 'proof' in theology because that task belongs more with the third part of the trilogy – the theological logic. *Something* can be said, however, about how an ecclesially appropriate theology emerges from the Scriptures on the basis of the unfolding divine design. At least we can say, for instance, that a way of deriving a theological criteriology which made of theology a system, or

---

28 *TD* II, p. 106.
29 *TD* II, p. 108.
30 *TD* II, p. 112.
31 H. de Lubac, *Histoire et esprit chez Origène* (Paris 1950); idem., *Exégèse médiévale: Les quatre sens de l'Ecriture* (Paris 1959–1964); H. U. von Balthasar, *Henri de Lubac: Sein organisches Lebenswerk* (Einsiedeln 1976).
32 *TD* II, p. 115.

separated out the epistemically more warrantable from the adventure of faith, would not do. Diminishing the dramatic nature of the revelatory event, it would by that fact alone declare itself a failure.

Two elements in theological method that a theology faithful to the intrinsic drama of the gospel *can* approve, however, are, first, the scrutiny of the historical facts of the drama-filled biblical events in all their uniqueness; and, secondly, the exploration of the way those facts contain 'a meaning that embraces, consummates and transcends every other projected meaning'.[33] Only we must be careful not to separate out a pre-dogmatic exegesis – which, untutored by revelation in its wholeness, will inevitably be reductionist – from a doctrinal theology that, thanks to its flawed exegetical preliminaries, can only judge the claims of Scripture and Tradition as excessive. Here, as in *The Glory of the Lord*, Balthasar counsels against too hard-and-fast a distinction between fundamental theology and dogmatic. Certainly, there must be 'an initial and basically human appeal about the fact's testimony' – or else the traditional Catholic insistence on a 'preamble of faith' showing faith's congruence with (speculative and historical) reason would fall to the ground. But the unity of the two is more significant than their distinction. To deny this is to lose, in aesthetics, the glory of the epiphany of Christ, and in dramatics, the scope and tension of his drama.

> A posteriori and a priori are inseparable here. This means that we are always presented with the *entire* phenomenon of Christian revelation within history: only the Whole can bear witness to itself and prove itself to be the unsurpassable reality it *must* be, if God himself, the Unique One, is involved in this unique train of events.

And applying to theological dramatics St Anselm's definition of God as 'that than which nothing greater can be thought' – a definition already pressed into service in the aesthetics to capture the concept of revelation, Balthasar goes on to say that, in the unfolding history of salvation, God must so demonstrate his presence that 'the drama of God and man' too can be shown to fall under this description.[34]

Since, within the unity of theological dramatics, it is the task of the *fundamental-theological* element to point to this totality, that element cannot but appear as the first sketchy appearance of the complementary *dogmatic-theological* component. We cannot show that the divine drama is the totality which can make sense of my, your, any and every existence without already introducing such themes as: the transcendence of the divine freedom which shows its power precisely by its enabling of lesser created freedoms to be themselves; the reality of the world's misery which cannot be abolished by speculation or revolutionary action but which so great a God can reverse incarnationally from within; the consequent discovery that God can be both himself and divinely other to himself – One who sends and One who is sent – and be so in perfect unity of dis-position, in a Third (the Spirit), and that man, in whom the Second

---

33 *TD* II, p. 116.
34 *TD* II, pp. 117–118.

achieves this redemptive transformation, is indeed called to the integral restitution of his nature (to resurrection of the body, and not just immortality of the soul); the union, in the way God saves, of concrete and universal – true of Israel, true of Christ, true of the Church; and the vocation of created freedom to fulfil itself in perfect responsiveness to the uncreated. Here Balthasar adumbrates what will be the great themes of the rest of *Theo-Drama* – but so as to suggest their apologetic power as pointers to the dramatic totality which the as yet unbelieving spectator in the pit is invited to step forward and enter, playing his or her own part.

We can, he says, *glimpse* this totality without being able to *survey* it. As a result while we cannot, in theology, assign some feature its place in an overall view (here again, Balthasar expresses his distaste for systems), we are able to suggest the consonance of some aspect of the faith with the glimpsed totality (allergy to systems does not mean withdrawal from 'totality thinking'). The correct verification procedure in dramatics is twofold: to *exclude* 'all the one-sided views that refuse to accept that all things can be integrated into the free God / world totality, as interpreted by Christian revelation', and to *include* 'everything that allows itself to be thus integrated'.[35] A Catholic theology (in both the confessional and the common-or-garden sense of that word) will 'ex-communicate' everything that opposes *communio* between divine and human freedom, and 'in-communicate' everything that promotes it. Heresies and theological errors typically question the 'divine integrative power' of God's love: even if they appear as 'Right-wing' deviations – biblicism or fideism – they smack just as much as 'Left-wing' scepticism of the 'self-righteousness of rationalism'.[36] And Balthasar applauds Newman's courage, in the University sermons, when he abandons the old High Church insistence on a limited number of (patristically established) *credenda* since he has caught sight of the idea of the

> *totality* of divine revelation . . . which is unfolded through history and yields the aspects of particular dogmas, yet, in its totality, is not altered or enlarged.[37]

The *Essay in Aid of a Grammar of Assent* will add to this that the totality becomes visible in the partial aspects (the individual dogmas) by way of convergence of indicators ('illation') – an approach that has the additional merit of throwing open the Christian 'Whole' as much to the uneducated as to theologians.

Now most of this is new – but not all. Among the early Christian Apologists and in St Irenaeus facets of theological dramatics already appear.[38] Who could deny that, say, the Gospels, or indeed the Old Testament histories (especially when taken in conjunction with the Prophetic books) are in some fashion 'dramatic'? The importance of the notion of 'God's Lawsuit' – a courtroom drama *par excellence* – for the biblical corpus has been demonstrated by the German Evangelical

---

35 *TD* II, p. 127.
36 *TD* II, p. 128.
37 *TD* II, p. 131; cf. J. H. Newman, *University Sermons* (London 1970), p. 336.
38 *TD* II, pp. 136–149.

Markus Barth.[39] The Swedish Lutheran historian of doctrine Gustaf Aulén revived the notion of Christ's dramatic struggle in his survey of theologies of the Atonement[40] – and defended his adoption of a theodramatic approach (without the name!) in a later monograph, much less known in the Anglo-Saxon world.[41] Balthasar approves of Aulén, but hints he can make a better job of theologising the angelic activity, Godly and diabolic, which the Swede left standing as a kind of inexplicable surd. And as to the drama of spiritual warfare, that is everywhere in the tradition, from the Synoptics, Augustine (the struggle of the two 'cities') and the Greek Fathers represented in the *Philokalia* to Ignatius Loyola and Lorenzo Scupoli. Nor should one forget works of Milton and Dostoevsky, Dante's *Commedia* and Bunyan's *The Pilgrim's Progress* – nor for that matter C. S. Lewis's *The Pilgrim's Regress* and *The Great Divorce*. Although these are not actually plays, they can still testify that theo-drama's 'speculative development' is Christian enough.

39 *TD* II, pp. 152–159; M. Barth, *Rechtfertigung: Versuch einer Auslegung paulinischer Texte im Rahmen des Alten und Neuen Testaments* (Zurich 1969); ET, *Justification* (Grand Rapids, Mich. 1971).
40 G. Aulén, *Den kristna försoningstanken* (Lund 1930); ET, *Christus Victor: An Historical Study of Three Main Types of the Idea of Atonement* (London 1931).
41 Idem., *Das Drama und die Symbole: Die Problematik des heutigen Gottesbildes* (Göttingen 1964).

5

The Two Freedoms

Mysteriously on stage

Theodramatic theology, then, as a development (if not an unannounced one) is assertorically Catholic. But its affirmations are not offered in an excessively cataphatic way. Balthasar's notion of the dramatic totality not only allows but also calls for the recognition of apophasis. He wants us to accept in advance the possibility that there will be pools of mystery we cannot drain.

> The raising of the many-sided intramundane drama to the level of theo-drama, which is essentially transcendent and unique, puts a question mark over even the most interesting dramatic categories, a question mark that must apply, ultimately, to every attempt to present this unique reality in the forms of speech.[1]

This drama, and this drama alone, is played out not only on earth but also in heaven. The earth/heaven distinction, remarks Balthasar, making good his implicit promise to do rather better than Aulén where the mythopoetic language of Scripture is concerned, is

> not only . . . a (dispensable) metaphor for the man/God distinction but also . . . an (indispensable) *sacrament* of the latter.[2]

'Heaven' is a created reality – the realm of the Angels – but it is from this 'location' which is other than earth that the divine dramatic activity is initiated. Without the heavenly dimension there would be no distance, and *therefore* no drama. Man, certainly, is, as that hero of the theological aesthetics Charles Péguy would say, *l'homme charnel*, man who belongs to the earth and is meant to be fruitful there. And yet

> all the same he remains essentially dependent on a blessing from a realm far above him that is inaccessible and cannot be manipulated by him. This is the paradox of a being which knows that it can only fulfill itself through grateful dependence on a grace on which it has no claim.

1 *TD* II, p. 17.
2 *TD* II, p. 177.

And the God of Scripture chooses to bestow this blessing, so much so indeed that God and man enjoy (and endure) a shared history which can be called, then, a

> shared history of heaven and earth, right up to the proclamation of the 'kingdom of heaven' on earth and the 'ascent into heaven' of the incarnate Word of God.[3]

Increasingly, as the revelation of Old and New Testaments unfolds, this ultimate stage-setting of the heaven/earth relationship is understood by reference to the events of revelation themselves. Otherwise put, the relation of heaven and earth itself becomes theodramatic – and the angelic hosts endowed with missions relevant to this context. As the Letter to the Hebrews has it, 'Are they not all ministering spirits sent forth to serve, for the sake of those who are to obtain salvation?' (1.14). And Balthasar cannot forbear from mentioning here how, as the full dimensions of the stage are identified in the moment of the humiliation and exaltation, descent and return, of the incarnate Son, there also comes into view an arena never intended in the original creation, the 'underworld' or *inferno* which is now 'man's ultimate possibility and condition'.[4] As the pupil of the mystical theologian Adrienne von Speyr, in whose spirituality the Descent into Hell plays so massive a part, Balthasar signals that no more in the dramatics than in the aesthetics will he leave this often neglected article of the Old Roman Creed out of account.

Still, the drama is not to be thought of as unilaterally initiated at all points from heaven's side. If earth were always passive, there could be no drama. Christology would subside into Monophysitism, the theology of grace succumb to extreme Predestinarianism. Earth, as the drama proceeds, will give birth to heaven – and, in this, heaven

> does not betray a weakness but rather manifests its fullness and its freedom to be itself, even on earth and *in* earth.[5]

It is the measure of the freedom given man from above that he can cause the kingdom of heaven to draw near, or stay away. 'Ultimately, therefore, the stage is entirely assimilated into the spiritual dimensions of the actors themselves.'[6]

The nature of the actors

We can now proceed, then, to enquire into the list of players in theodramatics, its dramatis personae. Actually, as Balthasar is quick to point out, this presents us with our first problem, or rather, pair of problems. The first, and less intractable, is a procedural difficulty. As anyone who reads a theatre programme knows, the list of dramatis personae is not especially informative unless read side by side with a synopsis of the plot, nor is a summary of the unfolding of the drama really illuminating except as a retrospective reminder, once we have left the theatre, of the depths revealed in the course of the play. And Balthasar admits that in one sense

3 *TD* II, p. 178.
4 *TD* II, p. 183.
5 *TD* II, p. 184.
6 *TD* II, p. 188.

we cannot say who the characters are without recounting what they do because their qualities are to be exhibited in the dramatic action and in no other way. So there would be something to be said for skipping a study of the dramatis personae altogether, and plunging directly into the heart of the play. And yet some general or formal statements about, for instance, the rôle of a tragic hero can helpfully be made before we get involved with the doings of this or that particular tragic hero in a given play. Always allowing that author, actor or director, may expand or extend the concept of the tragic protagonist in unusual or unexpected ways, to have *some* pre-understanding of what a tragic hero may be can in itself only aid the prospective playgoer. True, in theo-drama, since there is only one play of this kind to be had, we cannot obtain a formal acquaintance with the rôles to be played by looking at a wide range of examples; but this means that, in this *unique* case, we must get our formal grasp of who the chief figures are by, as it were, freezing the drama in its unfolding course and enquiring after the *nature* of the agents involved. Clearly, then, Balthasar's theo-logically dramatic account of the dramatis personae will correspond to what, in more conventional dogmatic theologies, is a theology of God as one and three, an ontological Christology of Jesus as one person in both divine and human nature, and a theological anthropology, an account of man in his relation to God. However, thanks to the demands of this theo-dramatic version of these topics, there will be no danger, as with a purely ontological theology, of treating divine nature, Godmanhood and human nature in splendid isolation from – respectively – divine action, theandric action and human action.

And that brings us to the second difficulty, one not so easily disposed of. Its resolution will occupy in fact the lion's share of the second volume of *Theodramatik*. As Balthasar remarks, in theo-drama, presumably, the main character is God, but then the question at once arises, Who else can act if *God* is on stage? In other words, the account of the dramatis personae of the divine drama must first and foremost come to terms with the problem of how finite freedom can act *vis-à-vis* infinite freedom without being swallowed up by the latter, which is simultaneously the problem of how infinite freedom can make room for finite freedom without surren-dering its own nature as infinitude. Of course we know that in ancient Greek drama no problem at all was experienced in the inclusion of both gods and men as simultaneous agents in a play's unfolding. But surely the philosphical critique of myth, in establishing how unthinkable is the idea of finite deity – gods who merely take a portion of the action – put paid to all that? It is hardly surprising that what Balthasar calls the 'age of the philosophers', from Plato to Plotinus, produced no such theological dramas as those of Aeschylus, Sophocles and Euripides, for, as he writes:

> here God was the 'sun of the good', the all-embracing 'Nature', the unapproachable 'One', sublimely superior to all the oppositions found in the world: consequently he could not step forth onto the world stage as a particular and special character vis-à-vis other particular and special characters.[7]

7 *TD* II, p. 189.

But the Christian cannot simply underwrite the philosopher's critique of myth just like that – something Balthasar has already made plain in Volume IV of *Herrlichkeit*. There, he affirmed that the world of myth, inasmuch as it discloses in imagistic form an inter-active relationship between this world and divine transcendence, put forth some perennially worthwhile forms of expression for a theological aesthetics. So here too while gladly accepting the purification of the concept of God brought about, in Greek-speaking antiquity, by rational philosophers, Balthasar insists that the postulates of those philosophers must themselves be critically assessed in the light of biblical revelation. And here the counter-claims of the Christian thinker recover dialectically the mythopoeic sense of the divine while assimilating the valid elements in the rational critique thereof. To Christian theology, the Absolute is essentially free, and free above all in the sense that:

> [it] has a sovereign ability, out of its own freedom, to create and send forth finite but genuinely free beings ... in such a way that, without vitiating the infinite nature of God's freedom, a genuine opposition of freedoms can come about.[8]

To some degree the apparent paradox whereby Scripture calls God everything (for the book of Sirach, 'The sum of our words is, He is the All', 14.37) while continuing to treat man as most definitely something can be resolved by appeal to the classical philosophical theology of the Church which, as Balthasar remarks, takes seriously the explicit or implicit philosophy human beings employ when thinking about the meaning of the world and of existence, and pursues its own thinking through of biblical revelation in the company of this 'mediating philosophical reflection'. A sound doctrine of the inter-relation of divine transcendence and divine immanence is essential. As absolute Unity, God cannot be designated as 'the Other' over against any finite thing; or rather, as Balthasar has put it in *Herrlichkeit*, he is so wholly other, so utterly beyond this-worldly discriminations, as to be, in Nicholas of Cusa's phrase, the 'Non-other'. Though when we think of our relation to God we must, to be sure, designate ourselves as other than him, he himself recognises us *in* him, not *outside* him – because all that we are, not least our freedom, we owe to that 'everything' of God's infinite freedom. In a formula of Archbishop William Temple of Canterbury, God plus the world equals God; the world minus God equals nothing. It seems appropriate here to cite an Anglican theologian, for Balthasar himself illustrates his point by quotation from that homely source, C. S. Lewis's *Letters to Malcolm*.

> Our reality is so much from His reality as He, moment by moment, projects into us. The deeper the level within ourselves from which our prayer, or any other act, wells up, the more it is His, but not at all the less ours. Rather, most ours when most His.[9]

---

8 *TD* II, p. 190.
9 C. S. Lewis, *Letters to Malcolm* (London 1977), p. 71; cited *TD* II, pp. 193–194. It should be noted, however, that in the final volume of the dramatics, Balthasar will query Temple's dictum, at least in its full force.

But beyond this contribution of rational metaphysics there is also the light that the revelation of God in Jesus Christ can throw on the issue. For Balthasar that revelation simultaneously sharpens the problem and deepens philosophy's attempted solution of it. On the one hand, the saving revelation *widens* the gap between infinite freedom and finite freedom in disclosing the abyss which separates the holiness of the first from the guiltiness of the second. On the other hand, the self-revelation of God as Trinity *deepens* the philosophical notion of the 'Other as non-Other' by taking the foundation of difference into God himself where it is precisely the distinction yet identity which holds good between God and his Word that makes possible the existence of finite centres of freedom called nonetheless to open themselves to divine infinitude. 'Called to' so open themselves but not necessarily, of course, actually doing so: only in the action of the theo-drama does it become clear how the Mediator, the Word made-man, in Balthasar's own words, indebted at once to Irenaeus and to Hegel, will

> recapitulate in himself the conflict between God's 'everything' and man's 'something' and, by so doing, sublimate and abolish it.[10]

Jesus Christ thus provides world history with its central question, 'Are you for this or against?', throughout all future time, heightening the dramatic vista to those apocalyptic proportions of struggle and judgment, heaven and hell, which *Theodramatik* will deal with in its closing volume, *Das Endspiel*, the 'last act'.

And so, simply by raising the problem of how God and man can act together, how infinite freedom and finite freedom can co-exist, has led Balthasar to look at the main agents involved in the production of theo-drama. On this expanded world stage we will have to do, in suitably dramatic form, with God, with man, and with the God-Man. First, with God whom Balthasar describes as

> the One responsible for the play, and yet . . . not responsible when man, in freedom, acts inappropriately [though] all the same, he stands by his original responsibility.

Secondly, with man, whom Balthasar thinks of as

> both singular and plural, thrown onto the stage, endowed with freedom, condemned to freedom and given grace to exercise it, with the power of becoming what he can on the basis of his own nature and constitution and yet unable to do this outside the divine freedom but only in it and with it.

Thirdly, with a Mediator whom Balthasar presents as

> indispensable and yet beyond all human calculation, in a pact with both warring parties and yet not a traitor to either; epitomizing the living drama in the very 'composition' of his being, torn asunder by his tragic situation and yet, thus torn, healing divisions.

10 *TD* II, p. 195.

And from this, so Balthasar concludes his 'definition' of the theme of infinite versus finite freedom:

> all else simply follows, beyond our wildest hopes, from the principle he has established; for, while he is the play's *peripateia*, [that is] reversal [or turning-point], the whole play by no means runs its course mechanically from then on: it continually reveals new, exciting, unforeseeable aspects of this reversal, and it goes on intensifying right up to the last scene.[11]

So far, then, Balthasar has merely established the outlines of this fundamental problem of a theological dramatics which of all presentations of the content of revelation cannot fail to address such issues as, How can the Creator share being – and so freedom – with the creature? How does the grace of God build upon nature and incorporate human freedom, rather than crushing the first and overruling the second? How are the two wills of the Redeemer, divine and human, simultaneously active in him without overthrowing the unity of his person? How can history be an *agendum*, consigned to man to make of what he will, and yet also be pre-determined in the divine elective counsel and brought proleptically to share its own goal in the death and resurrection of Jesus Christ? All of these are simply instances of the single *underlying* question: how is *finite* freedom interrelated with its own *infinite* source and goal?

Finite freedom: two concepts of liberty

Since what we are discussing is the interrelation of these freedoms as exhibited in the unfolding of revelation it is virtually a matter of indifference whether we begin by investigating the divine or the human. Beginning with God would be perfectly possible: not only is he, as Aquinas remarked, 'most evident in himself though not to us', but such a proceeding would enable us to highlight the presuppositions of finite freedom before going on to describe its reality. Actually, however, Balthasar will begin with man, on the ground that his is the only kind of freedom with which we are familiar. And this methodological option has the advantage of allowing us, hopefully, to show why man's finite freedom must postulate for its own exercise the infinite freedom of the Absolute, and, more specifically, in Christian revelation, the triune freedom of the biblical God. Beginning with man will do us no harm as *Christo*centric *theo*logians, for whom the goal of speaking is God in Christ as affecting man, so long as at all times we keep in mind that *interrelation* of divine and human freedoms which is theo-drama's primary datum.

Balthasar opens his account of finite freedom by pointing out that the concept seems at first sight self-contradictory. How can something be free if it is constantly chafing against restraint, the restraints given with the limitations of its own nature? And yet we do have a direct experience of freedom, an experience which can be expressed only in this apparent contradiction: we are at one and the same time free yet only moving towards freedom.

11 *TD* II, pp. 195–196.

Clearly, Balthasar will have to unpack this statement by distinguishing between two concepts of liberty. These he calls 'freedom as autonomous motion' and 'freedom as consent', and without much difficulty can show how this distinction crops up time and again in the tradition of the Fathers and mediaevals. Before expounding it directly, however, Balthasar draws attention, with help from the first volume of his theological logic, to freedom's ontological basis. In *Wahrheit* Balthasar had pondered on the co-originality of the discovery of the self and the world. By the very fact of knowing that I exist I also know that I am open to all being – a claim which he now re-conceptualises in terms of my coming to grasp, on the one hand, the utter uniqueness and in that sense incommunicability of my own being, and, on the other, the unlimited communicability of being at large. As an 'I' person, I am by that very fact ready to acknowledge that being is possessed by innumerable others who have just the same uniqueness or incommunicability that I do. Thus for Balthasar we should not say, 'I seem to be unique, but ultimately I am only one individual among millions'. Rather should we say, 'I am unique, but only by making room for countless others to be unique'. This is how finite personal being can be said to echo the being of the tri-personal God, for whom the incommunicability of hypostasis is one with the unity of essence in each divine person. In that finite image of the Trinity which is human being, uniqueness was given me so that, through the medium of the nature I share with my species, I can communicate with those others who have also been divinely 'called by name'. The point of mentioning all this here is to show how the primary 'given' of my existence is not what Balthasar calls a self-intuition or grasp of my own essence; rather do I make my most basic act of self-possession in and with my universal opening to all being whatsoever. And the relevance of *this* to our topic is that it reveals the primary sense of freedom, what Balthasar terms the first 'pole' or 'pillar' of freedom, and that is 'freedom of consent':

> a fundamental freedom . . . that enables us to affirm the value of things and reject their defects, to become involved with them or turn away from them.[12]

Such knowledge of the good as good, what the ancient Roman moralists called *bonum honestum*, means that while man only strives for what he perceives as good (even if it be in fact evil), such striving is not fundamentally self-interested. More primordially is it, in one of Balthasar's favourite words, drawn from the mystical tradition, 'indifferent', which in this context he paraphrases as meaning:

> *able to let the Good 'be', whether it be a finite or an infinite Good, simply for the sake of its goodness*, without trying to gain it for himself.[13]

The part, that is myself, with my self-possession, 'naturally', as St Thomas says, loves the whole more than itself; the right (to speak with Augustine,

12 *TD* II, p. 211.
13 Ibid.

Anselm, Bonaventure) is desired for the sake of its rightness, whatever 'enjoyment' may or may not be involved.

Whereas this first 'pillar' of freedom is unequivocally a given, something inescapable about the mode of our existence, freedom's other aspect – freedom as autonomous motion – has a less hard-and-fast character. For Balthasar the second sense in which we are free has to do with a moment subsequent to self-possession and that is self-realisation – for each human being can and must decide for themselves what freedom ultimately is and under what form it should be sought. In one sense this too is something we can hardly get out of: even the decision not to make decisions is precisely that, decision, and would reveal, subjacently, an entire vision of freedom if a dystopian one. But in another and more obvious sense, as everyday experience of other people, especially in a pluralist society, indicates, the manner of our self-realisation is up to us, and here the two basic alternatives, so Balthasar suggests, are libertarianism or absolute autonomy on the one hand and divine submission or theonomy on the other. Or as he himself puts it, more persuasively:

> a man may decide that, for the purposes of self-realization, the whole area must remain completely open (so that, if there were a pre-existent and fully realized absolute freedom, the path of finite freedom would only be distorted and its course frustrated); conversely he may see that finite freedom, if it remains alone and is posited as absolute, is bound to become the hellish torment of a Tantalus if it is not permitted to attain full development in the self-warranting realm of absolute freedom.[14]

And by appealing to the argumentation of the Fathers and the great Scholastics, in their synthesis of Scripture with Greek philosophy, Balthasar claims he can show that only the second *theonomic* way is viable.

And this is where he speaks explicitly of the two concepts of liberty: the freedom which consists in consent to the Good, freedom in the more primordial sense, on the one hand, and, on the other, freedom as autonomous motion, freedom in the secondary sense, what in modern philosophy would be termed the 'freedom of the will'. Balthasar points out that for the Fathers and mediaevals, by contrast with the moderns, this latter freedom is never defended simply for its own sake but as a vital presupposition of theo-drama. The aim of our spiritual ancestors was always to show how freedom, when understood as man's 'being from within himself', his *autexousion* or capacity for self-determination, needs to realise itself within the context of the *divine* freedom, and to do so in a process that is never-ending, at least on earth. It is here, with freedom as self-movement, the secondary pillar of freedom, that he begins his outline of a *theology*, rather than philosophy, of freedom. And just as in the second volume of *Herrlichkeit*, Balthasar's attempt to give theological aesthetics an orientation from Christian tradition, considered as issuing from the fountain head of the Fathers, opens crucially with St Irenaeus, so the same can be said here in the second volume of *Theodramatik*. Drawing on Book

---

14 *TD* II, p. 213.

IV of the *Adversus Haereses*, he records Irenaeus' apposite question as to why, at the beginning, God did not create angels and men to be sinless. The answer of the Lyonese doctor is that finite freedom must explore the whole realm of its possibilities if it is really to discover its finitude, its poverty, and so learn by experience that it can only fulfil itself by following the counsel of God. Balthasar calls Irenaean teaching here the 'developed form of the primary experiential concept of the New Testament' as that is found in, for instance, the parable of the Prodigal Son. And this he identifies as finite freedom's negative experience that, cut off from infinite freedom, it must go hungry and eventually perish. Fortunately, autonomous finite freedom operates within an encompassing Providence which restrains it at its limits. The sinner, having come to his senses through the experience of evil – for, as Gregory of Nyssa points out, the creativity of finite freedom includes the dubious privilege of creating something even God cannot create, namely evil, in our own wills – can now cling all the more firmly to the good.

The idea of human autonomy is by no means alien, then, to the Christian tradition. Man is, as Newman put it, echoing not only Gregory but Origen before him and Bernard after, 'the principle of creativity in the moral world'. Indeed, Balthasar in his exposition of Bernard's concept of freedom goes so far as to describe the freedom of autonomous motion (he also calls it 'rational spontaneity') as nothing other than human nature itself – though, so as to avoid a reckless Existentialism, he is careful to add that here we must qualify an account of that secondary pillar of freedom by reference to the primary pillar, freedom of consent.

And this, Balthasar reminds his readers, is something that the most classical divine of the Latin tradition, Thomas Aquinas, did not fail to do. St Thomas postpones his description of how the will is purely self-determined in its choices until he has explained that it seeks things only under the aspect of the good – and to that extent can be said to scan the whole range of being, which is the similitude of the divine goodness, in implicit search for the absolute Good, God himself. And so we come to that even more vital sense of freedom, freedom as consent.

In re-introducing this theme Balthasar furnishes the argumentative element which he promised in predicting that he could demonstrate the non-viable character of libertarianism or absolute autonomy, the mistaken definition of human freedom *over against* infinite freedom, whether the latter be taken as fictive or real. And this is the claim that, inasmuch as finite freedom is a 'given', it cannot get back to its origin, nor, insofar as it is indefinite or open, can it reach its goal – even by pursuing the sum total of goods and values to be found in this world. The question thus arises whether finite freedom will, in Balthasar's words:

> regard its being open as the opportunity to hand itself over to infinite free Being, to the Being who is the Giver of [its] free openness.[15]

In other words, within the open realm of being in its unconditional totality can there be a self-disclosure on the part of an infinite freedom? And if there can, might finite freedom prove able to fulfil itself *in* that infinite

15 *TD* II, p. 228.

freedom without either obliterating its own initial givenness as free movement or somehow succeeding in finitising infinite freedom, thus relegating God to the status of one factor among others in existence?

The answer of the New Testament is 'Yes' on both counts. Whatever may be the case with the Old Covenant, where the history of salvation is still *en route* from a condition of estrangement between man and God to one of *parrhêsia* or free mutual openness between them, in the New Covenant all heteronomy is overcome. As Balthasar puts it:

> In the preaching of Jesus and the post-Easter meditation upon it in the light of the Holy Spirit ... the womb of the Father's divine freedom opens so wide and so deep that we begin to suspect what 'the fulfillment of finite freedom in infinite freedom' might mean.[16]

It was the achievement of Christian Hellenism to place at the service of this evangelical discovery the formal model of the relation between the One and the Many found in different ways in both Stoicism and Plotinus, in order to show how finite freedom can only arise out of the primal freedom of God and, furthermore, only be sustained there. Just as in Plotinus, the other, over against the One, can only be 'other' because it itself is derivatively one, that is, participates in oneness, so for the theological faith of the patristic Church only because the will has its origin and sustenance in the divine freedom, in freedom itself, is it really free.

And here the key is the New Testament doctrine of the Holy Spirit, who is identified by St Thomas as the principal referent of the phrase 'the New Law' – which law thus loses the heteronomous character it possessed in the Old Testament. Considered as the love of God spread abroad in the hearts of believers, the Spirit liberates finite freedom so that it can embrace its own ultimate freedom, and he does so by initiating finite freedom into a participation in God's infinite freedom, into, that is, an inner participation in that freedom's specifically divine quality. This liberated freedom, which the Latin doctors call *beatitudo* (blessedness), *delectatio* (delight), *complacitum* (mutual agreement), or *consensus* (mutual consent), is for Balthasar above all the last, the term singled out for its appositeness by St Bernard. This is the freedom of 'consent' since, as he explains:

> on the one hand, finite freedom cannot be compelled by anything but itself to leave the path of infinite freedom and head for slavery, and, on the other hand, by definition, infinite freedom is free to impart itself to others; it is not in the power of finite freedom; it remains grace, that is, the freely given indwelling of infinite freedom in finite freedom.[17]

Extremely important to Balthasar at this point are Augustine's anti-Pelagian writings. In the *De Spiritu et littera* Augustine saw in a moment of breakthrough in insight that Pelagius' apparent elevation of the freedom of the Christian man above the level of the New Testament was in actual fact a sinking down to that of the Old. The relation between the

16 *TD* II, p. 229.
17 *TD* II, p. 232.

freedom given human beings by God and the commandments that God addresses to this freedom, remains, for Pelagius, an external one: it is still a case of the old law standing over against those who have not yet been liberated into enjoyment of the freedom of the children of God. The Spirit of grace, by contrast, facilitates a living freedom experienced as the charity which is 'sweet delight in what is right'. Among the Greek Fathers, the embrace of finite and infinite freedom is differently conceived. It is found not so much in the freedom of consent achieved by the Spirit in his transcendental liberation of the will through the grace of Easter and Pentecost as in the original constitution of the will as not only self-movement but also an unending movement towards its own origin in God. Here too, however, infinite freedom opens itself to finite freedom as the true context of the latter's self-fulfilment only in the divine self-manifestation in Jesus Christ.

Infinite freedom: depths of the divine Three

It is to infinite freedom for its own sake that we must now turn. In the extra-biblical world divine freedom is either, as with the Olympian gods, itself anthropomorphic and finite, or with the Neo-Platonists so much a suprapersonal norm that it enters into no living relation with finite freedom. Only in the Old Testament does it become clear that creation sets no limits to divine freedom. On his own sovereign authority, God steps beyond the divine realm in order to rule every aspect of the realm of the world, his almighty Wisdom penetrating all things. However, only with the New Testament is human freedom allowed inner access to divine freedom. Here for the first time infinite freedom establishes a reciprocity with finite freedom. In Jesus Christ, and especially in his being 'made sin' for us, infinite freedom demonstrates its amazing capacity to be itself even in a union with fallen nature, with guilty finitude. Here, on the Cross and in the Descent into Hell finite freedom is, in Balthasar's words, 'driven from its last refuge', and set on the road towards infinite freedom. As he writes:

> In concrete terms, infinite freedom appears on stage in the form of Jesus Christ's 'lowliness' and 'obedience unto death'. Thus he can call to himself the 'weary and heavy-laden' and summon even the clumsy and hesitant to be his disciples.[18]

And cautioning against such abuses of the self-revelation of infinite freedom as Ockhamist voluntarism, with its notion that God could will evil to be good, or Calvinist predestinarianism, which can hold an absolute reprobation of the non-elect, without any reference to foreseen demerits, Balthasar comments wisely:

> We need to keep ever before our eyes the way in which infinite freedom was pleased to appear in the midst of finitude, if we are not to be drawn aside into abstract (and hence falsely posed) speculative problems.[19]

18 *TD* II, p. 250.
19 *TD* II, pp. 250–251.

As God's 'Yes' to the world and the world's 'Yes' to God, Jesus Christ seals and implements the truth of the relationship between God and the world in terms of a Covenant between infinite and finite freedom.

Where infinite freedom is concerned, philosophy, theology's traditional handmaid, can, Balthasar thinks, to some extent instruct us. True, he sets his face against any metaphysical speculation which would find in the divine freedom a primal ground or – by way of referring to its un-plumbable, abyssal quality – 'non-ground' (*Ungrund*) beyond the divine nature, of the sort entertained in the Middle Ages by a Meister Eckhart or in the twentieth century by the Russian Orthodox religious philosopher Nicolas Berdyaev. Over against such thinkers, Balthasar maintains that anyone who says 'God' refers on the one hand to infinite reality, and on the other to that infinite reality's knowing and willing itself, grasping and affirming itself utterly, through and through. So far from the being of God containing something prior to his self-knowledge and self-affirmation which he must subsequently master, such a process of coming-to-be-oneself is characteristic only of what is *not* God. In God infinite being and infinite self-possession coincide; God's freedom is not something distinct from his nature, but is identical with that nature considered in its active quality, its defining activity.

But divine revelation adds more. Now we see not only that God is by nature free in his self-possession, but that for that very reason he is also free to do what he will with his own nature. Here Balthasar appeals to the dogmata of the Trinity and the Incarnation considered as throwing light on the revealed character of infinite freedom. God is so infinitely free that he can surrender himself as Father to share his Godhead with the Son, and as Father and Son to do the same with the Spirit. The Father is himself by giving himself to the Son; the Son is himself by allowing the Father to do with him as he wills; the Spirit is himself by understanding his 'I' as the 'We' of Father and Son. In other words, the absolute freedom found in God's self-possession is nothing other than his limitless self-giving. Looking at the divine mystery from the viewpoint of finite freedom one might have supposed that God's bliss lay primarily in his self-possession as infinite reality; but in God's own self-proclamation in Jesus Christ we learn that the bliss of absolute freedom lies elsewhere. It consists in *Hingabe*, 'self-surrender', that is, in *love*.

And this leads Balthasar both to the most doctrinally sensitive area of his theology (with the possible exception of his eschatology), and to his profound preferred solution to the riddle of how finite freedom can be integrated with its infinite origin and goal without thereby losing itself. And this is the claim that *between* the divine Persons lie great oceans of infinite freedom. In other words, the hypostases are not simply divinely free in that they possess each in his own mode the unique divine essence, which, in the way outlined earlier with the philosopher's assistance, is itself infinite freedom. Rather within a divine nature defined from start to finish by the modes of divine being which Father, Son and Spirit are, each of the Persons is *in himself* sovereignly free, even though at the same time the freedom of Father, Son and Spirit is also co-determined by the order of the Trinitarian processions in the relations of origin, and the unity of their substantial life in the relations of communion. Balthasar goes so far as to speak of the reciprocal 'petition' made by the Trinitarian Persons to each other, and to find in this the paradigm of all Christian prayer. Here, then, we have the root of Balthasar's controversial Trinitarian theologoumenon that while the divine nature may be unchangeable the manner of the interrelationships of the divine Persons is not.

And so the reason why Balthasar puts forward this idea is more than just a matter of wishing to inject a fuller theological realism into our account of the Incarnation, the Atonement and Pentecost – which could thus be dubbed the history of the Trinity and not simply the history of man with the triune God. In the context of the theme of infinite and finite freedom as opposing qualities of those involved in theo-drama, he finds here a way of showing how finite freedom (which he is as much anxious as any humanist to defend) need not fear its own obliteration or alienation when it enters the realm of the infinite. For 'letting-be' belongs to the very nature of infinite freedom, where each divine person subsists precisely *by being let-be*. Finite freedom can be what it fundamentally is, an image of infinite freedom, only when it aligns itself with the Trinitarian law of freedom as sheer self-surrender, and discovers that this law, so far from being foreign to it, is authentically its own.

Balthasar's theology of God the Son is especially important in this regard. That God should create a finite freedom other than himself without impairment of his own infinite freedom is only thinkable when we know that God in his own eternal being has already generated a Word, an infinite free centre of receptivity and expressiveness. As Balthasar sums up:

> Being totally dependent on divine freedom, the world can receive its possibility and reality nowhere else but in the eternal Son, who eternally owes his divine being to the Father's generosity.[20]

Or again:

> The 'nothing-out-of-which' the world came into being can only be sought in infinite freedom itself: that is, in the realms of creatable being opened up by divine omnipotence and, at a deeper level, by the trinitarian 'letting-be' of the hypostatic acts.[21]

Analogy between the world and God is possible in the last analysis only because the infinite distance between the world and God, itself negative, is grounded in the ultra-positive prototypical distance between God and God in the fruitful generation of the Word. This explains how Balthasar can call the Son made man the 'concrete analogy of being', and why too, returning explicitly to the theme of theo-drama, he can remark that:

> If a world is to come into being containing people endowed with finite freedom, requiring a drama to be played and a stage on which to play it, the Son alone can be its ground and goal; he alone can determine its entire course, irrespective, initially, of whether he himself will or will not appear in it as one of the main characters.[22]

20 *TD* II, p. 261.
21 *TD* II, p. 266.
22 *TD* II, p. 268.

Every production on the world stage must be judged ultimately by how, if at all, it has presented the coincidence of freedom and obedience which is the hallmark of the Word in whom the world was made, and this, looking ahead once again to the actual theo-drama which Father, Son and Spirit have produced in history shows how:

> when we come to discuss the individual human characters as role-bearers in the world drama, they will all be definable as persons within the total Person, as supporting roles to the title role.[23]

In playing a rôle as a person in Christ, the individual discovers the context for which 'autonomous motion' – the everyday experience of freedom – was made. At the same time, by locating the foundation of all finite freedom, all possibility of human dramatic action, in the divine Son, Balthasar can explain how in *fulfilled* freedom both uniqueness of personal identity *and* communion with others – those seemingly antithetical things – develop together. Since the Son, in his hypostatic distinctiveness, is infinitely unique, participation in him grounds the uniqueness of created persons who indeed must become the more defined in their uniqueness the more closely they answer the Father's call in Christ. At the same time, because this prototype, the hypostasis of the Son, really possesses the divine Being which is the source of being at large, the human person's self-opening to the prototype who grants him or her their uniqueness must also be the increasing abolition of all their dividedness, separation, from whatever else shares in being. So fulfilled freedom is not only entry upon true identity – becoming more myself; it is also communion – becoming more with others. Such communion is envisaged by Balthasar not in the manner of a simple personalism whose model is, so to speak, two persons looking at each other as they hold hands, but as the emergence of ever-new and unendingly varied dramatic plots – trails of developing and often unexpected interrelationships which, however, come together in the prototype who is both the foundation of the drama and its chief protagonist.

And this is, incidentally, the key to Balthasar's theodramatic ecclesiology. In concrete terms, the realm into which divine Providence ushers human freedom is the Body of Christ, a body which articulates itself in unique members or persons, each of which can only realise himself or herself through the exercise of ministries and charisms, ranging from the spectacular to the barely detectable, in a communal setting. In the words of Romans 8, persons in Christ are 'predestined to be conformed to the image of [God's] Son' inasmuch as, like Christ, they can be uniquely free to be themselves only insofar as they accept the dispossession of anything that is egotistically their own.

Exploring this ecclesiological theme would certainly not be a distraction from a consideration of Balthasar's Christology, for, biblically and doctrinally, the Head can never be without his Body, and, theologically, for such a Christocentric theologian as Balthasar wished to be in Barth's footsteps, all the theological treatises can and should be Christologically

---

23 *TD* II, p. 270.

expounded. Still, we must concentrate for the moment on theo-drama's chief presuppositions – which can now be seen to be 'the creation of finite freedom by infinite freedom' – termed by Balthasar 'the starting point of all theo-drama'.[24]

God 'latent' yet 'accompanying'

By virtue of the interrelation of infinite freedom with finite freedom, God is both 'latent' in his creation and yet also 'accompanies' it. What Balthasar is getting at is the way in which, while uncreated freedom is needed to liberate finite freedom (since the latter can only exist by participation in the former), a sort of divine 'withdrawal' is also prerequisite if 'between the giving of this gift and the use and exercise of it lies a certain interval that belongs to the human *autexousion*'[25] – to human freedom as relatively independent of God's. That God is present to finite freedom *incognito* – as the *latens deitas* of St Thomas's Eucharistic hymn, the *Adoro te* – makes it only too possible for the finitely free to enter on profoundly wrong choices in their deployment of freedom. It was indeed the divine plan that infinite freedom should follow errant man into utter alienation (the Son's Incarnation and atoning work), thence to bring it back to its Source in a new way. But this is simply the most dramatic illustration of how God as Providence *accompanies* human freedom, by a purpose which is 'maximal'[26] and to that extent *immutable* – though the word may mislead since what is at stake is his planning for the world the freedom to pursue his divine freedom, the freedom of the Holy Trinity.

For God's 'idea' of the world is at once infinite yet definite. It is infinite because

> in the Son, God reveals *himself*, and the model presented for man's participation and imitation is inexhaustibly richer than anything finite.[27]

It is definite because what could be better defined in its outline, harder in its edges, than the self-surrender of the Son, whose obedience (and here it might be helpful to glance at Balthasar's earlier 'theology of history')[28] is 'the internal norm of every human life and work'.[29] That combination – infinite and definite – explains, to Balthasar's mind, how the Letter of James could speak in its tacitly Christological ethics of 'freedom's perfect law' (1.25).

Balthasar's doctrine of Providence indeed, like so much in his work, is Christological in character – Providence is always 'progressive assimilation to the Son',[30] even if its Christ-oriented definiteness only gradually emerges. And as a few paragraphs ago we saw Balthasar's Christology about to give birth to an ecclesiology, so here, just because his account of

24 *TD* II, p. 271.
25 *TD* II, p. 273.
26 *TD* II, p. 279.
27 *TD* II, p. 281.
28 H. U. von Balthasar, *A Theology of History* (ET, New York and London 1963).
29 *TD* II, p. 281.
30 *TD* II, p. 282.

Providence is itself Christological, it would lead naturally (if the writer's design let it) into a description of the Church, Christ's Body.

> Whereas philosophy can envisage a providence only within the dialectic between the individual and the community of being – involving the dispute as to whether this providence is concerned solely with the universal plane or with the individual too – theology makes this dialectic concrete: it is a Providence that accompanies man toward the realm of the 'Body of Christ', which unfolds in unique members, each of them 'called' by name, 'foreknown' and 'predestined', with unique personalities which can only be realized in the form of ministries and charisms within the body-community.[31]

Ecclesial persons are uniquely free in themselves, since, with the Word incarnate, they are 'expropriated for the sake of the Whole'.[32]

Accepting freedom

Which brings us to the topic of what is involved in finite freedom's acceptance of its own true nature – the nature of a *gift*.

Someone has bestowed on us the 'Yes' of being. The 'given' of our being is no mere neutral Positivist datum but what the word implies. 'I am "gifted", the recipient of gifts.'[33] And the gift includes the awakening of a temporal and finite freedom by an eternal and infinite one – something that can only be understood, in the last analysis, by Trinitarian thinking.

> In and through the human 'I' there is manifested an Absolute 'I', who has from eternity generated an equally Absolute 'Thou' and, in the Holy Spirit, is One God with him. It is precisely this process of generation, this giving and receiving of self, and this oneness of both in the Holy Spirit that causes the absolute preciousness – we call it *holiness* – of Absolute Being to shine forth in its limitless self-affirmation and freedom. To himself, God is never 'just there' in the Positivist sense: rather, he is always the most 'improbable' miracle in that the utter self-surrender of the Father-Origin truly generates the coeternal Son and that the encounter and union of both truly cause the one Spirit, the hypostasis of all that is meant by 'gift', to proceed from both.[34]

Such Trinitarian thinking cannot do without the Christological and soteriological action which will occupy the next two volumes of *Theo-Drama*. As Balthasar writes, in what may be regarded as a commentary on St Paul's confession, 'I live by faith in the Son of God who loved me and gave himself for me' (Galatians 2.20):

> I only appreciate fully that God is my 'highest good' when I learn (in the Son) that I am a 'good' to him, affirmed by him; this is what

31 *TD* II, p. 283.
32 *TD* II, p. 284.
33 *TD* II, p. 286.
34 *TD* II, pp. 286–287.

guarantees my being and my freedom. And it is only when I learn
that I represent a 'good' and a 'thou' to God that I can fully trust in
the imparted gift of being and freedom and so, affirmed from and
by eternity, really affirm myself too.[35]

The 'affirmation' that much contemporary Western popular psychology
commends is rather more mysterious, evidently, than commonly believed.
What 'affirms' me is the knowledge that it is *God* who gives me to myself
– as a chain of testimonies from Christian tradition – Nicholas of Cusa,
Pierre de Bérulle, Fénelon, the giants among them – would have us see. It
is no pre-existent essence that comes to be by the gift of a share in the self-
bestowing divine act of being. It is I myself. What is gifted is not simply
my existence, as a way of participating in that inexhaustibly creative being.
My nature is penetrated to its very foundations by that way of being that
is mine. The gift then is not of being *simpliciter* but of being, more
specifically, an 'I', and, yet more wondrously, an 'I' that can not only call
on infinite freedom as 'Thou', but be addressed by that freedom as myself
a 'thou'. Now the appropriate response to a gift is gratitude to a giver, but
here the gratitude can be of no ordinary kind.

> We render thanks for our selves ... by responding, giving an
> answering word ... to the fact that we have been called 'thou'. We
> do this by progressively incarnating the word of thanks in our lives.
> This in turn is the progressive self-realization of finite freedom
> within the context of infinite freedom. More precisely, it is the
> realization, by the finite 'copy' (*Abbild*) of the definitive model
> (*Vorbild*) exhibited by the infinite prototype (*Urbild*); in this way finite
> freedom can truly participate in infinite freedom.[36]

Balthasar will return to that ancient language of man's 'imaging' of his
'archetype', rendered more nuanced by the agglutinative properties of
the German language, before he lays the theme of freedom aside.

Meanwhile, however, Balthasar is obliged by the terms of reference he
has made his own, to offer some comment on the topics of *prayer* and
grace. Finite freedom is the gift of the infinite: that explains at once the
rationale of worship, praise, thanksgiving, which are our immediate
response to this gift. But the 'progressive incarnation of the word of
thanks' includes more than this; it entails, as we heard, finite freedom's
fulfilment in the realm of infinite freedom – a realm which, if it really is
free, can only be *solicited* for its grace, its further self-gift. Here we
encounter then prayer not as doxology but as petition. To the philosophical problem raised by such prayer, *either* 'the Absolute is rigidly
immutable – in which case finite freedom can pray for nothing but
conformity with the infinite Will, and prayer, merely has the psychological
effect of promoting such conformity' (that appears to have been Kant's
position in *Religion within the Limits of Reason Alone*); *or* God 'is
"changeable" and thus, from our vantage point, finite and mythological',

---

35 *TD* II, p. 287.
36 *TD* II, p. 291.

Balthasar replies by a strictly theological answer, invoking as he does the saving covenant freely bestowed by the Holy Trinity.

> The 'good gifts' for which, in the spirit of the Covenant, man asks and which he infallibly receives (Matthew 7, 7–11) are ... nothing other than the 'Holy Spirit' of God, and this the heavenly Father cannot refuse his beseeching children (Luke 11, 10–13). If they are really his children, that is, belonging to his Covenant, they are already supported in prayer by the Holy Spirit who prays within them (Romans 8, 15 and 26ff.).[37]

Petitionary prayer understood as a sharing in the Trinitarian circumincession of Father, Son and Spirit easily slips free from the horns of the dilemma on which rationalist philosophers would impale it.

This is not simply a re-interpretation of what we are doing anyway in praying: it is an understanding that challenges finite freedom's acting in a way that explains (for Balthasar) all the conversions, personal revolutions and dramatic changes of vocation in Church history.

> Primarily and radically, finite freedom must succeed in relativizing its finite goals and aspirations insofar as they arise from the center of a finite, empirical 'I' or 'we'. It must allow everything it regards as good to be measured against an ultimate standard that lies on the yonder side of its finitude. It must slip out of its masks, roles and costumes, quit the world's stage on which it is accustomed to act and appear before the sole Master of the world play. He is, in the first place, simply infinite Freedom; what he will decide and do is a priori unknown to us, nor can it be deduced or even guessed from anything in the finite world.

And so

> Finite freedom must become unmade, must come to have no path of its own, must attain calm composure or indifference: this is the categorical precondition if it is to receive a vocation and destiny (going beyond the philosophical relation to the Absolute) from the hands of infinite Will.[38]

Such 'unmaking' does not lead Buddhistically to a pathless divine abyss for the self; rather does the Father refashion a finite centre of freedom in his Son, giving the person a 'path' of his or her own. This 'path' is sufficiently specific to constitute a unique life-pathway for the self, and yet like all such paths it refers the individual to the overall unity of creation in Christ. When finite freedom at last commits itself to infinite, that is not just for its own flowering. Infinite freedom takes the finite and introduces it into the initiative God took for the world's salvation. Despite Balthasar's reservations on the score of Eckhart's writing, he makes his own Eckhart's teaching on the unique *Weise* – here translated 'path' – each of the elect is to receive from God, his or her 'life-idea', what the New Testament will

---

37 *TD* II, pp. 302, 300.
38 *TD* II, p. 304.

call a 'charism' and Church tradition a 'vocation', the discernment of which lies at the heart of that supremely formative document in Balthasar's own life, the *Spiritual Exercises* of Ignatius Loyola. To find the 'treasure' of my mission I am justified in leaving behind everything – as so many parables and dominical sayings in the gospel imply.

Surely, though, such parables and sayings concern more fundamentally the Kingdom of God – which is a corporate, not an individual, reality? This consideration is perhaps what leads Balthasar to emphasise at once that my 'life-idea' can only be an aspect of the total idea for the redeemed creation God has in Christ. Our 'charism' cannot be sundered from the mystery of Christian initiation by Baptism and Confirmation: this basic truth of the Catholic catechism is no doubt what spurs Balthasar to link the gift of a 'life-idea' to that rebirth in God through Christ and his Spirit in the virgin-mother Church – a theme which will concern him not only in Volume III of *Theo-Drama*, where the interrelation of Christology, Mariology and ecclesiology is central, but also – and even more so – in Volume V, where the aim of the world's creation by the Holy Trinity is seen as our final entry into the Trinitarian life.

In this discussion, so Balthasar believes, the concept of *grace* has in fact emerged without our giving it that name. (It follows from the attempt to produce a Christian dogmatics in theodramatic form that we should not expect the matter of such a dogmatics to fall into the divisions of School divinity, or for its constituent parts to bear the titles of the traditional treatises.) Balthasar is curiously reticent when it comes to writing a theology of grace – it may be advantageous, he muses, not to pursue the topic cataphatically in too much detail, better to use an apophatic discourse which consists in saying what grace is not.[39] And indeed Balthasar's clearest statement *de gratia* is a negative one, when he writes:

> the creature is not 'in' grace, grace is in fact withdrawn ... when it endeavors to rest content with the freedom it has received and even to regard this freedom as originating in itself, imagining that, in virtue of its transcendent structure, it can open up the realm of self-transcendence through its own efforts.

If we ask what *positively* being 'in' grace is, the only answer we are given is that a graced creature must be one that 'follows through its indebtedness' (to infinite freedom) in the 'direction' not only of its 'origin' (by ceaseless gratitude) but also of its 'goal' – its home in God.[40]

The same determination – to replace (in, at any rate, the theodramatic context) the language of grace with that of the 'two freedoms' – is apparent in Balthasar's detailed excursus[41] on the theme of the 'image and likeness' of God in man which serves as the bridge to his brief 'dramatic anthropology'. Among the orthodox Fathers and Doctors there have been many ways of understanding those key terms of the book of Genesis. Balthasar, emboldened by the precedent offered by that star of the Catholic Tübingen

39 *TD* II, p. 312.
40 *TD* II, p. 314.
41 *TD* II, pp. 316–334.

School Franz Anton Staudenmaier, adopts an interpretation in terms of freedom (both men, one in the Romantic period, the other in the late twentieth century, were sensitive to the apologetic need to present the Church's faith as a gospel of liberty). 'Image and likeness' must be re-expressed 'in terms of finite freedom's nonheteronomy within the absolute character of infinite freedom'.[42] Thus far into *Theo-Drama*, we are hardly surprised to hear it.

42 *TD* II, p. 333.

6

Dramatic Anthropology

Since it is the Son-*made-man* that we are talking about, Balthasar must naturally flesh in the *human* side of the Saviour's composite reality. For an account of finite freedom in general is not yet an account of man in particular. The holy Angels too, after all, are finitely free, and if we may imagine, in solar systems beyond our own, the manifold crowning of creation in other rational species, they also will fit the bill of Balthasar's theodramatic theory so far. But immersed as we are in the factuality of the human condition, it is not these other possibilities that interest us, but the drama of man which, in the Incarnation, God has made his own.

> The relationship between infinite and finite freedom may constitute the basic formal datum of every theodramatic theory, but once man appears in all his concreteness, this drama becomes suddenly, abruptly real. So real that we cannot even attain an external vantage point from which to contemplate and evaluate it; we are caught up in the drama, we cannot remove ourselves from it or even conceive ourselves apart from it.[1]

Defining man?

It is a feature of the human *essence* that it cannot be seized except in the midst of dramatic *existence* – and yet the chief dimensions of that essence, in all their inner tension, *can* be seized there nevertheless. Volume II of *Theodramatik* ends with a wonderfully compact theology of man – pre-Christian, Christian, and post-Christian – where those dimensions, and their accompanying tensions, are set forth with a concision which would take an entire course of lectures on natural and supernatural anthropology for its full unpacking.

By way of preamble, Balthasar notes how, for so many religious and philosophical traditions, this animal that is so much more than an animal is *not really at ease*. It is not just that a being that belongs with the rest of cosmic nature, so far as its physical and sensuous life is concerned, has gone beyond that nature in its intellectual and spiritual capacities by a

1 *TD* II, p. 335.

kind of subtle prolongation of natural instinct (that was Nietzsche's opinion). More than this, that intellectual and spiritual life is frequently at war with its own instinctual basis (do we not affirm in the abstract the eirenic qualities that may make a man a social failure, and admire in the concrete the ambition and even ruthlessness that makes another a success?). Humankind is not simply an especially refined version of cosmic stuff. While we cannot deny our own biology, and its implications for our nature, biological data alone are woefully inadequate for suggesting the character of our self-realisation. The more we meditate on this hiatus, the more we appreciate how

> in spite of the fact that man is bound up with the world, there is
> something a-cosmic about him.[2]

And where, in culture and religion, the difference between God and the world is clearly espied (for under the sacred canopy of the pagan universe of the ancients the distinction between them did not fully appear), then the human person, discovering the God who is thus different from the world, gives that truly ultimate One his fullest allegiance – and in so doing emphasises his or her a-cosmic vocation. But is not this 'treason against the world'?

Balthasar does not propose to resolve this disparity. Instead, he argues that it cannot naturally be resolved. No combination of the elements of the human jigsaw that lie to hand can be produced which will make sense of the whole. No synthesis of the totality is possible for us, and in attempting one we would only truncate some essential aspect of the humanity whose wholeness we want to defend. God alone can make us make sense – and dramatically so – of the mystery of man.

> In a Christian theodramatic theory we have the right to assert that
> no other, mythical or religio–philosophical anthropology can attain
> a satisfactory idea of man, an idea that integrates all the elements,
> but the Christian one. It alone can release man from the impossible
> task of trying, on the basis of his brokenness, to envisage himself as
> not broken, without forfeiting some essential aspect of himself in
> the process.

Specifically, the way theodramatics places so precious a key in our hands is when it

> releases [man] from this burden by inserting him, right from the
> start, into the dramatic dialogue with God, so that God himself may
> cause him to experience *his* ultimate definition of man. This does
> not mean that man is dispensed from the effort of planning and
> fashioning himself, but he is shown the way to do it and the ultimate
> destination he should have in mind.[3]

The divine Creator, in his philanthropy, or loving kindness towards man, wills that man, and therefore the world, should make his home in God,

2 *TD* II, p. 343.
3 Ibid.

and freely so, in such a way that man can become what, without God, he could never be. To identify aright the human rôle – man's true dramatis persona – will turn out to mean positioning him on a 'Christian system of co-ordinates', for the two principle keys to the divine integration of the human puzzle (God as Creator, and God as He who loves mankind) are available in their fullness only in the religion brought by Jesus Christ who is at one and the same time the First-born of all creation, through and for whom everything was made, and the Only-begotten Son in whom man, and the creation with him, is predestined to enjoy the glorious freedom of the children of God.

Pre-Christian discoveries

Only when we see man's dramatic performance *vis-à-vis* the mystery of Christ do we see him for who he really is. Yet Balthasar is not so Barthian as to suppose that no elements of valid anthropology are visible at all to the pre-Christian world. Just as in his theological aesthetics, he regards the myth, philosophy and religion of classical antiquity as serving revelation both negatively (by showing up the inadequacy of human resourcefulness) and positively (in the media they offer it for its glorious epiphany), so here likewise, until Christ steps forward onto the stage, the action is incoherent, yet certain traits of the One in whose image and likeness we were made have already come to the fore.

Awareness of man's roots in the cosmos is the first of these. 'Anthropology' is a modern concept: 'In pre-Christian times the question of man is only posed in connection with the question of the whole of being'.[4] Balthasar stresses how the ancients situated man within a triad of elements: the divine; the cosmos; and, not least, the *polis* or 'city' which mediated between a cosmos not yet fully distinguished from its divine Source and the individual human person.

> The *polis* is the meeting place of the divine *nomos* of justice, which governs the cosmos, and that wisdom which 'ought' to govern man, which alone can guarantee justice in a particular state.[5]

The combination of the divine, the cosmic and the 'political' had a chemistry suggestive in different ways both of solids and of liquids. It was solid in that it gave pagan man a certain security. It was liquid in that the three ran into one another in an 'uncanny' fashion – for, as Greek tragedy demonstrates, failure to negotiate aright the interrelation of these elements can have disastrous consequences. Antiquity knew various attempts to synthesise what could be too unstable a combination of forces. In Hellenistic cosmopolitanism, the *polis* is expanded till it coincides with the cosmos. In the emperor cult, the cosmos is drawn into the *polis* so that the emperor's law is that of the gods. But while these will have some later Christian resonance, in the ideas of a transcendent 'City of God', based on creation and redemption, and of the 'imperial' Christ – *Christos Pantokrator*, Balthasar's eye, ever acutely theological, focuses rather on

4 *TD* II, p. 346.
5 *TD* II, p. 351.

the significance of what is surely the oldest of such 'syntheses', the parallel between the human microcosm and the macrocosm of reality at large. The theodramatic possibilities lying latent in this notion are twofold. First, because man is 'the epitome of the cosmic tensions and oppositions' – as Scotus Eriugena and Hildegard of Bingen will stress, and this is true; second, because the soul is related of its nature to 'the comprehensive unity of the world' – as St Thomas will emphasise in his notion of the soul as 'in a way, everything', *quodammodo omnia*.[6] Here the universe shelters man and indeed, according to Hildegard (whom Balthasar treats as the high point of this approach) is itself created 'hominiform', with a view to man. But Thomas qualifies so unified a view of the macrocosm–microcosm relation with one of his subdued yet potentially devastating Scholastic tags: our affinity with the universe is *quantum ad aliquid*, 'the case only in some respect'. Man is related more directly to God than he is to the world: it is not of the cosmos – even if we factor in its divine Source and its mediation in the *polis* (in Christendom, the *Ecclesia*) – that he is made 'to the image and likeness'. Stepping out from beneath the shade of the world (Balthasar regards the writing of Nicholas of Cusa as a milestone in this development), man looks around him in a consciously anthropological way for the first time. And it is now that the three innermost tensions of his being – spirit/body, man/woman, individual/community – declare themselves really insistently for the first time.

Three polarities

All three have it in common that they: (a) require of us a constant movement between the poles which the two terms in each pair represent; (b) find in death the supreme and brutal question-mark; and (c) for both of these reasons (antinomy and finitude) point us beyond themselves in the direction of a possible resolution that can only be transcendent in their regard.

Now the term 'polarity' in Balthasar's corpus derives from its use by his master from days at the Jesuit house of philosophy at Pullach, outside Munich: Erich Przywara. In his anthropological writings, the Polono-German Jesuit at once attempts a synthesis of all the wide-ranging material that comes under the head of 'Humanities' and at the same time tries to show how the aim of organising this material into a single 'form' (*Gestalt*) will surely fail: not (as might be thought) because – quite simply – there is too much of it, but for the more interesting reason that the internal tensions it reveals cannot be appeased.[7] As we shall see, Balthasar goes further – arguing, daringly, that the Christ event dramatically *heightens* the tension between the opposed poles, such that the human *agôn* must swing onto a new level before a solution comes into view.

---

6 *TD* II, p. 354, with reference to a chain of citations from Aquinas' work: *Quodlibetal Questions*, 4, a. 3; *Summa Theologiae*, Ia., q. 91, a. 1, c., and q. 96, a. 2; ibid., Ia. II ae., q. 17, a. 8, c. and ad ii; *De potentia*, q. 5, a. 10.

7 E. Przywara, *Humanitas: Der Mensch gestern und morgen* (Nuremberg 1952); idem., *Mensch: Typologische Anthropologie* (Nuremberg 1958); see also his commentary on the Ignatian Exercises, *Deus semper maior: Theologie der Exerzitien* (Vienna–Munich 1964²), I, pp. 49–68.

Spirit and body: here neither dualism nor monism will serve our turn. As Balthasar has already noted on the question, Is man essentially a cosmic being, or a metacosmic one? the 'natural polarity' whereby (looking from the dim beginnings) genetic development comes to its climax in mind or (looking back from the end of the process) the creative spirit modifies its own material infrastructure for its own purposes can also come across to us as an 'unnatural dichotomy' – and frequently does so:

> Man can be the ultimate blossom of nature, the epitome of the world, while at the same time, despite his bodily being, he remains pro-foundly alien to the time–space world of nature and strives to regain the lost original world.[8]

And when spirit and passions conflict in particular agonistic situations (so well summarised by Paul in Romans), our awareness of our simul-taneous 'greatness' and 'misery' (unsurpassably described by Pascal) becomes acute indeed. We can, if we wish, say optimistically that we are boundary beings, placed in a fascinating locale between beast and angel. But the liminal territory where we find ourselves looks suspiciously like a no-man's-land as well. Extreme spiritualisation is as de-naturing for us as extreme sensualisation – even if the latter be, all things considered, worse. We cannot rely on the serene accomplishment of a beautiful balance within ourselves between spirit and senses; instead, we must struggle, by virtue of our freedom, to make of ourselves a 'responsible spiritual-physical being'. And so

> the unity of the contrary movements can only arise out of a dramatic engagement.[9]

The fact that this 'unity' will have to be negotiated in the face of death (and how can it circumvent *that*?) points us to the ultimately Christological nature of the solution – in the risen Lord.

Man and woman: here is the second polarity, that a 'man is always in communion with his counter-image, woman, and yet never reaches her' (and vice versa of course, with woman and man). It might be supposed that, inasmuch as the human person is spirit, he or she would rise above the difference of the sexes. Balthasar, however, will have none of this.

> When the Adam of Genesis fails to find a partner among the animals, it is not because he lacks communication from spirit to spirit: what he misses is the relationship in which bodily things are com-municated spiritually and spiritual things bodily.[10]

The equality of man and woman is a nuanced affair. From the second of Genesis' two creation accounts, where Adam loses a 'rib' that Eve may be, Balthasar infers:

8 *TD* II, p. 358.
9 *TD* II, p. 364.
10 *TD* II, p. 366.

man retains a primacy while at the same time, at God's instigation, he steps down from it in a *kenosis*; this results in the God-given fulfillment whereby he recognizes himself in the gift of the 'other'.[11]

So a kenotic or self-sacrificing kind of 'priority' for Adam determines the texture of the equality which holds good between Adam and Eve. Here is (with a vengeance!) a possible source of tension – but note how for Balthasar everything divinely done in regard to the First Adam is ordered to the fulfilment of its meaning in the Second, Christ.

Balthasar takes more seriously than many modern students the assertions of the Fathers that in their state of original righteousness the proto-parents would not have known sexual arousal and the woman defloration as we know them now. The tension in which they lived with a cosmos they (by nature and by grace) transcended was such that the animal phenomenon of dying after mating – now, after the Fall, true of ourselves too, as Fichte and Hegel point out – in no way touched them. What form their union by eros would have taken he cannot say (he notes elsewhere it would be beyond the powers of lapsarian sexologists to describe);[12] what he definitely affirms is that to dispose of patristic commentary on these matters as quasi-Manichaean is superficial and trivialising.

Individual and community is the third and least intrusive, in the pre-Christian context, of anthropological polarities. Because the full meaning of what a 'person' is emerges only with Christianity, the tension between the communal and individual is simply, in the ancient world, not acute. It exists at the social periphery, for instance among the resident aliens and slaves without rights (and a liberation theology would rightly wish to ponder longer the significance of this than does Balthasar). But it is found only adventitiously, in special circumstances, by way of an act of expulsion of a citizen from the *polis* (and even the law of sanctuary, binding all communities, comes to his aid). The exception to these generalisations is one absolutely central to Greek tragedy: the fate of the hero or the king outstandingly endowed with knowledge of the 'divine law' who for whatever reason falters, such that his authority to promulgate the law of the city, and represent its order to the gods, is called into question.

Seen philosophically, however, tensions were bound to arise. It is intrinsic to the nature of humankind that each human being (male or female) perfectly embodies the concept of humanity – yet part of that concept is that every one who instantiates it does so as an individual, and therefore to the exclusion of others. As Balthasar points out:

> This very incommunicability is the precondition or reverse side of all spiritual communication. Not only does it require the reciprocal knowledge and recognition of the other as 'other' but also the freedom to detach oneself from the totality of the world (and hence from the community) and encounter the latter creatively, out of the uniqueness of one's own self.[13]

11 *TD* II, p. 373.
12 H. U. von Balthasar, *The Christian State of Life* (ET, San Francisco 1977), pp 92–95.
13 *TD* II, p. 388.

Moreover, the individual bound to the community, indebted to his fellows, experiences the further tension that, *by the same token*, he also has access to God. 'By the same token' because in Balthasar's inter-personalistic version of the inference to God's existence found in Transcendental Thomism all knowers know God implicitly in each and every mental act inasmuch as such acts spring from an original self-awareness where it dawns on us that we are '"gift" and "gifted", something which presupposes a "giving" reality'[14] – and where that realisation dawns on us precisely through another human being (our mother). 'Shared humanity and nonmediate presence before God are [therefore] inseparable in every individual.'[15] And it is not good enough to say, under the menace of dying, that the soul, the metacosmic, is what is essential to man. The question of death enters all three polarities in some shape or other to render them the more irresoluble. I write *'the more irresoluble'* since for Balthasar it is no use chivvying pre-Christian man for failing to solve the problem of basic anthropology: without divine provision of fresh resources it *could* not be solved.

Dramatic intensification

The irruption of the gospel makes things worse before it makes them better. The 'problem' begins with the revelation attested in the Hebrew Bible.

> The first sentence in the Bible, read against the total content of what it has to reveal, announces a sovereign freedom on God's part that is entirely different from that found elsewhere in the history of religion. It proclaims the creation of the world in its entirety – heaven and earth – out of nothing by the power of God's word and puts an end to the tendency of cosmos and physis to merge into the *theion*. Both cosmos and man are now on the same side: they are creatures vis-à-vis the God who creates them. This axis determines the entire, new system of coordinates and cuts through all the 'similarities' between God, world and man.[16]

As Gregory of Nyssa avers in his *On the Making of Man*, the difference between the divine and what is only like it is that which sunders uncreated from created.[17] True, the divine transcendence, now disclosed in its full extent for the first time, does not exclude God from his cosmos but, on the contrary, makes possible his intimate immanence within it. Never-theless, a more-than-cosmic God ceases to be a 'measure' by which man can judge his own qualities (or lack of them). Now 'he himself must submit to being measured and judged by God'[18] (a key notion, that, to the opening volume of Balthasar's theological logic).

---

14 *TD* II, p. 391.
15 Ibid.
16 *TD* II, p. 395.
17 Gregory of Nyssa, *De hominis opificio*, 16.
18 *TD* II, p. 396.

Creation *ex nihilo* indicates the absolute freedom of God who did not need to create in order to prove himself to be either Power or Love. (He is already inseparably both as the Holy Trinity, and, as Balthasar has already noted, it is because God's giving to his creatures is *motiveless* that it is 'good and full of meaning – and hence . . . beautiful and glorious'.)[19] The human creature must now seek its origin in the abyss of divine freedom – and this is a dizzy-making thought, for it implies that the image of God in man 'loses all objective visibility and ascertainability'.[20] Balthasar has already opted, in his excursus on the *imago Dei* idea, for the view that the 'image' lies in the created mirroring of uncreated freedom.[21]

Yet we cannot suppose (certainly Scripture does not) that simply constituting man as a free agent is the end of the story. This (the rational free creation) is only the first word, a word that renders its recipient receptive to words yet to come. As opening up the natural realm of truth, goodness, beauty, it is already inexhaustibly rich. And yet compared with the supernatural revelation that is to come, its richness is merely that of a promise. For subsistent Being himself is to open to man his own free inner life. In supernatural revelation, for which the 'free self-opening of one human subject to another' is the only comparison that does not entirely limp,[22]

> the Absolute bends down toward the creature, but it only reaches the creaturely level, substantially, by lifting the latter up, beyond itself and its entire natural substance, to its own level, giving it access and citizenship in the sphere of the Absolute.

And Balthasar marries the conflicting opinions in mid-twentieth-century Catholic theology as to whether such revelation is propositional or personal, when he goes on

> If it is to be a self-communication of the Absolute, it must be both ontological (substantial) and verbal (addressing the mind, explicatory): 'participation in the divine nature' without verbal communication is just as unthinkable as verbal communication without substantial participation.

Put less technically:

> If man is destined to share the divine nature, he must also be called to it in a way that is recognizable as such.[23]

And the effect of this is a dreadful heightening of those polar tensions we have explored. When Mother Nature loses her subsistence in favour of the only Self-subsistent, God, then:

> at the very moment when the creature addressed by God is lifted above itself, up to a nature that is essentially foreign to it,

19 *TD* II, pp. 272–273.
20 *TD* II, p. 397.
21 See above pp. 79–81.
22 *TD* II, p. 399.
23 Ibid.

hypercosmic and absolute, it plunges down into a hypocosmic abyss, which, however, is shown to be none other than the same abyss of God's freedom and power that lifts it above itself.[24]

The tension between the cosmic and the metacosmic was known to the pagans – yet not the principle of revelation thinking that, however great a similarity God reveals as between himself and the world, the dissimilarity is far greater, nor the spin put on that by Balthasar's mentor Erich Przywara when he wrote, in Balthasar's summary, that 'the more the creature is found worthy of intimacy with God, the more deeply he becomes aware of God's uniqueness and incomparability'.[25] Balthasar's own original contribution appears when he goes on to say that more (even) is involved: if and when the free divine self-communication to man happens, by the effective bestowal of the Word:

> the individual who receives the word acquires a new quality: he becomes a *unique person* . . . The 'person' only shines forth in the individual where the absolute Unique God bestows an equally unique name on him (unique because it is chosen by God), a 'new name which no one knows except him who receives it'.[26]

In one sense, only (Old Testament Jews and) Christians, then, together with those pagans who have received uncovenanted grace that assimilates them to the revealed economy (and with that grace, a mission), can be called 'persons'. Let us note, however, before the hands of liberally minded individuals are thrown up in horror, three qualifications to this statement. First, in one sense this is simply a verbal stipulation or, as Balthasar says, a 'question of terminology'. Secondly, it in no way impugns the dignity of that spiritual (and therefore rational) subjectivity of human beings as knowing and loving agents which is what common discourse takes a (human) person to be. If one wishes to retain the common usage, and yet be Balthasarian, it suffices to maintain that there are 'two forms or grades of personhood'.[27] And thirdly, 'every human being' can share the 'distinction' of enjoying a 'relationship of intimacy with God' – the relation which warrants the special use of the term 'person' in the first place – 'to some degree'.[28] Balthasar will expand his controversial notion of personhood in Volume III of *Theo-Drama*; here, however, we can note that it is required by the concept of theodramatic dramatis personae that not everybody can be regarded as players to the same extent, and indeed at a limit some are not at all – and in this sense the differentiated concept of what it is to be a person Balthasar proposes here is absolutely integral to his project.

It is often said today that, in a secularised society, the notion of 'sin' is losing its meaning. Balthasar would find this confirmatory of his presentation, since, on his view, only persons in the strong sense – those

24 *TD* II, p. 400.
25 *TD* II, pp. 401–402. Balthasar does not name Przywara here, but that this *is* a précis of his thought is undeniable. See my *Word Has Been Abroad*, pp. xiii–xiv.
26 *TD* II, p. 402, with an internal citation of Apocalypse 2.17.
27 *TD* II, p. 403.
28 *TD* II, p. 402.

who have received a supernatural identity, vocation and mission – *can* consciously sin. (Of course, *people* can still be *guilty* – but, as the linguistic evacuation of sin language suggests, that is not quite the same.)

Only where the biblical word of God is addressed to man

> as a 'commandment' that addresses the very core of his personality does the desire arise within him to act against it: 'Sin, finding opportunity in the commandment, wrought in me all kinds of covetousness.' The commandment is a function of the relationship between One who specially chooses and one who is specially chosen, that is, ultimately it is the function of a love relationship in which God grants us a participation in his own sphere, reserved to himself: 'Be holy, for I am holy'.[29]

If supernatural personification itself makes sin possible, how should we *not* expect the saving revelation to intensify dramatically any pre-existing tensions in anthropology!

That such tensions are perfectly contained in the God-man, Jesus Christ, shows, however, that they are not unbearable. The New Adam is now the exemplary man (though we must note that he is so in his human fullness which includes, importantly, the Resurrection). The polarities Balthasar has explored – spirit and body, man and woman, individual and community – are not abolished but they are creatively related by a 'new rhythm'. On *body and spirit*: previously, body was called to ascend to the level of spirit and spirit to descend to that of body (without *both* movements our humanity would be either too animal or too deracinated), but now the descending action of God in the Incarnation makes smooth that often jagged rhythm Christologically.

> In the new supernatural rhythm in which God becomes incarnate right down to the lowest depths and out to the farthest bounds, the physical is 'divinized', permeated with God's Pneuma, transfigured and 'transferred' into the kingdom of the Son, and hence of God. The Platonic Eros, striving upward from the bodily to the spiritual and divine, is overtaken in the event of Agape and brought to share in a fulfillment that goes far beyond its own upward thrust ...[30]

This is something which happens when humankind allows the Son to shape it Eucharistically into his 'body' (cf. I Corinthians 12.27). On *man and woman*: here the 'closed anthropological cycle of the sexes' where procreation was linked to guilt as well as death is opened up to a strange superfulfilment.

> The reciprocal fruitfulness of man and woman is surpassed by the ultimate priority of the 'Second Adam', who, in suprasexual fruitfulness, brings a 'companion', the Church, into being. Now the 'deep sleep' of death on the Cross, the 'taking of the rib' in the wound that opens the heart of Jesus, no longer take place in unconsciousness

29 *TD* II, p. 405, with internal citations of Romans 7.8, and Leviticus 19.2.
30 *TD* II, pp. 412–413, with an allusion to Colossians 1.13.

and passivity, as in the case of the First Adam, but in the consciously affirmed love-death of the Agape, from which the Eucharist's fruitfulness also springs.

Sexual fruitfulness becomes now essentially a metaphor – albeit an enacted metaphor, one lived out (literally) in human flesh – of a 'unique fruitfulness that bursts through the cycle of successive generations . . .'[31] On *individual and community*: in Christ, the individual – the *person* – receives a uniqueness that is dependent on no community, and yet this uniqueness is designed precisely to enrich the community of Christ's body with its many members. The individual–community polarity is transcended in the 'communion of saints' which itself rests, once again, on the incarnation of the Word and his continuing communication to the Church's members in the Holy Eucharist.

But the danger, for man in the Christian era, is our imagining that these fresh vistas opened up by the grace of Christ, inseparable from his Godmanhood and saving economy, are actually *postulates of human nature*. Such a misunderstanding is for Balthasar the root of the Gnosticism and Titanism which so marks the history of the post-apostolic period – above all in a 'post-Christian' society. It is characteristic of post-Christian man that

> in passing through Christianity [he] has grown used to the heightening of his creaturely rhythms and wants to hold on to them as if they are his personal hallmark, a gift that now belongs to him entirely.[32]

Thus secular eros claims the imperativeness of Christian agape; secular evolutionism covertly incorporates in its idea of matter that of divinely creative power; secular humanism treats man whom Christian revelation has disclosed to be now 'born of God' as himself ultimate, divine. The Prometheanism Balthasar studied in his earliest major work, *Apokalypse der deutschen Seele*, drew its nourishment, he now maintains in this new work of his late maturity, 'from the anthropological "heightening of tension" introduced by Christianity'.[33] And here Balthasar revisits these wartime products of his early studies in *Germanistik*. He sees as 'Titanic' not just the literature and philosophy animated by the Prometheus principle but also writing and thinking structured by the 'Dionysus' and 'Thanatos' principles as well.[34] For since what is ultimate in man cannot be mastered by the categories of reason however Promethean its grasp (as with Kant and the Idealists), the inevitable discovery which follows of man's 'suprarational natural vitality' generates Dionysianism. But Dionysianism in turn finds that the 'I' is fulfilled only in the flow of circumambient life – which calls forth a new 'supreme' principle, 'Eros–

---

31 *TD* II, p. 413.
32 *TD* II, p. 417.
33 *TD* II, p. 421. Compare H. U. von Balthasar, *Apokalypse der deutschen Seele*. I. *Der deutsche Idealismus* (Salzburg 1937), reprinted in 1947, with a new preface under the title *Prometheus: Studien der Geschichte des deutschen Idealismus*.
34 Idem., *Apokalypse der deutschen Seele* II. *Im Zeichen Nietzsches* (Salzburg 1939); ibid. III. *Die Vergöttlichung des Todes* (Salzburg 1939).

Thanatos', a theme which 'in this intensity, was unknown to antiquity and could only reach such a pitch under Christian provocation'.[35]

Thus late Western thought is filled with parodies of Christian belief. Balthasar treats under this rubric Hegel, Feuerbach, Marx, but most tellingly Sartre and Nietzsche in whom

> the 'gratis' quality of the divine self-giving in Christ, this eternally overflowing love, is perverted into meaningless 'superfluity' and hence absurdity.[36]

All these ideologies are in flagrant contradiction with each other because they miss that 'mid-point' which only the gospel can exhibit. As false versions of transcendence they necessarily ruin the finite human spirit. So too, in the post-Christian epoch, political 'edifices' arise which parody the (necessary) claim of the Church to attest the absoluteness of God's loving plan by false totalitarianisms of their own – or at any rate by attempting to pursue with purely immanent resources a future common good in hope.

The same inability to cope aright with anthropological tensions typifies post-biblical Judaism tempted by an excess of communitarianism in Marx, of sexuality in Freud, and pulled in two directions at once by a mysticism of the here and now in Hasidism, and the yonder in Cabbalistic Gnosticism.

> As yet, the Jew has not been granted the picture of the Risen Christ, the attained totality, the 'pledge' of a totality that still awaits us.[37]

This still barely described key actor, Jesus, will predominate in *Theo-Drama's* next volume.

---

35 *TD* II, p. 423.
36 *TD* II, p. 424.
37 *TD* II, p. 427.

PERSONS IN THE DRAMA:
THE PERSON IN CHRIST

7

The Agency of Christ

So far what has been said about Jesus Christ in the setting of theo-drama can appear to be, and in one sense is, wildly aprioristic – very much a Christology 'from above' – though we should bear in mind that Balthasar presents his theodramatics as an implicate of his theological aesthetics, and so can take for granted what is said there about the humanity of Jesus and its transcendent, Trinitarian dimension, under the heading of the 'objective revelatory form'. In point of fact, however, he takes the opportunity provided by the third volume of *Theodramatik*, *Persons in Christ*, to engage more fully with the modern critical study of the New Testament and to offer, somewhat surprisingly, a 'Christology from below' which will confirm, illuminate and supplement what can be inferred of the character and activity of the God-Man from the experience of the concrete interaction of divine and human freedom found in the Church.

What Balthasar means by a 'Christology from below' is not of course a value-free investigation of who and what Jesus of Nazareth considered himself to be, and how his claim might be assessed. For Balthasar, such neutral presuppositionless enquiry is not only an epistemological chimaera; it also has nothing to do with authentic theology or, rather, fails to meet the scientific demands of Christian theology, its internal requirements of cognitive appropriateness to its own subject matter. A 'Christology from below' is not, then, an approach to the Jesus of history which brackets Christian faith, though all the material discussed by students of the Jesus of history, whatever their background, is germane to such a Christology. Rather is a Christology from below an investigation of the genesis of Christological faith within what Balthasar calls the 'ellipse', the bi-polar orbit, of study and thinking which connects the Easter faith of the first disciples with the object of their faith, Jesus who became Christ.

Balthasar's hundred-page methodological study of *Leben Jesu Forschung*, 'life of Jesus research', engages with or at least alludes to most of the major names in such studies, and not only in the German-speaking world, from David Friedrich Strauss in the 1830s to Martin Hengel today. As in *Herrlichkeit*, his first concern is with retrieving the form which Jesus' humanity took in and of itself, though now, in dialogue with such scholars, he naturally gives closer attention to the exegetical debates, while, at the same time, so as not to lose touch with the specifying approach of theological dramatics, laying more weight on New Testament apocalyptic, the element in the written deposit of the apostolic age which more than any other shows the intra-mundane drama where Jesus was an actor expanded into a theo-drama that embraces both God and man, heaven and hell. While not denying the rôle of early Christian creativity in applying to Jesus fresh ideas, concepts and titles – the building-blocks of the various theologies found within the New Testament canon, Balthasar makes it clear that, in his judgment, the effect of such constructive activity was not to overlay something originally much less impressive but to bring out the content of the phenomenon of Jesus in something like its full dimensions for the first time. As he writes, with Strauss' epoch-making *Das Leben Jesu* in mind:

> The decisive question ... is: Has this process articulated an original 'form', identified its significance and revealed its true outlines – or has it taken what was originally a relatively form-less core and clothed it in successive garments, which ultimately yield a ... [mythical *Gestalt*].[1]

Or, thinking this time of Bultmann, he aks whether

> If we compare the weight of the full gospel kerygma with some pre-Easter substratum (a hypothetical reconstruction of extremely meager proportions), the former is so overwhelming that the latter can be dismissed as insignificant as far as faith is concerned[2]

– a question which, if answered affirmatively, would effectively return us to Strauss' position, for an Easter kerygma suspended over such a historical void hardly deserves any other name than that of a myth. Or, and most simply, apropos of Martin Kähler who, writing between Strauss and Bultmann, and despite his enormous influence on the terms of subsequent discussion, never faced the question of the underlying justification of exegetical research: 'To what extent is the object of this proclamation a historical "fact"?'[3]

Balthasar's answers to these questions will constitute, then, the exegetical foundations of his Christology. He prepares them by establishing a number of salient points. (It is relevant to note that each succeeding point takes us further back in time towards the *Urphänomen* of Jesus himself.) First, and in dependence on Hengel, in the mere quarter-century which separates the death of Jesus from the close of the Pauline corpus, we find already formed the ideas of Jesus' pre-existence and divine nature, his rôle in creation and sending by the Father. Secondly, and within a few years of the first Easter, Jesus' disciples made use of a wide range of Old Testament paradigms to interpret his teaching and the events of his passing over to the Father – from which, leaning on the exegete Gerhard Delling, Balthasar draws the conclusion that already during his

---

1 *Theo-Drama. Theological Dramatic Theory*. III. *Dramatis Personae: Persons in Christ* (ET, San Francisco 1992), p. 64. Cited below as *TD* III.
2 *TD* III, p. 67.
3 *TD* III, p. 77.

earthly ministry Jesus had presented himself as 'the complete exegesis of the word of God'. Thirdly, though distancing himself from the views of Harald Riesenfeld and Birger Gerhardsson on the proto-rabbinic nature of the group Jesus gathered around him, Balthasar accepts a more modest Germanic form of that Swedish thesis to the effect that, within the 'socio-logical continuity' of those who professed faith in him even before Easter, Jesus supplied for his disciples material suited to their original preaching of the Kingdom during his lifetime in the shape of consciously fashioned *logia* – dominical 'words' or sayings. Fourthly, and given that even in the pre-Easter period such disciples must have been called upon to say *something* about the person who had despatched them on their mission, Balthasar makes his own some words of Walter Grundmann:

> It is quite impossible to give an intelligible account of how a story about Jesus, which attached no saving significance to his person, could have given rise to a proclamation that is solely concerned with his saving significance.[4]

These four points taken in their convergence indicate what Balthasar terms 'continuity in discontinuity', though it should be noted that Balthasar is also interested in 'discontinuity despite continuity' – for, as he remarks, the crucifixion, death, burial and Resurrection of the Lord both separate and unite. These events, that is, both transform the figure of the pre-Easter Jesus and at the same time reveal that figure's ultimate significance.

What Balthasar has so far established is that the theologically ambitious ideas, concepts and titles found in the Christology of the New Testament may well be rooted in, rather than projected onto, the behaviour and attitudes of this Jesus who became Christ. And this brings him to confront a series of questions such as, first, What is the relation between Jesus' pre-Easter claim and the Easter event? Secondly, what did Jesus take as the goal of his efforts? Thirdly, did he expect the transcendent in-breaking of the definitive Kingdom of God during his own lifetime? And finally, in what frame of mind did he face his approaching violent death? From his discussion of these four questions – which takes place, once again, in a polylogue with many other exegetes of diverse standpoints, Balthasar singles out two concepts which, when juxtaposed, yield the key to Jesus' understanding of his own mission. And, as we shall see, it is on the basis of the idea of the *mission* of Jesus that Balthasar will construct, in a most original way, his doctrine of the *person* of Christ.

What then *are* the two concepts thrown up by a search for the Jesus of history which has already established, at least to its own satisfaction, the continuity in discontinuity between the pre-Easter Jesus and the Easter Christ, concepts that, taken (as is not normally the case) together, can yield Balthasar such far-reaching results? They are Jesus' sense of time on the one hand, and, on the other, what Balthasar calls the *pro nobis* – a portmanteau term which covers such formulae as 'for us', 'for you and for the multitude', 'for our sins' – and stands for the redemptive aim of Jesus' activity.

4 *TD* III, p. 86.

Jesus' use of the time-categories of apocalyptic was entirely his own: as a result Jesus' eschatology was both totally futurist and absolutely realised, an apparent paradox whose resolution Balthasar will shortly provide. Jesus *both* looked ahead to a reality that is infallibly coming, *and* did so in the 'calm security' of someone living entirely for his mission here and now. He did not merely live with a view to what he called 'that hour', but anticipated it by living constantly in the immediacy of the mission given him by the Father. Jesus enjoyed, then, a unique theological sensibility for time, and this means that the prophecy of an imminent in-breaking of the divine Kingdom into the temporal order of this world need neither be written off as a sheer mistake nor sanitised by being presented as a misunderstanding on the part of his disciples. For it is perfectly possible to suppose, and indeed makes best sense of the evidence to assert, that Jesus saw the time of this world *within* the unity of his own destiny, rather than, as with any other human being, locating and measuring his destiny within the flow of world-time. And thus what for him was fulfilment in the glorious Resurrection and the Parousia of the Son of Man could be for the world simply a movement towards fulfilment – thus making possible, of course, the time of the Church.

To this concept of Jesus' unique sense of saving time Balthasar now adds that of the *pro nobis* – the notion of a redemptive thrust to his activity, including there most importantly his death, summed up in the pre-Pauline formulations of the earliest apostolic *paradosis* on the Eucharist and the Resurrection in I Corinthians 11 and 15 respectively. There we read of the giving of his body *huper humôn*, 'for you', his dying *huper tôn hamartiôn hêmôn*, 'for our sins'. The exegetically inescapable conclusion that Jesus possessed a unique sense of time illumines this unavoidable datum of the earliest dogmatic tradition and is in turn illuminated by it. Jesus' consciousness of his mission was that he had to abolish the world's estrangement from God in its entirety – that is, to deal with the sin of the whole world. It is in the light of the *pro nobis* that Jesus' attitude to time becomes clear. For on the one hand, he is entirely dedicated to the Father at every moment of his earthly life; his earthly work and prayer form part of his redeeming task which is not, then, concentrated solely in the future, on the Cross. Precisely this gives Jesus his constant serenity, and enables him to speak of the Father's righteous love, its mercy and its demands, as a reality here and now. But, on the other hand, his life cannot, as Balthasar puts it, 'follow along "wisdom" lines; it must have an "apocalyptic" rhythm'. The decisive part of his earthly mission is still to come; his life is moving towards a 'baptism', towards the 'cup' he must drink and which will prove in the drinking humanly unbearable, stretching him beyond all limits. As Balthasar writes:

> His life is running toward an *akmê* [a culminating point] that, as man, he will only be able to survive by surrendering control of his own actions and being determined totally by the Father's will ... For this surrendering of control to the Father is essential if, in this hour, the single, indivisible event that [the *pro nobis*] requires is to take place: he must bear the totality of the world's sin ... being 'made to be sin' ... becoming 'a curse' ... by the all-disposing will of the

Father. If we can define the core of apocalyptic as the imminent expectation of God's final judgment of the old world, and therefore the change of aeon to a new world, we can say that this apocalyptic dimension ... is most definitely concentrated in him, his person, his span of life (including his death), his destiny. He has to deal with the world and its time on the basis of his unique, temporally circumscribed, human existence: his final 'hour' contains the entirety of world-time, whether or not the latter continues to run, chronologically, 'after' his death.[5]

We catch a faint echo of this stupendously dramatic, indeed world-shaking event when we consider what is involved in our own dying. As our individual life story comes to its consummation in the presence of God, eschatological reality cuts across intramundane time. And while this is only of significance for the individual, it does provide us with some understanding of how the unique death of Jesus could open up a fulfilment that slices into history at an angle – but a fulfilment, this time, of a *universal* kind. Or, to cite Balthasar himself again:

It is in virtue of the 'pro nobis' of *this particular* death that we are drawn into the situation in which all things are fulfilled in the kingdom of God.[6]

Although Balthasar reserves his full theology of the Atonement for the volume of *Theodramatik* which concerns the central dramatic action of Incarnation and Passion, he lifts the curtain here sufficiently to give us a glimpse of the most important of that drama's leitmotifs. And that is the idea of *Stellvertretung* – at once representation and vicarious substitution. In the Pauline Letters, Jesus takes the place of others in various senses: cultically, as the sacrificed Passover Lamb, the expiation on the Day of Atonement, sin offering and whole-offering; juridically, in terms of the sacral law, for God has condemned sin in his flesh and nailed to the Cross the bond that stood against us; from the point of view of slavery, for Christ himself enters slavery in our place; and from that of his obedience, which wipes away the disobedience of Adam. And all these ways of saying that Jesus has accepted the weight of the world's sin, together with other forms of the *pro nobis* found in notably I Peter and Hebrews, are essential if we are to understand his attitude towards his 'hour' – if, in Balthasar's own words we are adequately to

explain the abyss that opens up before his eyes: it is a 'hiatus' that robs his own time of any synchronicity with any other time, including that of his disciples.[7]

Here 'quantitative dis-chronicity' – a *quantity* of time out of joint – implies 'qualitative dischronicity' – a *quality* of time out of joint. Since Jesus is the 'way', he must be the first to open a path through the trackless region of atonement, as the Writer to the Hebrews saw so clearly. This

5 *TD* III, pp. 110–111.
6 *TD* III, p. 113.
7 *TD* III, p. 115.

enables Balthasar to present his solution to the exegetical riddle of the
Son of Man. Did Jesus identify himself with that transcendent figure or
not? That he should have seen himself as the herald of a yet greater
redemptive agent in no way accords with his attitude to a future already
breaking in upon the present, and yet, as Balthasar puts it:

> If, nonetheless, he said 'Son of Man' instead of 'I', it would show
> how stupendous and unimaginable he found the relationship
> between the two sides of his own self: on the one hand, he was
> someone living on earth with a particular mission that, humanly
> speaking, he could carry out; and, on the other hand, he was
> plunged into a mission that had been eschatologically stretched
> to the breaking point through the experience of the 'hour'
> (Passion–Resurrection), with an outcome that, at present, was quite
> unforeseeable.[8]

The recovery, albeit with an all-pervasive Balthasarian flavour –
discernible in the handling of such themes as death, freedom, power and
evil – of a thoroughgoing Anselmian doctrine of redemption is, in
Balthasar's view, essential to a full-bloodedly theodramatic account of
the Cross. To reduce the Cross, as does for instance Hans Küng, to no
more than a demonstration of God's gracious solidarity with sinners is to
make of it no more than an audio-visual aid, teaching, moreover, a lesson
about a God who actively pursues reconciliation that had already been
learnt by many people in the Old Testament. In reality, however, the actual
event of reconciliation is dramatic in the extreme, both within the
Godhead, as between God's wrathful justice and his merciful love, and
between God and man, for the Covenant must be fulfilled on both sides,
not just from God's but from man's too. But here, over against the classical
Protestant version of this doctrine, a Catholic employment of the notion
of representation has to take into itself that of humankind's incorporation
into Christ, since the action and suffering of our representative must have
an inner, ontic effect – and not merely an external, forensic, one – on those
human persons involved in theo-drama, in whose place he stands.
However, to speak at all of the one nailed to the Cross as both the
representative man in solidarity with sinners and God's Word and Son,
given up by the Father, is of course to anticipate Balthasar's movement of
thinking in a Christology from below which has not yet reached its goal
in the affirmation of Jesus' divinity.

The key concept in Balthasar's move from an account of the Jesus who
became Christ to his affirmation of the eternal divine origin of Jesus Christ
is *mission* – and that need not surprise the Thomists among us since for St
Thomas (as already mentioned) the *missio* of Jesus is the human continuation, or embodiment in space and time, of the eternal *processio* of the
Word from God. But Balthasar's way of reaching Thomas's conclusion is
utterly his own.

What we have established so far within the ellipse of Easter faith seen
as a testimony to that faith's object, Jesus who became Christ, is that Jesus

8 *TD* III, pp. 116–117.

possessed a sense of mission both eschatological and universal. Within the dimensions of his human existence, including his death and so surrender to the Father's future vindication, he was to complete a task that would affect all creation. This necessarily implies, so Balthasar points out, that not only was the mission unique, so also was the missionary, the One sent. Whereas in the case of the prophets their human being and their divine function were distinguishable, here we are dealing with someone who never was and never could have been anything other than the One sent. And so the question is raised whether, in Balthasar's words, he can

> be 'sent' in such an absolute sense that his mission coincides with his person, so that both together constitute God's exhaustive self-communication?[9]

The idea of mission, of being 'sent' or of having (in some heightened solemn sense) 'come', 'come out' or 'forth', is not only Johannine but also Synoptic. In the Parable of the Wicked Husbandmen, moreover, all three Synoptic evangelists agree in distinguishing between the earlier sending of 'servants', and the final sending of the 'son'. But it is in John above all that Jesus' knowledge of himself coincides with his knowledge of being sent. He does not do the Father's will incidentally but lives from it, for apart from it he can do nothing. The One who sends is seen to be present in the One who is sent. The latter is so dependent on the One who sends him that his entire being is in motion towards him: he is returning to him. Anyone who has a part in the Son must himself be sent out from the Son's source, that is, be born of God, born anew. All of this implies something more radical than the appointment of any mere *shaliach*, any messenger. Where a person is entrusted with a mission so substantial that he is summoned to put his very existence at its disposal, the person thus sent might become to a degree identified with the mission. But Jesus speaks as if the Father loved the person of the Son *only because* this person is identified with his mission, 'For this reason the Father loves me, because I lay down my life' (John 10.17). It is for all the world as though the imparting of mission here coincides with an imparting of being. 'This *is* my beloved Son [perhaps, originally, "Servant"]: listen to him' (Matthew 17.5, and parallels).

Using this concept of mission as a key term, Balthasar can put forward what he calls a Christology of consciousness and, on that basis, a Christology of being, two ways, the second deeper than the first, of looking at the work and person of Christ. The Christology of consciousness explores the coincidence of Jesus' mission-consciousness with his person. This mission, itself more than human, for to reconcile the whole world with God is not a simply human undertaking, is in no way heteronomous *vis-à-vis* the person of Jesus. It is not imposed from without like a law, for his 'I' is identical with it. On the other hand, it has, apparently, always been present in his consciousness; it is not something he has conceived and taken upon himself as a private individual. Rather, he *is* the task of

9 *TD* III, p. 150.

fulfilling this universal design; it is for the sake of his mission that Jesus is this particular human being. And both person and mission are experienced as springing in unity from the source that is the Father. The task given him by the Father, to express God's Fatherhood through his entire being, by means of his life and death for the world, totally occupies his self-consciousness. 'Who he is' is exhaustively expressed in his being from the One who addresses him as 'My beloved Son'.

This might appear to make Jesus completely independent of other figures in the theo-drama, undermining Balthasar's claim that it is through a constellation of figures that the Author, aided by the synthesising work of the Director, directs the audience to the ultimate meaning which is his goal. But, on the contrary, Balthasar draws from his account of Jesus' 'absolute' mission-consciousness inferences important both for his Mariology and for what he has to say about other figures who co-act with the Jesus of history. For, on Mary, given that it would appear essential for self-consciousness to be awakened by a 'thou' and subsequently initiated into a world of spiritual tradition, then, if Jesus' self-consciousness coincided with his sense of mission, the Mother who initiated this Child into an I–thou relation for the first time must have played a unique rôle in awakening his mission-consciousness likewise.

> Without this spiritual handing-on, which takes place simultaneously with the bodily gift of mother's milk and motherly care, God's Word would not have really become flesh. For being-in-the-flesh always means receiving from others. Even if the One who receives the word of tradition is himself 'the Word from the beginning', from whom all genuine tradition takes its origin, he must accept this earth-grown 'wisdom' as a form – in the terms of the world – of his Father's will and providence. So we see that the Incarnation of the Word that brings the promised fulfillment, or the 'new and eternal Covenant', has an inherent need of an antecedent history that we call the 'Old Covenant'; in Mary, the (Abrahamic) faith that characterized this Covenant becomes a contributory element in the Incarnation.[10]

And again, on other figures in the Jesus story:

> The mission of Jesus has no conceivable temporal beginning. But as it unfolds through historical time, it enters increasingly into history. It awaits God's signal for its fulfillment not only purely from within: it also awaits it from without, because the mission will be fulfilled essentially in a fulfillment of history; the Father's will is encountered in history no less than in interior inspiration. [Thus for example] from all indications, the Baptist's appearance and fate served as a sign to Jesus that he should begin his public ministry.[11]

And in all this, Jesus' continuous handing himself over to the Father through the inner and outer events of his life is presented by Balthasar as no mere passivity, but on the contrary as a kind of action which, humanly

10 *TD* III, p. 177.
11 *TD* III, p. 178.

speaking, demands more of the subject in terms of self-possession and initiative than would the pursuance of self-imposed precepts and goals. I write 'humanly speaking' because the free obedience of Son to Father is achieved in fact through the Holy Spirit. The coincidence of Jesus' primordial freedom with the will of the Father points back to a mysterious supratemporal event where Father and Son co-originate in the Spirit the sending forth of the Word in the likeness of sinful flesh. Appealing to the Filioquist pneumatology of the Catholic Church, Balthasar proposes therefore to throw light on the consciousness of Jesus in relation also to the Spirit. Just as, on the basis of his eternal origin, the Son has received power to breathe forth the Spirit, so similarly, in his Incarnation he already has within him a docility *vis-à-vis* the Spirit. The Spirit is *in* him in fullness as the Gospel of John testifies (3.34), so that the Son can surrender himself to this guiding Spirit without any sense of heteronomy. Nor does this in any way render otiose the human will of Jesus, for such sublime inspiration arouses in the person inspired – as the example of artistic inspiration would show – a deeper freedom than that involved in arbitrary choice, and thus enables more of the person to be stamped on it: something Balthasar tries to illustrate from Mozart's *Die Zauberflöte*. Jesus uses his temporal human freedom to ratify and hold fast to the eternal, divine free act in which he has consented to the Father's will to save, according as he is inspired to do by the Holy Spirit who is the presenter of the Father's commission.

How can such a missiocentric theology of the consciousness of Christ provide the basis for a theodramatic theory? First, in the identity of Jesus' person and mission we have the realisation *par excellence* of what is meant by a dramatic character: a figure who by carrying out his rôle attains or discloses his true face. In theo-drama, Jesus will be therefore not only the chief character but also the model for all other actors.

Secondly, it is only the identity of character and mission in Jesus Christ which makes the *world*-drama a *theo*-drama. For *this* identity derives from the fact that the agent concerned has been given a mission not accidentally but as a modality of his eternal personal being. Only the mission of the Son brings in its train the mission of the Spirit – to begin with in Jesus' 'state of emptying', the *status exinanitionis*, from Incarnation to Cross and Descent into Hell, thanks to the Father's sending of the Spirit upon the incarnate Son (something which Balthasar links to the moment in the immanent Trinity when the Son receives from the Father the power to share in breathing forth the Spirit), and then in Jesus' 'state of exaltation', the *status exaltationis*, from Easter to Pentecost, when the Spirit is sent from the Father and the exalted Son upon the Church and the world (something which Balthasar connects with the participation of the pre-existent Son in the Spirit's actual spiration). And this alone opens up the triune God's involvement in the entire world-drama. For this play is not 'theodramatic' simply as organised by God and produced for him in his presence. God himself has actually appeared in it in Jesus Christ the Son of the Father who possesses the Spirit 'without measure'.

But then, thirdly, the mission Christ is given of expressing the Father in human form means that he has to embody mankind's whole dramatic situation in its relation both to itself and to God. He has to express the likeness of God within the shattered image. He is, in Pauline language, the Last Adam, who is to give meaning to the entire play. Through not only his personal destiny in Cross and Resurrection but also, by way of the entire ensuing world drama which he affects, he becomes, in Johannine language, the Omega which, as the Alpha, he was always meant to be.

So far we have not touched on Balthasar's theology – also mission-centred – of the *being* of Christ, under which rubric Balthasar situates his notions of the unity of person in Christ, his twofold nature or being, and the relation of the totality of human nature as well as individual human beings to Christ and his work. These are, of course, the principal themes of the classical ontological Christology as found, say, in Maximus the Confessor and Thomas Aquinas, on both of whom Balthasar will draw. But all is changed by being re-presented in theodramatic guise. It is Balthasar's theology of Christ as a person which is most unusual. For he argues that the concept of personhood not only originates, historically speaking, in Christology and its Trinitarian dimension, but (more than that) philosophically and theologically remains *even today* unavailable without reference to Christ. Although, as we saw in the Prolegomena to *Theodramatik*, the conscious subject knows he is human in a unique and incommunicable way, *quantitatively* different from all other conscious subjects, yet no fundamental ontology can show him that he is *qualitatively* different from all others – show him *who* he is, rather than *what* he is. In the web of provisional evaluations and re-evaluations which makes up human life, even at the deepest level of interpersonal relations, no unquestionable, non-precarious assurance can be given me as to my qualitative identity. That can only be given, if it ever *is* given, by the absolute Subject, God, and until given I remain a conscious subject, certainly, but not a person.

> It is when God addresses a conscious subject, tells him who he is and what he means to the eternal God of truth and shows him the purpose of his existence – that is, *imparts a distinctive and divinely authorized mission* – that we can say of a conscious subject that he is a 'person'.[12]

Consequently, for Balthasar others can claim to be persons only by virtue of some dependent relationship with Jesus Christ. Though we cannot speak in their case of an identity between mission and 'I', we *can* say that as conscious subjects they are endowed with a part or aspect of his universal mission. The sending of the Spirit will imply a genuine distribution of rôles to actors in the form of missions or charismata. This is why the Johannine Christ can declare it good that he goes from the disciples, for only thus is his drama opened up for his fellow-actors and actresses and becomes the stage for the action of the reciprocal indwelling of God and man. Set in motion by the departure of Jesus, this is a per-during event in which new players can continually act their parts – appearing on stage and leaving it – without their personal acting being

12 *TD* III, p. 207 (italics added).

condemned as sheer futility. We become persons only by receiving from God a mission in Christ, which is why for Balthasar initiation into the life of the Church entails nothing less than ontological transformation.

Nor is this surprising if in conclusion we return to the start of this chapter and reflect that our coming forth as free creatures has its archetype in the generation of the Word. If the analogy between the Son's eternal begetting and our own creation can provide a bridge both to the *Son's* becoming a creature and to *our* evangelical rebirth from God, then, when the Son becomes man, that analogy between divine and human being takes on concrete existence in the Logos made flesh. Hence our deepest identity as the children of God can only be found in a re-orientation on Jesus Christ of our rôles in the world play. Absolute freedom has prepared a personal path for each of us to follow freely, in the liberated freedom which alone permits true self-realisation. Yet the Kingdom of God – which is 'present' in Christ and to the Church is 'coming' – has to assert itself by fighting in the rest of the world drama still to be played. In this continuing *agôn* there remains a constant temptation to follow the course of this world as defined by powers hostile to God. Balthasar's eschatology, in the concluding volume of the theological dramatics, will map out what this struggle over the world entails, describe our essential involvement in it, and that final judgment upon us which has as its foundation the fact that, risen as we are in Christ, we are able – whether we realise this capacity or not – to engage in that *actio* in which the *bonum* shows itself to be, in the full sense, the *transcendentale*, that is, action in which the fruitfulness of the Sacrifice of Christ is shown forth, the very thing that *Theo-Drama* sets out to display.

8

The Feminine Counterpart

Our Lady

As already mentioned, it is integral to Balthasar's project that the dramatis personae are precisely that – persons in the plural, even though there is no playing on this stage without reference to the Son whose human rôle is Jesus. Salvation is no mere dramatic monologue, which one man might act, but a genuine *inter*play, reflecting the discovery of theological aesthetics that revelation strikes us via a *constellation* of figures. Admittedly, conscious subjects – who are, we recall, not yet for Balthasar 'persons of theological relevance', or 'coactors in theo-drama' –

> cannot enter this acting area of their own accord; even less, once they are admitted, can they choose their own theological role. But ... [nonetheless] this area is one which, through Christ, creates and maintains freedom in God; and if man freely affirms and accepts the election, vocation and mission which God, in sovereign freedom, offers him, he has the greatest possible chance of becoming a person, of laying hold of his own substance, of grasping that most intimate idea of his own self – which otherwise would remain undiscoverable.[1]

Election, vocation, mission: these will be, then, the tell-tale signs of Christ's counterparts – of all other theological persons. Though prepared in God's foreknowledge, players other than Christ receive their vocation in a special moment of salvation history and they are, characteristically, not only unsuspecting but, in their own estimation, ill-equipped for their tasks. Scripture's stress, however, lies on God's operation, not man's response; and yet in being servants of their mission the actors chosen are not submerged beneath a burden but enjoy a boundless freedom of a new kind.

In theodramatics the ontological difference between the hypostatic union of divinity and humanity in the unique case of Jesus Christ and the union of grace in the saints – a traditional thesis of Catholic divinity – is rendered as a distinction between, on the one hand, the Christ whose

---

1 *TD* III, p. 263.

consciousness 'coincides with' his universal Trinitarian mission, and, on
the other, those conscious subjects to whom he gives a mission as well as
the 'grace and authority' to appear on the Father's stage. But just as the
divine transcendence at large makes possible the divine immanence, and
thus the participation of creatures in the being which God is, so here too
this very difference makes possible a sharing by the other actors (and
actresses) in the universality of Christ's mission. Balthasar expresses this
in terms of a kind of self-diffusion of the theological person, which annuls
their purely private existence as individuals and gives them an essentially
communal rôle. 'The theological person radiates as far as his vocation
and mission reaches',[2] providing space for the salvifically relevant action
of others in dependence on, but also by analogy with, Christ himself. Here
the structure of the conscious subject is wondrously crowned, for it
already belongs to human nature that the individual soul is, in Aquinas'
words 'in some sense everything', turned in open-ended sympathy
towards other realities – and notably other human beings. Ancient thought
intuited this in the notion of the corporate personality of the leader or the
king, in whom the community finds personification. Christian dogmatics
will marvellously confirm this idea in its own concept of the essential
interrelation of the elect community and specially chosen theological
persons within it.

Of these *Mary* is the chief example. She is not just one defining point in
the circle of figures around Jesus: a dot, so to speak, which by joining to
other dots helps to outline the contours of his mission. In introducing her,
in the context of theological dramatics, Balthasar speaks of Mary's
theological personhood (i.e., constitutive rôle) in five succinctly expressed
ways. First, in Mary the faith of Israel, from Abraham on, is so concentrated that it can bear to receive the culminating divine promise. Second,
that promise is in fact fulfilled with her bringing Jesus Christ, and his
universal mission, into the world. Third, it follows from this that – para-
doxical as it may seem – her *personal* mission is the fount of all *universality*
in the Church. Fourth, as such, Mary's mission embraces those of the four
christological 'pillars' of Balthasar's ecclesiology: the missions of Peter,
Paul, John and James, seen as embodying a quartet of fundamental
features in the work of Christ. Fifth and last, Mary's mission enfolds the
other womanly missions crucial, on Balthasar's view, to the original gospel
– which are those of Mary Magdalen, the *apostola apostolorum* who brought
the news to the future office-bearers, and of Mary of Bethany, she who
chose the 'better part'. Mary, then, is the first of the 'theological persons'
(human beings with their 'characters' thus changed thanks to the differing
but complementary dramatic interventions of Father, Son and Spirit) with
whom, in this work, Balthasar has to deal. His systematic discussion falls
under the rubric of 'Woman's Answer' – her answer, namely, to the Word
of God.

Just as the setting of Balthasar's discussion of the great figures of biblical
salvation history is Providence in general (for in Israel–Church mission is
always ultimately for the wider world), so here too he places this unique

2 *TD* III, p. 271.

woman's 'answer' in the context of the male–female polarity at large. The latter is a reality of the cosmic creation which, in humankind, extends right up to the level of the divine image in man, since that image exists in differentiated form in males and females. And while in paganism the divine Paradigm of the world perpetually fêtes itself in the *hieros gamos*, the union of 'God' and 'Goddess', in the Judaeo-Christian tradition the very way that absolute Origin is symbolised – as the *Father*, the separate source (not Mother, continuous with her child) – means that the Father's Word must take flesh as a man (not a woman) if his mission is truly to represent the One who sends him forth. At the same time, however (and here an element of truth in the pagan myths is recovered), the Word made not only *human* but *male* needs his *Gegenüber*, his female 'other'. As with Adam, his latent feminine complement is to 'come forth from within him, as his "fullness"' – a reference to the ecclesiology of the Letter to the Ephesians (1.23).[3] It follows that Balthasar's Mariology is situated somewhere between his theological anthropology (with its account of man and woman as, in diverse yet mutually supplementing senses, the image of God) and his ecclesiology of the Church as Bride of Christ. And this is indeed what we find.

Balthasar plays on the etymological fact that, in German, 'word' (*Wort*) is masculine whereas 'answer' (*Antwort*) is feminine to suggest the nature of the complementarity between the human male and the human female. In the second of the two creation accounts furnished by the editor of Genesis, Adam names the animals but there is no proper *answering response* until Woman is taken out of Man.

We encounter the same notion in what may be called the metaphorical ontology of seeing (and not just, then, that of hearing). In the light of the Germanic phoneme *litz*, 'look', a *face*, *Antlitz*, is evidently something that *faces*, and so is looked at.

> Man looks around him and meets with an *answering gaze* that turns the one-who-sees into the one-who-is-seen.[4]

To say that Eve is drawn from Adam's side is, mythopoeically, to affirm that the unity of Adam and Eve, Man and Woman, the word and its answer, the look and the face that returns it, is in no way an external one. To say that *God* fashioned her with his own hands is to assert – again, in the language of mythopoetics, that their meeting is not just a matter of natural sexual correlation but takes place in the spiritual freedom which only God can give.

Now Balthasar comes to an extremely important point for his entire theological doctrine, and this concerns the crucial rôle of woman in the creaturely expression of that fruitfulness which is one of his principal designations not only of the divine nature but also of the inner-Trinitarian communion – the way the divine nature is concretely appropriated and expressed. Though the command to 'be fruitful' is addressed to both man and woman, without woman's 'answering fruitfulness' the fruitfulness of

---

3 *TD* III, p. 284.
4 *TD* III, p. 285 (italics added).

man, however primary it may be, is also impotent. Here we must notice that, following Barth, Balthasar quite explicitly does not take 'fruitfulness' in the theological anthropology of Genesis to be either (specifically) sexual or even (more generally) at all concerned with procreation. In the *large* sense of the term, then, only woman can bring man's fruitfulness to its fullness; only she can be, in the words of I Corinthians (11.7) man's glory. In a Trinitarian analogy, her 'procession' *from* Adam is prolonged in a 'mission' *to* Adam, and this I take to be more particularly a *Pneumatological* comparison, for on Balthasar's account of the Spirit, the latter proceeds everlastingly from (the Father and) the Son, yet in the saving economy the Son allows the Father to render him dependent on the Spirit. While simultaneously insisting that none of this must obscure that other truth by which we rightly regard man and woman as *individually* images of God, Balthasar can nonetheless move to a conclusion of the greatest moment:

> Since it is woman's essential vocation to receive man's fruitfulness into her own fruitfulness, thus uniting in herself the fruitfulness of both, it follows that she is actually the fruit-bearing principle in the creaturely realm.[5]

Indeed the creature, for Balthasar, is more deeply feminine than masculine, precisely *as creature*, that is, *vis-à-vis* God.

> Insofar as every creature – be it male or female in the natural order – is originally the fruit of the primary, absolute, self-giving divine love, there is a clear analogy to the female principle in the world.[6]

And so even at a natural level every rational creature has a sort of mission to be on the alert for receiving the seed of the Word of God, so as to bear that seed and bring it to developed form.

The christological position of womankind must be located, then, at the intersection of these two axes – that between man and woman on the one hand, and between God and the world on the other. Insofar as the Word is God, he in no sense needs completion by another. But inasmuch as he is human, and, specifically, in humanity's masculine gender, he needs, like Adam, the fullness of an Eve. When we speak of Jesus as an individual man, we naturally think of him as relating to woman as a particular person. But when we consider him as Word incarnate, mandated to reconcile with the Father the whole creation, we see that this female helpmate bears necessarily a social character – for she represents that humankind which *vis-à-vis* God is itself 'feminine'. Hence the co-inhering mystery of (the individual) Mary and (the corporate) Church.

The fact that the Incarnation is quite specifically a *redemptive* Incarnation adds a further nuance, and a major one at that. Not only does the Word enter the human race through that process of conception, pregnancy and birth from a woman which, in the time after the Fall, is intrinsically linked to corruption and death. He also needs to redeem his 'helpmate' since his

5 *TD* III, p. 286.
6 *TD* III, p. 287.

task as the Second Adam, liberating mankind from 'futility' (Romans 8.20), includes the bringing about of what Balthasar terms:

> that ultimate relationship between man and woman that is dimly anticipated in the paradise legend and set forth as a final destination in the 'marriage of the Lamb' in the Book of Revelation.[7]

Looked at theodramatically what this means is that Mary (and in and through her the Church, the social dimension of the New Eve) must go through all the 'states' which humankind has known in its basic relation to God so as to bring their highly dramatic potential to redeemed expression.

> She must share in mankind's 'original *status*', but also in its fallen *status*, since she must display solidarity with humanity in the concrete. Finally she must share in the 'ultimate *status*', which her Son has initiated and, in his Resurrection, has himself assumed once for all.[8]

As Balthasar points out, this statement draws attention to the inevitability of the Church's working out *some* doctrine about Mary's origins and final destiny – historically realised as that inevitability was *de facto* in the dogmas of the Immaculate Conception and the Glorious Assumption.

While Mariology and ecclesiology are as inseparably related in their joint dependence on Christology as are the main female figures of Mary and Church, Balthasar insists that, Mary's membership of the Church notwithstanding, ecclesiology must yield pride of place to Mariology in the hierarchy of the theological disciplines.

> There is no question of a collective, not even the 'faithful people', producing the Redeemer-Messiah out of itself, in virtue of its own faith. The fact that the Church can become the 'Mother' of those who believe in Christ always presupposes that Mary conceived the Messiah and brought him to birth.[9]

So Pope Paul VI was justified in declaring Mary, at the close of the Second Vatican Council, to be 'Mother of the Church', for she is, in the words of St Peter Damian 'source of the living Source, origin of the Beginning'.[10]
At the same time, however, Mary's maternal rôle *vis-à-vis* Christ and the Church is one of *selflessness*, thus turning her primacy over against the Church into an endless enabling in the Church's favour.

It will readily be seen that there is nothing simplistic about the foundations of Balthasar's Mariology. For woman is at once the answer to man's primal word and yet a being equal with him; she is ordered to the man, becoming a person in dialogue with the other-gendered, and yet she is also ordered to the child, a principle of generation for the human race at large. Balthasar speaks of her, accordingly, as escaping definition, a

---

7 *TD* III, p. 290.
8 Ibid.
9 *TD* III, p. 291.
10 Peter Damian, Sermon 45.

process that oscillates (from the Virgin Bride to the Mother of the Church, from the answering Person to the Source of the race).[11]

So far from having a stereotypical view of the male/female polarity he denies that it can be summed up conclusively in any formula. Pervading the entire living creation as it does, it can only be approached 'by allowing each pole to shed light on the other'.[12]

Coming to Mariology itself, then: rather than laying down a law that reflection on our blessed Lady 'must' have this or that *point de départ* (for each is limiting – to start from Mary as *Theotokos*, for instance, may lead to overlooking her rôle as the representative 'answering' one), Balthasar prefers to draw attention to the fact that Marian theology cannot dispense with a *story*, for it is a demand of woman's ontology, her very nature, that she requires a span of time, a narrative space, in which to develop from 'receptive bride' to the mother who both bears and nurtures a child. Somewhat startlingly, Balthasar declares that narrative – at least in the sense of giving attention to the sequence of individual historical events – is more important in Mary's case than in Jesus', for the latter's missiological consciousness develops in a 'straight line', whereas Mary's rôle is ever changing in accordance with the needs of her Son 'whose helpmate she is'. From the mysteries of the Infancy, through the public ministry to Calvary and the Cenacle, her journey follows a zig-zag route – hence the emergence of the apocryphal lives of Mary of the patristic period or the mediaeval *Vitae*, and their more chastened modern equivalents.[13] The need to construct a coherent story line, Balthasar seems to say, cannot be avoided even in Mariological studies which examine the materials in the light of some major principle in theological doctrine, or historically, via the chief epochs of the Church's Marian meditation.

Balthasar insists that while the *veneration* of Mary in the Church grew exponentially, Marian *doctrine* remained always the same. Like Newman, engaged in courteous polemic with Pusey, he finds already in the ante-Nicene age not only an awareness that Mary guarantees the true humanity of the Word but also a mysterious identification of Mary and Church – the two great themes of all Catholic Mariology. But it soon turns out that what Balthasar means by the continuous identity of Marian doctrine is the undisturbed abiding, in the heart of the Church, of the *core-affirmations* of that doctrine. He would not deny, indeed he asserts, that further implications required time for their unfolding. The need to reconcile the absolute primacy of the divine saving initiative with the divine recognition of the creature's 'feminine' fruitfulness, its deepest being as responsiveness to the Word, produced that long-lasting debate in Catholic divinity between 'Maculists' and 'Immaculists' about the Conception of Mary. The difficulty of connecting appropriately the operation of the Saviour and the co-operation of the Woman whose consent to the Word must be consent to all its resonances, all the consequences of the

11 *TD* III, p. 293.
12 *TD* III, p. 292.
13 Here Balthasar has in mind such studies as Paul Gächter's *Maria in Erdenleben: Neutestamentliche Marienstudien* (Innsbruck 1954) and F. M. Willam, *Maria, Mutter und Gefährtin des Erlösers* (Freiburg 1963).

Incarnation, generated that disputatious family of concepts which deal with Mary's assistance to Christ's mediation. And recalling how a sea of titles for the Mother at the Cross rises (with, say, *co-redemptrix*) and falls (with, perhaps, *auxiliatrix*), Balthasar speaks, in this same marine or at any rate riverine metaphor of

> the ebb and flow, through history, of Mariology's tides; a flood of lofty attributes, titles and venerations is almost necessarily followed by an ebb that restores the level; but the ebb-tide can also seep away, leading to a forgetfulness that is unworthy of theology.[14]

In an audaciously broad sweep, Balthasar considers the history of Marian doctrine to be essentially summed up in two movements. The first, running from the sub-apostolic period to the central Middle Ages, considers her position in relation to Christ and the Church (and thus her place as co-redemptrix). The other, spanning the period from the central Middle Ages to ourselves, looks at her situation 'between the aeons' of saving history and so her Conception and Assumption (as well as, Balthasar claims, her perpetual virginity). Though the second phase inherited its materials from the first, it contributed a novel 'speculative restructuring'.

Reviewing the patristic and early mediaeval evidence for the parallelism between Mary as Mother of the Head and the Church as Mother of the Body, Balthasar, quite properly in our context, puts his own theodramatic slant on the texts surveyed. A Christological approach to Mariology, where Mary stands with Christ over against the Church, cannot be set against an ecclesiological model where she belongs with the Church *vis-à-vis* Christ, for the (theodramatic) truth is that

> the more personal and unique Mary's relationship with Christ is understood to be, the more she represents the concrete epitome of what we mean by 'Church'.[15]

This follows from the principle that the zone of theological *personhood* is co-extensive with the realm of *mission*. The title co-redemptrix simply translates the *compassio* of the Mother of the Crucified as helpmate of the New Adam. 'Simply' – yet Balthasar is aware of and excoriates (underestimating perhaps the rôle of literary trope and genre in such matters) the ramified distortions to which an exaggerated Mariology can be prone.

This, however, does not prevent him from regarding the Mariological contribution of the Second Vatican Council as in some respects meagre – the relation of the faithful to Mary is too much presented there in *moral* terms. This is the want which, by rethinking Mary's place at the 'turn of the ages', a theodramatic Mariology will happily supply. For Balthasar, Mary's Immaculate Conception is required by her dual mission as not only Mother but also companion, 'Bride', of the Word:

---

14 *TD* III, p. 297.
15 *TD* III, pp. 304–305.

as a Mother, she has to mediate – in the requisite purity – everything human that her Child needs; as her Son's 'companion' and 'bride', she must be able to share his sufferings in a way appropriate to her, and what most fits her for this task is her utter purity, *which means that she is profoundly exposed and vulnerable.*[16]

Turning the tables completely, in other words, on some modern Eastern Orthodox critics of the 'Latin dogma' – the Immaculate Conception, so far from endangering Mary's solidarity with sinful humankind, makes that solidarity possible, rendering her a 'genuine citadel of compassion'.[17] If Mary's original righteousness does not, then, sunder her from the Old Testament world of needy sinners, it is her virginal conception of Jesus which signalises that, nonetheless, she is the pivot on which the succession of the ages turns. Given the inescapable connexion of sexual reproduction with transience and death, the Virgin Birth points towards the immortal divine life of the age of salvation. In a subtle discussion of Mary's *virginitas in partu* Balthasar seems inclined to accept this proposal of theological doctrine: the true birth-pangs suffered by the Messiah's Mother were the belated ones she knew at the Cross. Eschewing speculation on the 'how' of the unbroken hymen (did the Child who opened the womb reclose it, or were, more simply, the natal passages expanded?), Balthasar points out that for the Fathers the 'revirginising' of the harlot *Ecclesia ab Abel* – the wayward people of God – in Mary was as wonderful as her miraculous preservation of intactness in giving birth.

The age of the New Covenant is that of the heavenly Kingdom anticipated. Hence, necessarily, the Assumption. Or, as Balthasar puts it, with reference to the Marian dimension of the Woman of the Apocalypse (ch. 12):

> The Woman is oriented to eternity. She is oriented to eternity in herself (in virtue of her heavenly attributes), in her Child (who is 'caught up to God'), in her adversary (who has fallen from heaven) and in her offspring, 'those who keep the commandments of God and bear testimony to Jesus'. So the question of her translation (*transitus*) to heaven arises automatically.[18]

But how is the question to be answered? Though Balthasar considers that the patristic homilies on Mary's assumption may have a second-century core, his acceptance of the doctrine of her glorification proceeds on, once again, theodramatic lines. It is, for him, an implication of 'various aspects of Mary's mission' in those aspects' mutual illumination, their convergence. From four aspects of that mission – her sharing in our originally righteous nature, her physical and spiritual participation in the Incarnation, her co-suffering with the Redeemer, and her relationship to

---

16 *TD* III, p. 323 (italics added).
17 We can note, however, the crucial difference in Mary's mercy compared with that of Jesus: as the Lamb of God, the incarnate Son 'must get to know the bitter taste of sin from the inside', whereas the Mother of the Word 'recognizes' that bitter taste only 'in the effect that sin has on her Son', ibid.
18 *TD* III, p. 336.

the Church as our Mother, it follows that she is 'utterly whole and holy in soul and body', and this is what the dogma of 1950 expressly says.

The Marian Church

Balthasar's theodramatic ecclesiology takes its rise from consideration of the 'tremendous concentration' which the redemptive Incarnation involved. If from the world's vantage point, the man Jesus is an icon of the Holy Trinity (for 'in himself, through the Spirit, he represents the Father'), from God's he is, in a much less customary usage, the 'icon of the world'. That is, he represents 'all human nature's conscious subjects on the basis of the real substitution he undertakes on their behalf'.[19] If, in this fashion, then, the divine Son has broken through the limits of Israel, the stage on which his purely human complement and partner must represent him and continue his work must be as wide as the world. Because the figure of Jesus is a concrete one, so too must be his (ecclesial) counterpart, and to this extent the Church will appear as a continuation of the Synagogue. But as, additionally, the Church of the Gentiles, with a mission on a universal scale,

> the Church ... always transcends her particular form at any one time, for her goal is the fruitfulness of Christ, which is aimed at the whole of mankind. Thus transcending herself, she participates in the universality (or catholicity) of the work of reconciliation that God has designed and implemented for the whole world.[20]

Catholic theologians frequently speak of the Church as a 'person' or as having 'personality', attempting to hone conceptual terms that will capture the force of the more imagistic vocabulary of 'Mother' and 'Bride'. Balthasar wishes neither, with Augustine, to absorb the Church's personality into that of Christ (so that Head and body form the *totus Christus*) nor with Origen to posit the Church as an independent hypostasis, the heavenly Jerusalem, our Mother, whom the Logos leaves when he leaves the Father's side to cleave to his fallen spouse, the unredeemed. Rather, with such contemporary ecclesiologists as Heribert Mühlen,[21] he thinks in terms of a construction at once Christological and Pneumatological, and therefore Trinitarian – though inevitably the peculiar perspective of theo-drama distances his presentation from that of *Una Mystica Persona*. It is on the basis of their 'inter-related and inter-penetrating missions' that the disciples of Jesus can say 'We' *with* him by his Spirit, and yet at the same time offer their loving service *to* him, and, through him to the Father. Though no Christian can ever say 'I' in the Bride's name, Scripture (Balthasar is thinking of the closing verses of the Apocalypse) does give the Bride a voice of her own, with and in the Spirit but yet distinct from him. Perhaps the key lies, once again, in the mystery of Mary, in whom the Church was inchoately present and in whom 'she'

19 *TD* III, p. 341.
20 *TD* III, p. 342.
21 H. Mühlen, *Una Mystica Persona: Die Kirche als das Mysterium der Identität des Heiligen Geistes in Christus und den Christen. Eine Person in vielen Personen* (Paderborn 1967²).

remains a 'person' with, accordingly, a mission greater than that of even the sum of her members.

The Church too – unsurprisingly, if Mary be its archetype – has a dramatic identity. In Balthasar's ecclesiology the drama arises from the tension between 'event' – the gracious moment of her divine founding, and the renewal of that moment at key-points in her life or that of her members, and 'institution' – the ongoing common life structured by day-in, day-out preaching, sacramentalisation and (in particular, in this context) the activity of her office-holders, the hierarchy. So far from counterposing institution to event, or seeing the institutional life of the Church as an unfortunate necessity following from the fact that we cannot always be at the level of spiritual existence implied by great religious events, Balthasar sees the institution as *what makes the event possible*. This he does by rethinking the entire life of the Church in terms of its Marian matrix, its archetype in the Woman who was both Mother and Bride.

> What renders the 'bridal' and 'maternal' Church fruitful … ? The answer lies in the creation of the Church as an 'institution'. Far from being the antithesis of the nuptial 'event', the institution actually makes it possible for this event to be a here-and-now reality at every point through history. The institution guarantees the perpetual presence of Christ the Bridegroom for the Church, his Bride. So it is entrusted to men who, though they belong to the overall feminine modality of the Church, are selected from her and remain in her to exercise their office; their function is to embody Christ, who comes to the Church to make her fruitful.[22]

So the question is, How, concretely, is the Church as Christ's mystical partner, his Bride, rendered fruitful by the Lord who comes to her in the institution? Balthasar suggests five partial, but cumulatively impressive, responses. Essentially, these are five ways of pointing up the congruence of a Church with a mystical finality living nonetheless via an institutional existence.

1. First, the *Incarnate* Word appropriately has a *similarly incarnate* spiritual humanity as his *Gegenüber*.

   > The 'Bride' (the 'We') who is this Man's partner, as a social entity, must have a bodily constitution; not one chosen at will by herself, but one that is an integral part of her unalterable essential structure, matching the inner, pneumatic vitality infused into her.[23]

2. Balthasar's second point is the assertion that owing to the mutually pre-supposing character of 'life' and 'form' in the Church, the 'abiding structure of offices' within her is a necessary condition for sharing the event of her birth from the side of Christ. There can be

---

22 *TD* III, pp. 353–354.
23 *TD* III, p. 355.

no *Recht-fertigung*, no justification, which bypasses the *Rechts-Ordnung*, the ecclesial order of justice. Even canon law is relevant to evangelical *Rechtsein*, 'right being'.

3. Just as the Holy Spirit is not only the intimacy of the inter-subjective relationship of Father and Son, but, for the Christ of the economy, an objective 'rule' to which he owed obedience throughout his ministry, so the Church too has not just subjective holiness, in Mary and the saints, but objective holiness as well – in the office of those duly commissioned, defective disciples though they themselves be, to fashion other imperfect human beings into that perfect *ecclesia mariana immaculata*.

4. Though set free in Christ, we are so only on the basis of a new slavery to the love of God represented by the Cross. The discipline which Church office imposes on others as on itself is therefore an inevitable precondition of liberation in Christ.

5. Drawing on Newman's distinction between 'prophetical' and 'episcopal' tradition: on the one hand there is a prophetical sense of faith alive in the whole people of the Church, but on the other the Church of office has a distinctive rôle to play by reason of its own episcopal tradition. Considered as a contributor to that wider tradition, the episcopal, on Balthasar's view, *guards* the prophetical, *evaluates* it and *keeps it pure*. Considered as its tributary, it *attends to* it and *learns from* it.

Use has been made, in the post-Conciliar period, of Newman's notions in regard to the learning task of even – and especially – the teaching Church, most notably in the 1859 essay *On Consulting the Faithful in Matters of Doctrine*, to justify the individual's dissent from magisterial teaching. But this is not the emphasis of Balthasar's remarks. His ecclesiology is meant, rather, to invite the individual

> to examine, in faith, his own conscience, which is only a Christian conscience if it lets itself be guided by the great stream of revelation – interpreted by tradition and official Church teaching and preserved in Scripture – and enters into it. Given all this, it is possible for the official Church to make demands, according to the mind of Christ, that seem unintelligible and extreme to an individual or group; there is nothing strange in Christ leading us along the path of the Cross not only in person but also, most definitely, through the institution he himself has appointed.[24]

As no play is without its context, so here we have the ecclesiological a priori which makes possible our perception of the dramatic action to come.

<hr />

24 *TD* III, p. 359.

9

Roll-call

Before leaving Christ's feminine counterpart – Mary and the Church made in her image, and attending to what must always be the heart of any soteriology, the Passion of Christ, Balthasar takes a final roll-call. Who shall be the principal dramatis personae of this (paradoxically) supreme *action*?

Here he must consider: (1) the Israel that, in saying No to God at the 'center of the tragedy of God and mankind [the Cross]' is in that moment both negated and fulfilled in the genesis of the Catholic Church; (2) the 'nations', also called to enter the theologically dramatic action, but not with the key rôle that Israel enjoys (or endures); (3) the 'Christian individual' called to be a witness to the Passion of the Lord and in that sense a co-martyr with him; (4) angelic and demonic 'powers' of which Scripture is so full; (5) the Trinitarian persons who, above all, provide the drama.

In point of fact, Balthasar does not keep very strictly to the brief implied by the situating of these subjects between the Christological and stauro-logical sections of *Theo-Drama*. The lengthy disquisition on the mystery of Israel, and his development of motifs about the Church other than those already treated under the heading of *ecclesia mariana*, may strike us as simply the offloading of material necessary to a twentieth-century dog-matics but lacking any obvious location in a theology, at once foundational and dogmatic, that is offered as, in turn, an aesthetics, a dramatics and a logic. But we must remember that in *Theodramatik* Balthasar is concerned above all with the missions that agents assume or are given in view of the working out of the divine drama whose *dénouement* is the Cross of Christ and that, for *his* theology, mission and identity are co-related terms. Taking a 'roll-call' (my term) of those involved is a natural preliminary to Balthasar's theology of the events that saved the world – but if identity be intimately bound up with mission, a certain largeness of temper is appropriate to the definition of who the agents are.

Israel

Balthasar's view of Israel is, thanks not least to his dialogue with Buber and his study of Barth, a complex one. As Balthasar explains, the Church's message to Jewry can never be a simple exemplification of her mission to 'the nations'; Jewry does not belong to the nations, since, as the Messiah whose name she does not yet recognise himself put it, 'salvation is from the Jews' (John 4.22). The Church cannot, in dualistic fashion, sever Christendom from the stem of the 'cultivated olive tree' (Paul's metaphor for Israel in the Letter to the Romans). To do so could only cause the inner withering of the engrafted wild olive of the Gentiles, and the putting forth of poisoned fruit in anti-Semitism. But at the same time, Balthasar also attacks what he terms the 'monism' which would simply identify Israel and Church as one continuous 'People of God', thus reducing Christ to just a factor in that total process and producing in the meanwhile such distortions of the gospel substance as Christian 'holy wars' and their contemporary equivalent, liberation theology. The fact is that Israel said No as well as Yes to fulfilment in Jesus Christ – and like Eric Peterson and Gaston Fessard (among Catholics) as well as Karl Barth, Balthasar considers that this state of affairs will continue until the Eschaton. That opinion is not based on empirical assessment of the practical possibilities of 'Jews for Jesus': it is a theological opinion – a 'theologoumenon' – based on the principle that without a *dialectically* situated Israel where (namely) *most* Jews reject Baptism though *some* accept it, the Cross would be deprived of its 'historically manifest form' as *both* divine judgment on God's erring people *and* their redemption.

But here we must be careful. It is not, to repeat, all Israel that rejects Israel's Messiah. Indeed, St Luke's Gospel opens with a portrayal of *some* of Israel's representatives welcoming him with (in Symeon's case, literally) open arms. So the true position is more nuanced, or, in that term of Barth's, dialectical.

> First, Israel refuses to step over the threshold to which – Christianly speaking – its paths had been leading (for New Testament thinking and speaking constantly presuppose and use these paths); secondly, in the form of the 'remnant', it *does* actually step over the threshold, with the result that, having stepped over, it is no longer simply one with its past but genuinely enters into a 'synthesis'. A dividing wall has been torn down, which is none other than the wall of Israel's particularity; it was this wall that, in spite of Israel's universalist tendencies, prevented the 'nations' [from] joining Israel to become a homogeneous whole.[1]

But even where the massive majority of Jewry is concerned, Balthasar refuses to speak of 'the synagogue' as cut off from Christ.

> We can liken the two 'peoples' [Church and Synagogue] to the two malefactors and say that the crucified Jesus, with his hands out-stretched to both of them, expresses his solidarity both with the one turned toward him and with the one turned away from him. He shows solidarity with the latter precisely in that, in his person, he embodies the role allotted to all Israel in the poems of the 'Suffering Servant': he suffers on behalf of others.[2]

1 *TD* III, p. 366.
2 *TD* III, p. 398.

Difficult as it is to establish the positive significance of the action of Israel's majority in rejecting the Messiah, Balthasar throws up his hands in horror at Franz Werfel's immediately post-war suggestion that Providence *condemned* Israel to say No to God, to accept an 'evil role', so that the saving drama of the Lamb of God could go forward, for the salvation of the world.

But if Christians have difficulty in determining the sense of the continued existence of an Israel defined by contradiction of the claims of the Crucified, we can at least note how problematic Jews themselves find the issue of their own identity. Is the racial component in Israel of absolute or merely relative importance (an issue already raised by the election of Abraham to be father of many peoples ...)? Does Israel look back more fundamentally to a founding origin, defined by Torah, or to a future destiny, given voice through the prophets? The indecisiveness of Jews themselves, confronted with these questions, suggests to Balthasar that an even more basic question has been obscured, namely:

> whether Israel's election–vocation–mission can be fulfilled in a linear manner, as it were, or whether at a certain point it must transcend itself qualitatively if it is to attain fulfillment at all.[3]

Such self-transcending, then, must not be thought of as annulment of Israel's privileges, but the form they were destined to take from the beginning. Abraham is the father of all believers. But he is so (this at any rate is how the Letter to the Hebrews interprets his 'blessing' by the pagan priest king Melchizedek in the book of Genesis)

> only ... insofar as he bows to Melchizedek, the symbolic anticipation of Christ ... Israel is therefore rooted in Christ and must bow before the Pauline mystery, indicated in Abraham's encounter with the 'king of righteousness, king of peace'. Israel's particular progenitor (in whose loins was Levi, that is, the Old Testament priesthood) bows down before the universal Priest, the Church's foundation stone.[4]

The nations

Nothing could be clearer from Scripture and Tradition than the reality of Israel's theodramatic rôle, however we finally envisage it. When Balthasar turns to consider the place of the pagan nations on the world stage he finds himself wondering whether *as such* they possess a rôle at all. For Scripture, the nations are, in their uniqueness of identity, only elected insofar as God uses their leaders or people to teach a lesson to Israel.

> As for the 'nations' ... while they are watched over by a general (supernatural) providence, they are not given a distinct theological mission and personality prior to Christ's call; and even after being

3 *TD* III, p. 371.
4 *TD* III, p. 424, citing Hebrews 7.2 and alluding to verses 9 and following of that chapter.

called by him, they cannot receive such mission and personality except within the unity of the Church.[5]

This statement is more significant than at first it sounds. It does not simply rule out what Balthasar terms 'national messianism', of, at any rate, a *pagan* kind (the qualifying clause in the passage just cited leaves ajar the door for some special mission of a *baptised* nation). More than this, it enables Balthasar to take up a position in the debate triggered by younger members of the school of Karl Rahner who claimed for the religions of the nations 'ordinary' – that is, intrinsic – status in the work of salvation.[6]

Following the grain of Scripture Balthasar is happy to acknowledge that, from the first moment of creation, it has been the will of God that all men should be saved (cf. I Timothy 2.4) – a statement which warrants the comment of the Second Vatican Council's Declaration on Non-Christian Religions to the effect that 'all nations form but a single community' insofar as God's 'providence, the proofs of his kindness and his saving purposes extend to all men'.[7] In a world so described, the natural and the supernatural are, even for Gentiles, intertwined strands. Yet the Old Testament roundly excoriates 'the gods of the nations' as mere human projections, in contrast to the living God of Israel 'whose essential *freedom* vis-à-vis man has been experienced in history'.[8] Balthasar underlines the word 'freedom' because he is arguing not only that the Rahnerian 'solution' sits ill with the statements of Scripture on the topic of pagan cultus but also that it compromises the divine liberty to address human beings as and how God wants. The theorem of a 'supernatural *existentiale*' whereby humankind at large has received

> an anthropológico–theological constitution in which grace, verbal revelation and a universal salvation history are implanted in a transcendental, a priori manner[9]

is too much of a straitjacket in which to confine the God of surprises. Moreover, owing to the mutually contradictory quality of the various world religions (Islam and Hinduism, for example, are far more intellectually opposed to each other than is either to the gospel), we could no longer, on the Rahner School view, speak of the divine 'plan' of salvation: so competitive and jarring a medley can scarcely be dignified by the name of a *design*. Whatever else they are, the nations, each with their traditional cultus, are not theological persons in the theo-drama, for no divinely given rôle is theirs by right.

We should note that there is nothing mean-minded about Balthasar's rejection of this latitudinarian theology of religions. If the grace of God is less predictable than Rahnerians think, it may also be, at times and in

---

5 *TD* III, p. 422.
6 Balthasar is aware that the influential study by H. R. Schlette, *Die Religionen als Thema der Theologie* (Freiburg 1963), goes beyond Rahner's own stated position, but still objects to the latter as a mistaken reading of the – in itself perfectly true – thesis of grace's universality; see especially n. 31 on *TD* III, p. 416.
7 *Nostra aetate*, 1.
8 *TD* III, p. 415.
9 Ibid.

places, in excess of the light given to Israel. 'He can raise up . . . sages and prophets from among them, to whom even Israel has to listen and from whom it must learn.'[10] Thanks to the natural desire for God, for the vision of God which our divine imagehood entails, and thanks also to the generosity of God's grace, he has left traces of himself scattered throughout the field of the world. *But* such 'traces' are not to be identified with pagan humanity's 'objective religious systems': the nations are not by name assembled at the Cross of Christ.

The Atonement, indeed, 'signals the end of the other religions'.[11] As the Church gathers converts from the nations she does not assemble second-class citizens who, compared with Jewish Christians, are salvation history's disenfranchised. Jesus Christ gives to the nations everything and more that Israel could have told them. 'Uniquely, his person concentrates and embodies God's entire word to the world.'[12] And on the Cross he will accomplish a work absolutely catholic in its effect for all mankind (for 'catholic' *means* 'universal'), rendering otiose and *passé* the salvationally mediatorial attempts of the other religions.

Even if – as for the present writer is certainly the case – one finds unpersuasive Balthasar's (would-be) historical account of the slow death of non-Christian religiosity since the Enlightenment, the two dogmata of incarnation by hypostatic union on the one hand and unconditionally comprehensive atonement on the other sufficiently ground his basic claim.

What Balthasar has done in this section is to combine a theology of missionary activity drawn from his erstwhile *Nouvelle Théologie* Jesuit mentor and colleague Henri de Lubac[13] with his own theology of the rôle of Christ *vis-à-vis* history as the 'whole' *vis-à-vis* the 'fragments'.[14] For conversion to the gospel

> is not the 'complementing' of something already possessed but rather a total 'turning around' in which what is fragmentary is *left behind*; it will be found again but only within the totality, on the far side of a hiatus.[15]

The grounding of the Church's 'rôle'

Before finally leaving the topic of corporate humanity in its theodramatic rôle-taking, Balthasar adds a final word on the ultimate grounding of the Church's part. The foundation of the Church is Jesus Christ who by the combined particularity of his own human being as the rabbi from Nazareth, on the one hand, and, on the other, the universality of his outpoured Spirit as the risen Lord establishes her in her jointly 'personalizing' and 'socializing' role.

10 Ibid.
11 *TD* III, p. 420.
12 *TD* III, p. 419.
13 Henri de Lubac, SJ, *Le Fondement théologique des missions* (Paris 1946).
14 *Daz Ganze im Fragment: Aspekte der Geschichtstheologie* (Einsiedeln 1963; 1990); ET *Man in History* (London and Sydney 1967)/At *A Theological Anthropology* (New York 1967).
15 *TD* III, p. 421.

The community is built on and nourished by a particular, life-giving body that, paradoxically, has been universalized (while remaining particular); on this paradox, Catholic ecclesiology, with all its tensions, rests.[16]

That the Church is, in her Christic foundation, a universal community that is also intensely particular in its realisations explains in advance all those features of her life such as the combination of hierarchical ministries yet full personal membership, liturgical spirituality yet personal piety, unicity of doctrine yet plurality in theologians' personal output, which ill-advised commentators would treat as problematic blips to be ironed out by ('left-wing' or 'right-wing') reform.

This essential relation of the Church to the mystery of Christ enables Balthasar to speak of her – with so many Catholic theologians of the nineteenth and twentieth centuries – as his *Sacrament* – and to connect the seven sacraments of Catholic tradition thereto. Though the Church must continually re-actualise her own being by her actions, that being is more fundamentally received from Christ. As Balthasar is well aware, in a sociologically oriented age like our own, it is all too easy to let a general theology of the sacraments degenerate into an account of the sacred signs as essentially *about the Church* – ourselves – whereas they are first and foremost *about God in Christ*. As he puts it, though it is only

through the Church that the sacrament mediates Christ, for the individual does not simply 'take' the sacraments entrusted to the Church: he 'receives' them from her

still,

what the individual sacrament mediates is not the Church but Christ's self-dedication to the Church, so that the individual may be drawn into the Church's mission.[17]

The sacraments celebrated by the Church would not be sanctifying for us unless the Church first received the Christ whose signs they are – and from that primordial act of reception of the incarnate divine Word Balthasar deduces the threefold office of the Church, a teaching office (for this is really the *Word*), a priestly office (for this is really the *incarnate* Word who gives himself), and a pastoral office (for this incarnate Word is really *divine*, and so the bearer of the authority of God).

Perhaps less successful (because more artificial) is Balthasar's attempt to divide up the seven sacraments in terms of whether they concern more the *nature* taken by the Word in his incarnation or the *event* enacted by the Word in his redemptive sacrifice. He himself admits the fragility of such a thesis. We may note, however, *en passant* the brilliant theology of the apostolic succession which calls ministerial order the visible perpetuation in the Church, by means of a specific organ, of that act whereby, in handing himself over to the Church, Christ makes her in her very being

16 *TD* III, p. 426.
17 *TD* III, p. 430.

his Church – once-for-all in founding the apostolic ministry, but also new every moment in its grace-borne acts.[18]

And yet the Church is not given solely for the celebration of signs that make us holy. 'Her goal is the entire human world.'[19] It is because the Church is missionary that she is who she is, just as Jesus' *missio* from the Father makes him the human form of the *processio* which constitutes the Son in his inner-Trinitarian being. But where the Church's mission is practised as mere activism, her being is de-natured. To be light for others she must be light in herself. For Balthasar the Church's appropriation in depth of her inner resources is crucial to outer fruitfulness.

> The intensive apostolate of the religious begins with the preparatory phase of the novitiate, and that of the priest begins in the seminary, just as Paul's tremendous influence began in Arabia, and all the Church's great founding figures emerged out of solitude.[20]

When a Church energised by contemplation becomes active, we begin to see sparks fly: the would-be transforming impact of the Church on a hostile or at best indifferent world cannot but be dramatic. Here anything is possible – from persecution leading to extermination to an 'inculturation' so successful that, by a purely Pyrrhic victory, the gospel is swallowed up by the world.

Despite Balthasar's high doctrine of the Church he insists that her mode of being, as we know it, is purely provisional. Just as, in Balthasar's Trinitarian theology, in the lowly state of the Son's 'economy', between Annunciation and Descent into Hell, the Holy Spirit is the 'objective rule' for his action, so that, with the Resurrection and Ascension the Son may resume – but this time for all humanity – his eternal rôle as, through the Father, Giver of the Spirit, so in Balthasar's ecclesiology, the Holy Spirit takes 'objective form' in the ecclesial institution, above all, in the sacrament of Order, so that believers may be trained up for that immediate presence of their incarnate Lord which is for them the life of the Age to Come. In this sense the Church's provisionality testifies to her unique status in the Holy Spirit and is not so much a caveat entered against a high ecclesiology as it is the latter's definitive proof.

And yet Balthasar *does* recognise a more negative aspect of the provisional Church, which consists in her inclusion of both tares and wheat, hairy monsters from the deep as well as fish fit for the table. However secure the meta-historical foundations, sin renders the historical life of the Church precarious, and this Balthasar links to the envy and jealousy which the possession of any striking charism can arouse. The (genuinely) attractive quality of some aspect of the message of an individual or group within the Church can become, tragically, more important to people than her organic unity. Here, for Balthasar, lies the genesis of schism.

18 Cf. *TD* III, p. 439, where we read: 'what is institutional in [the Church] is the means whereby the Holy Spirit maintains her living origin, that is, the presence of Christ and the Christ-event, as an ever-present reality within her'.

19 *TD* III, p. 435.

20 *TD* III, p. 436.

If the Church is a 'theological person', then, for a theodramatic theory it follows as night day that there cannot be a multiplicity of churches. If the Church is an actress (not an actor, for this is the *Bride* of Christ) she must be a single theological persona. Perhaps between, say, the Eastern Orthodox and the Catholic Church there is but 'impaired communion', not true schism: in that case, a single theological person acts in both. In any other sense, *when considered as corporate realities*, the other ecclesial communities are not – for Balthasar – actually on stage. (We shall proceed in a moment to consideration of how the individuals that compose them – and make up the fellowship of the Catholica itself – can nonetheless be 'persons in Christ'.) Ecumenically, Balthasar is a pessimist. Ill-will, grievance, misunderstanding – all these can be diminished or even removed, and such moral fruits of the twentieth-century Ecumenical Movement are far indeed from negligible. But organic reunion with those who have defined themselves over against the 'visible symbol of unity' (the Petrine office of the Pope) is, to his eyes, a chimaera.

The Christian individual

But this in itself argues nothing against the witnessing potential of the individual on the theological world stage. The Christian individual – as that arch-enemy of Hegelian totality-thinking, the Danish 'father' of Existentialism, Sören Kierkegaard, noted – is never just an 'example' of community. If, as the Gospels attest, Christ was so particular as to be, in this world, and indeed among his disciples, a *lone* figure, this teaches Christians a lesson.

> Though [the Church] is Christ's community of love, she consists of individuals who live their lives following the solitary Christ.[21]

Balthasar points out how Paul, the doctor of Christ's mystical body, and John, the apostle of love, appear to have endured 'isolation' at the end of their lives (cf. II Timothy 4.16 and III John 9–15, interpreted as Diotrephes' attempt to exclude the Beloved Disciple from his church). But such 'apostolic isolation' corresponds to the essential solitariness of each Christian's confession at Baptism. (No one can believe for me, or, in the case of infants, for those who 'sponsor' me.) The incongruity of these juxtapositions disappears when we remember that the origin of the Church's fellowship lies in the Trinitarian fellowship lived out by Jesus in extremest form in the loneliness of the Cross. Summarising and applying to the loneliness theme his basic soteriology Balthasar explains how the Christian individual cannot always expect support – not even the support of seeing any result from his or her suffering.

> The experience of utter forsakenness is an integral part of the Son's mission; it remains a form of the closest relationship, even when it appears in the mode of God's turning away from him. And it is precisely in this relationship of forsakenness that the solitary, isolated Son exercises the most fruitful phase of his apostolate. For it

21 *TD* III, p. 448.

is now that he gives birth to the Church. Christian fruitfulness, which takes place in solitude (even to the extent of forsakenness), cannot be experienced by the one who thus bears fruit. It takes place within a trinitarian fellowship that, as far as subjective experience is concerned, vanishes into nothing at the boundary; objectively, however, it is never more effective than then.[22]

The Christian individual responds to Christ by lonely witness, then – and yet his or her witness is always given *in the Church's name*. What the individual Christian represents is not Church authority (unless, of course, he – or in certain circumstances she – has received a mandate so to act), but what Balthasar calls 'the unabridged role of the Church in a non-Christian or anti-Christian environment'.[23] And the theologian here can call on the work of the actual dramatist (as Balthasar now does by appeal to Reinhold Schneider): a diversity of lives, and not just those of official martyrs and confessors alone, can reveal in word and deed the 'innermost essence of what we mean by "Church"'.[24] Balthasar's choice of examples is itself revealing of where he locates theological drama at its highest tension in individual lives. He considers on the one hand those who are inadequately seconded by the Church in the stand they take – with particular reference to those who, upholding Catholic faith and morals in their fullness, find a local church establishment unsympathetic or opposed. And on the other hand, following Schneider (who was writing in the pre-Conciliar period in modern Catholicism), he treats of those saints who had to confront representatives of the State (and not necessarily evil or corrupt ones at that). For, as Schneider's work shows, the proper pene-tration of culture by the gospel is a delicate business.

> What most fascinated me in this work was the omnipresent drama of the encounter between two missions that are equally original and yet stand in a deadly mutual conflict: the mission of the one who is entrusted with the task of administering the earthly realm and the mission of the saint as the real symbol of the kingdom of God that descends into the world.[25]

But what of individuals who belong (socially, outwardly) only to that 'earthly realm' and not at all (to all intents and purposes) to Christ's Church? If subjects, however conscious and rational, can only be persons in Christ, and Rahnerian 'anonymous Christianity' be rejected, is not their lot parlous? Balthasar replies that the experience of finite freedom, and notably of how such freedom is both a gift from 'the other' and its divine Ground and also a responsibility – a *mission* – to others in turn *does* foreshadow something of the divine and Christological mission through which alone individuals enter theo-drama. Unlike radical progressives who would have the Church celebrate the world in its cultural secularity (itself, of course, something else again from its sheer createdness which is

22 *TD* III, pp. 450–451.
23 *TD* III, p. 452.
24 *TD* III, p. 453.
25 Balthasar, *Tragedy under Grace*, p. 11.

indeed 'very good' [Genesis 1.31]), Balthasar believed, however, that in
unpropitious Enlightenment circumstances,

> we are experiencing the drastic practical results of [the Positivist]
> loss of meaning; and above all we are also realizing how the loss of
> the religious dimension in the social sphere (that is, its privatization)
> makes it difficult for the individual to experience it as a reality in his
> own life.[26]

Angels and demons

The biblical drama, for Balthasar, has no secondary angelological plot
and yet both angelic powers and principalities hostile to God are
presented in its central scenes, such that no script deprived of them could
be fully recognisable as the Bible's own. The references of Scripture to
these beings are fragmentary and difficult fully to decipher, but extra-
biblical testimonies – Balthasar has in mind the 'encounter with beings . . .
who manifest a "felicitous" fullness' in Rilke's *Duino Elegies* (for the good
angels) and (for the evil) awareness even in atheistic writers of the
demonic as meta-psychological power – admonish us not to interpret
such realities out of existence.

For Scripture, while the God of Israel is utterly without competitors, he
is not alone. Heaven is socially inhabited by denizens in contact with earth.
If in the 'call vision' of Isaiah, the glory of God is flanked by the seraphim,
the Gospels show an amazing concentration of angelic presences – hardly
surprising if 'in Jesus the kingdom of heaven has come near and begun to
descend upon the earth'.[27] And yet the angels that minister to the Logos
incarnate, characteristically and by that very fact, yield place to him. With
the evil angels, by contrast, the situation is quite other. They come to
confront him. 'Satan' may originally have appeared before God as a
licensed prosecutor (that is what his name means), whose rôle is to bring
the divine righteousness into (even) higher profile. But thanks to the
providentially catalysing influence of thinking about the spirit realm
outside Israel, he emerges, by the New Testament period, as a being for
whose activity God is not responsible. Quite the contrary! The Saviour
himself struggles with him, masterfully in the Wilderness, desperately in
the Garden, and counsels his disciples in the *Pater noster* to pray for
deliverance from this 'Evil-doer' or 'Perverted One'.

Balthasar's account of the ontology of the angels (good or evil) proceeds
by way of argument with Karl Barth. Barth's theology of the holy angels
is not quite orthodox from a Catholic standpoint (above all in its refusal
to ascribe to them an original freedom of choice, for God and their supernatural vocation, or against). But Balthasar can affirm much of what his
Protestant compatriot has to say on the basis of Bible and Tradition: these
creatures, fusing as they do with their function of adoring God are to that
extent perfectly worthy of our imitation. But before imitation comes

26 *TD* III, p. 460.
27 *TD* III, p. 474.

presence: God is never found by us without them since when heaven bends down to earth there they are, giving God's relation with us 'cosmic contour and concreteness'.[28] But Balthasar strenuously denies that a spiritual creature could inherit all the perfection God had destined for it simply by virtue of existing in its own nature. Here he is speaking up for the authentic Thomas of Henri de Lubac, but also for the Fathers of whom Aquinas is the continuator.

> Even if we concede that the angel loves God necessarily, by nature, with a 'natural love' – which can be designated as *amor amicitiae* [the love of friendship] and belongs to the innate nobility of its nature – this love must first be ratified by personal freedom if it is to reach God in himself: *eminentius quam natura, ex amore gratuito* [more eminently than by nature, from out of gratuitous love].[29]

The trouble is, here as elsewhere, that while Barth, in his theological development, moves ever closer to the nature/supernature distinction, he never actually reaches it, and so the light which should fall on the topic of the holy angels from the axiom of Catholic divinity that God creates the world (nature) for union with himself in Christ (supernature) is in his case imprisoned at source.

Balthasar's reservations about the Barthian account of the good angels pale almost into insignificance in comparison with what he has to say of Barth on the Devil and *his* angels. Barth's decision to devise for the diabolic angels a new ontological category, neither the uncreated nor the created, but *sui generis*, a potentiated nothingness, is dismissed by Balthasar as either sheer myth-making or a disastrous return to the sources of German Idealism for which the fall of the angels is but a diminution of divine fullness, to be explained and justified by the redemptive process as a whole.

As free spirits the angels can be called persons. If – as Scripture confesses – they were created through and for the incarnate Son to whom their missions in salvation history were subject, then they can also be called 'persons in Christ'. But to say they are also dramatis personae of the play that theological dramatics studies is to go further – and perhaps questionably so. For, as Balthasar points out:

> it is not *their* drama that is being enacted but the drama of God and man (and, in man, the world).[30]

And yet the drama of the angels is not unconnected with that of humankind. The majority of the Fathers take it for granted that the angelic drama has reference to the single drama of the world whose centre and *dénouement* is the Lord's Pasch. They speak of the angels as asked to exercise their primordial freedom either by resisting the temptation to envy when faced with the Adam who was God's created image, or by

---

28 *TD* III, p. 479, citing words of Barth in the *Church Dogmatics* III/3 (ET, Edinburgh 1961), p. 494.
29 *TD* III, p. 482.
30 *TD* III, p. 489.

resisting the temptation to pride when invited to bow down before the Second Adam, the kenotically incarnate and crucified Lord. Balthasar indeed tends to the view of the seventeenth-century Spanish Scholastic Francisco Suarez, to be followed in nineteenth- and twentieth-century Germanophone theology by, respectively, Matthias Joseph Scheeben and Michael Schmaus, that the holy angels received grace only in prevision of the merits of Christ.

It is Balthasar's intention to give the biblical witness priority over speculation: he is by no means fully in sympathy with the metaphysical angelology of Aquinas who used his treatise on the angels to set up thought experiments in the philosophy of mind. But this is not to say that he is unconcerned with what we may term the angelic structuration of the 'cosmic setting' of salvation! While not following Karl Rahner in the latter's subordination of angelology, via Christology, to anthropology, he applauds Rahner's brave determination to revive a theology of the angels' cosmic rôle.

> The fact that the angels operate from heaven can mean that they are not only entrusted with momentary tasks but can represent heaven's whole approach and closeness to the material cosmos. So they can be given authority and power over all realms of creation but especially over men's individual and social history (as personal or national 'guardian angels'). If, right from the outset, heaven and earth were created to be mutually complementary in the theo-drama, it follows that heaven's representatives have an inherent relation to the material world ...[31]

It is easier to think of the angels at the Liturgy – but that is because we ourselves (unlike them) find it hard to be liturgically minded (adorers) while we are engaged in action outside church. Communication with them can indeed only take place in an 'atmosphere of prayer', for they are heaven's representatives. Yet the undividedness of their attention to God in both worship and mission means that they accompany us outside the ritual liturgy as within it.

Are, then, the demonic angels also persons? Here Balthasar's doubts are the inverse of his self-interrogation on the blessed angels. That the Tempter and the demonic spirits have a rôle in the Gospels is manifest. The cast must, then, include them, for where would at any rate the Synoptic evangelists be without Jesus the exorcist? But are they on that account 'persons in Christ'? Hardly, since that implies a subject's positive relation to their persona's destiny and mission, which are gifts of grace. So, in that case, are the fallen angels persons at all? Balthasar thinks probably not – with the Evangelical Emil Brunner, the Orthodox Fyodor Dostoevsky, the Catholic Joseph Ratzinger. As with a character in C. S. Lewis's theological science fiction novel *Perelandra* (also published as *Voyage to Venus*), they are 'un-persons', personal being in a condition of inner collapse, living dissolution. Rejecting (as he had earlier done in the theological aesthetics) the notion of a mystical body of Satan, for evil is of

31 *TD* III, p. 494.

its essence disaggregating, Balthasar describes the relation between the many demons and the single Satan as 'anonymous and amorphous' for this reason.[32] That the New Testament speaks of their subjection by the victorious Christ, rather than their conversion, once more testifies to their apparent lack of 'inner, personal history'.[33] But then Paul, like Balthasar, is 'more interested in victory than in the vanquished'.[34]

God the Trinity

Balthasar is now reaching the end of his roll-call, and it is time to remind us, in a few brisk pages, of the true centre of the action whose unfolding we are to witness in *Theo-Drama*'s succeeding volumes. For though Jesus Christ is, in the divine mission with which he is identical in creation and salvation, not only the necessary reference point but also the ontological foundation of all theological rôles whatsoever, the centre of the theodramatic action is the entire divine Trinity: *Deus Trinitas*. And here the question arises

> Is the play 'theodramatic' only insofar as it is organized *by* God and produced *for* him and *in his presence*?[35]

This is something which, no doubt, a straightforward philosophical theism might happily assert. Or, alternatively, can God actually appear in the play? Notably, can he

> enter a drama that takes place in the world, and play a part in it, without becoming mythological?[36]

This is the theodramatic equivalent to the question raised in Volume IV of the theological aesthetics when Balthasar asked whether there was any way that the true transcendence of God asserted by philosophy could recuperate the real involvement of the divine in the world presumed by myth – and found the answer in the biblical revelation.

In point of fact, if the Son comes on stage in theo-drama as man, the answer has to be 'Yes', for the Son, even as man, is always the Trinitarian Son, who defines himself by reference to the Father and is interpreted aright only through the Spirit. It is in his unique person that the divine *ousia* is displayed in its trihypostatic quality.

But how can one person reveal three? As Balthasar puts it, does not this render the word 'person' equivocal and even unintelligible? His apologia for the Holy Trinity proceeds in this way. The mission which personalises the conscious subject that is Jesus has to be divine, since only a divine person can 'measure up to' God's Cause, and be the agent of God for universal salvation on earth. But as soon as we know that this divine One is One *who was sent* we realise that there must be at any rate twofold personality in God. Balthasar completes the picture by bringing in the

32 *TD* III, p. 498.
33 *TD* III, p. 500.
34 *TD* III, p. 501.
35 *TD* III, p. 506.
36 *TD* III, p. 505.

Holy Spirit. The Son who is sent cannot truly be said to *obey* if we only think of the Father's eternal decision to send him, since that 'decision' is his own eternal decision likewise. However, the Son *can* be said to obey the Father if the Spirit

> presents him with the Father's will in ever-new ways and with ever-greater clarity, even though he already has this will within him in the form of his readiness to obey.[37]

And in a wonderful summary of the Spirit's place in God Balthasar explains:

> What hovers between Jesus and the Father as the mediation of mission is the economic form of the eternal unanimity between Father and Son, which becomes a distinct witness to both of them and with which both of them seal their Yes. It is, as it were, their 'We', which is more than the sum of their 'I' and 'Thou'.[38]

Is it true to say that in salvation history's drama the Trinity was 'progressively' revealed? On the one hand, Balthasar insists that before Jesus Christ no one could have thought of the Trinity. Triads of cosmological principles in Hinduism are not the divine Trinity, no more is Hegel's attempt to synthesise the monotheism of the Jew with the polytheism of the Greek. In this sense there is no 'Old Testament Trinity'. On the other hand, since the three persons essentially interpenetrate, there could be no revelation of God (the Father) in Israel which was not a revelation of the triune God – albeit informally. The difference Christ makes is not, however, *merely* one of formal explicitation for

> the Word had not yet stepped over definitively to man's side, to be recognizable as a divine Person, and the Spirit that rested on man had not yet finally penetrated his heart ...[39]

And even in the realm of the 'development' that, according to Catholic divinity since Newman, follows on the disclosures of Son and Spirit from Annunciation to Pentecost, Balthasar prefers to speak not chiefly of an accumulating armoury of concepts but of the play's mediation of ever-deeper *insights* into the mystery of God. And in a marvellous passage Balthasar rounds off his account of how the God who is *above* the drama (literally, in the physical staging of the theatre of Calderon!) is actually also *within* it:

> The Father seems to remain above the play since he sends the Son and the Spirit; but in fact he could not involve himself more profoundly than by thus sending them: 'God so loved the world that he did not spare his only Son, but gave him up for us all' (John 3.16 and Romans 8.32).... The Son dedicates himself to the world's salvation just as eternally as the Father does; from before all time,

37 *TD* III, pp. 510–511.
38 *TD* III, p. 511.
39 *TD* III, p. 513.

he pledges himself to carry out the world plan, through his Cross, for the good (the 'very good') of the world. And even after accomplishing his earthly mission, when he seems to 'wait' for the end (Hebrews 10.13), he fills this period of waiting with his kingly (I Corinthians 15.25) and even bellicose (Revelation 19.1ff.) activity. Thus, having overthrown the last enemy, he acts as Judge, subsequently to hand the kingdom over to the Father. As for the Spirit, the incorruptible 'witness' who registers all things objectively, he is also the 'love of God poured forth' (Romans 5.5) throughout the entire drama; he is profoundly involved from within, right to the very end, and 'with sighs too deep for words' he moves the tangled drama on toward its solution, 'the glorious freedom of the children of God' (Romans 8.22ff.).[40]

For Balthasar the teaching of Nicaea I on the *homoousion* of the Son is already implied in this conspectus of the New Testament plot as is also – he will go on to explain – the procession of the Holy Spirit taught at Florence. First, on the Nicene dogma:

If he-who-is-sent has essentially to reveal the love of him-who-sends, and if he is identical with his divine mission, he must (as the personal bearer of this mission of love) be the divine, that is, eternal Offspring of him-who-sends, whom he himself calls 'Father' in a sense that bursts all analogies . . . The Old Covenant spoke of God's 'bowels' (*rachamim*) trembling with compassionate love: this is precisely what is revealed to the world when the Father surrenders all his love, embodied in the Son.[41]

Unless the Father generates the Son, how could the Son be the Reconciler of all the world? And then, on the Spirit, Balthasar maintains (as the *Theologik* will develop at far greater length) the twin Florentine dogmas of the procession from the Son within the more primordial proceeding from the Father.

Insofar as Jesus is the fruit of the Spirit's overshadowing of the Virgin, he naturally has the Spirit within him; but insofar as the Spirit is sent *down* upon him explicitly (in 'bodily form' [a reference to the Baptism, over against the Annunciation]), the Spirit is 'over him' (*ep' auton*: Matthew 3.16; Luke 3.22).[42]

When these two acts of the biblical drama are rendered in ontological form – the form they have received in the dogmatic tradition – what we find is that

the *being* of the Spirit in him – the Incarnate One – is the economic form of the *filioque*; and the Spirit who *comes down* upon him, hovers over him and drives him is the *a Patre procedit*.[43]

---

40 *TD* III, p. 514.
41 *TD* III, pp. 518–519.
42 *TD* III, p. 520.
43 *TD* III, p. 521.

All of which means that 'the spectrum of modes of the Spirit's presence admits of different modes of immediacy between Son and Father', in dependence on what Jesus' mission needs at some one time, or in some particular situation – and this is the deepest explanation of the inward variety in the Saviour's response to his destiny and call.

Of course the epiphany of God is mediated in created being. In one sense, it is owing to finite being's imagehood, or at any rate 'vestigial' likeness to God, that the persons can epiphanise on the stage. The final volume of *Theo-Drama* will consider the implications of this more fully, but Balthasar already drops the vital clue that

> being, in its hierarchical stages and degrees of interiority (existence, life, feeling, thinking and loving) simply cannot be anything but a trace, an image, of eternal, triune Being; and the more vibrant, communicative and fruitful it is, the more clearly it manifests this relation.[44]

But this cosmological and, above all, anthropological presupposition of the Trinitarian dramatic action is not, for Balthasar, primary. What comes first is the presupposition of that action which is the nature of the divine Trinity itself. Only the God who is himself everlasting plenary communion can 'get involved in his world ... without becoming entangled in its confusion'.[45] Transcendent, above the drama, and immanent, within it, he 'can simultaneously remain in himself and step forth from himself' – and in doing the latter, as the Gospels record, he stepped in fact into what was not merely non-divine but anti-divine.

Conclusion

Concluding his investigation of the Trinitarian nature as freedom, conducted as that enquiry was in the light of the New Testament revelation – in which, likewise, the other 'players' in theo-drama are to be assessed, Balthasar can only repeat that his original intuition (Christianity is, first and foremost, *drama*) was correct.

> The Christian God, in his identity, is able to be the 'One', the 'Other' and the 'Unifying'; even at the formal level, therefore, he is the most dramatic of all gods. Furthermore, when he produces a world out of himself and takes responsibility for it, this process, corresponding to the archetype from which it springs, is bound to be sublimely dramatic.[46]

Applying what we now grasp of the dramatic self-involvement of the Holy Trinity to the original dramatological 'trios' of the prolegomena volume, Balthasar reminds us how we distinguished a 'trio of creativity' – author, actor, director – from a 'trio of realization' – 'presentation', audience, 'horizon'. If we could see from the start that the first are

44 *TD* III, p. 525.
45 *TD* III, p. 529.
46 *TD* III, p. 531.

conceptually tailormade for Father, Son and Spirit ('a perfect metaphor for the economic [he will shortly add 'immanent-economic'] Trinity'),[47] the second set are, he suggests, equally apt for theological purposes: they show the 'way in which this Trinity, guiding and fashioning the world drama, draws it into itself'.[48]

47 *TD* III, p. 532, cf. p. 534. The American translator uses the term 'triad' – doubtless because of its overtones of *Trias*, the Greek for 'Trinity'.
48 *TD* III, p. 535.

THE ACTION

10

Scene of Action

Balthasar's theology of the Atonement is entitled, appropriately enough for a theodramatics, 'The Action'. Naturally, no theology of the Atonement can take the form of a pastoral idyll, for the salvation of humankind was hammered out with nails on wood. Alternatively, violently wrought though it was, the Atonement's outcome could easily be presented in terms of a serene reconciliation. Justified by the all-merit of the redemptive Sacrifice, humankind forgiven, divine wrath appeased, God and man are now at peace. This is not at all Balthasar's view. For him, the paradoxical result of the atoning ('at-one-ing') work of Jesus Christ is a hitherto unheard of intensification of the human hostility towards God.

> We are faced with a titanic rejection on man's part; he resists being embraced by this very mystery of the Cross. This anti-Christian aversion is something new; it has only existed since the coming of Christ . . . It is only when heaven is wide open that hell too yawns at our feet.[1]

But while this is previously unheard of, it is not altogether unexpected. The tinder was already laid in the construction of human freedom if the second and third volumes of *Theodramatik* are to be believed. Human beings are free *vis-à-vis* God and even over against him; and yet they are fully free only as 'persons in Christ'. This is an inherently unstable state of affairs, and when divine action is brought to bear upon it in the saving work of the Son it is hardly surprising to find it becoming explosive. Like a lens concentrating the rays of the sun, the combustible elements react by conflagration. This Balthasar takes to be the inspired meaning of the New Testament book under whose 'sign' he places his soteriology, the Revelation of St John the Divine.

Balthasar's reading of the Apocalypse is summed up in a single sentence, when he writes:

> Christ's completed work gives him power to break the seal of world history and unveil it; yet this very opening of the seal brings

---

1 *Theo-Drama: Theological Dramatic Theory*. IV. *The Action* (ET, San Francisco 1994), p. 11. Cited below as *TD* IV.

about a growing sense of fear and foreboding as the end of time approaches.[2]

As simultaneously the climax and an overview of both Testaments, the Apocalypse is a book about both judgment and salvation. And if in the first 11 chapters of the book judgment occupies centre stage inasmuch as the conclusive salvation is somehow allowed to stay latent, from Chapter 12 onwards it is the very efficaciousness of Christ's saving work which seems to summon opposing powers to a 'battlefield' for their last confrontation. A struggle is going on, and actually intensifying even as the Lamb himself stands victorious, bearing the trophies of victory. Hence the Seer can alternate between depiction of the heavenly Church's triumph and the Church militant's agony. Balthasar makes his own both Adrienne von Speyr's comment in her *Apokalypse* that faith just *means* 'living within the tension between the Old and the New Covenant', and her cinematographic simile for how nonetheless St John can show the consummating end:

> Since all must be fulfilled, there must also be this momentary fulfillment of eternal pain (like a 'still' taken from a film), and of this too the saints must have knowledge.[3]

The Johannine Apocalypse is, then, quintessentially Christian because typified by a ubiquitous dramatic tension. For Balthasar, the Revelation justifies in advance the master-theme of Augustine's *City of God*: salvation history manifests a 'law of heightened resistance' whereby two 'cities' increasingly diverge as the counter-divine one takes on, as if in parody, the forms of its heavenly enemy. And all of this fulfils the predictions of Jesus himself about the world's response to the disciples.[4]

The apocalyptic drama occupies the entire stage of theo-drama as a whole – namely, heaven and earth, though its 'earth' is 'more theological than cosmological':[5] a world whose face is turned away from God. In a 'rebirth' of Old Testament images – the phrase comes from that great theologian of Anglican Catholicism, Austin Farrer[6] – divine judgment on the earthly city swells to monstrous proportions. As Balthasar points out, here divine blessings fall to earth as penal acts of divine justice, for the Lamb's atoning work is blasphemed and ridiculed by men. Accordingly, 'these punishments conceal heaven's love for the guilty earth',[7] on the principle that good fathers correct what is wayward in their children.

And if the stage setting takes in all heaven and earth, the timescale includes all the events of revelation. Against the perduring backcloth of an 'eternal present' constituted by the Lamb slain in intention from the beginning of the world, the reality of time irrupts with ever more momentous consequences into that of eternity. Balthasar's interpretation

2 *TD* IV, p. 18.
3 A. Von Speyr, *Apokalypse* (Einsiedeln 1976²), p. 464.
4 As in Matthew 10; John 15.1–16.4.
5 *TD* IV, p. 25.
6 A. Farrer, *A Rebirth of Images: The Making of St John's Apocalypse* (London 1949).
7 *TD* IV, p. 26.

of the sequence of symbolically portrayed events in the Apocalypse is no doubt as plausible as others on sale in the exegetical marketplace. He maintains that the author made no veiled references to particular happenings in secular history or governmental powers in the history of politics, but that nevertheless he shows us 'utterly concrete principles' clashing by night.

Balthasar emphasises the perversely brilliant counterimage which evil offers God. The seven-headed beast, itself a parody of the seven-fold Spirit, 'was, and is not, and is to ascend from the bottomless pit and go to perdition' (Apocalypse 17.8) – a grotesque echo of the God who 'is and who was and who is to come' (1.8).[8] While the beasts counterposed to the Incarnation are destroyed by Christ (19.19–21) and the final enemy – the dragon – is reduced to nothing by God alone (20.9), the fall of Babylon, that symbol of the human city organised not only without God but against him, is precipitated by the beast itself, together with its instruments, the rulers – something which Balthasar interprets as a disclosure of evil's self-devouring, self-destructing character (18.1–24; 19.17–21).

From the centre of history, the incarnate and crucified Logos both reigns and fights, so that he can rule universally. The much-disputed millennium, when Satan is 'bound' and the saints co-reign with Christ Balthasar takes, with Augustine, as a reference to the age of the Church while also allowing this peculiarly Johannine concept its own consistency. In a statement important for his hagiology, Balthasar declares:

> The saints and the blessed exercise a bodily presence and influence on the earthly Church that is not shared, to the same degree, by the 'rest of the dead' (cf. Apocalypse 20.5). The binding of Satan is thus only the necessary counterpart to the saints' exercise of power together with Christ; it can be regarded as a different perspective on his fall from heaven.[9]

By 'bodily presence' Balthasar does not mean, presumably, that all glorified souls are in that condition which Catholic doctrine ascribes to the blessed Virgin as the *Assumpta*, but rather that, thanks to the special efficacy of the intercession of the saints, the *density* of their continued earthly rôle is that much greater. Even this 'millennial' reign is, however, succeeded by struggle, a final intensification of the struggle between the pro-God and the anti-God cities – whereupon evil's 'innermost potency' is consigned to self-consuming torment.

The framework of this drama – the opening vision, with John's seven letters to the churches of Asia, and the closing scene of a transfigured city, radiant with God's glory – show how this histrionic material is to be used. The aim of the book is paraenetic – to encourage the Christian disciple, and each local church, to sustain their evangelical existence and mission, even amid great hardships, in the knowledge that, through the Church, earthly realities will one day be transformed into heavenly. For the seer, carried forward to the vantage point of the End:

8 Cf. *TD* IV, pp. 450–451.
9 *TD* IV, p. 41.

What is already true in the Church, in the hiddenness of faith, that is, that God himself and the Lamb are her temple and her light, is now fulfilled openly and publicly (21.22ff.). Similarly, the Church's doors were always open to the world; she was always the light of the world, and the riches of the nations were already hers yet in an invisible manner; now, however, this will be manifest to the eyes of all (21.23–26).

And that is possible, in the last analysis, for reasons not ecclesiological but Christological. It is the One who declares himself 'the first and the last, the beginning and the end' (22.13) who is the

complete framework for that entire drama that embraces world history and the end-time.[10]

In his reflections on the Johannine Apocalypse, Balthasar explains why he has placed his soteriology (opening out as this does onto his eschatology) under the sign of this mysterious book. The last text in the New Testament canon not only presupposes the salvific events which the rest of the New Testament mirrors and describes; it also integrates within itself those prophetic and apocalyptic elements in the Old Testament canon which are most pertinent to a theological dramatics.[11] Its particular dramatic form is admirably suited to its content, which can indeed be regarded as the unfolding of that form. More especially, the images of the Apocalypse constitute a kind of dogmatics in themselves – an overall, and authoritative, interpretation of the gospel in its illumination of human history from the beginning to the end – and as such stand over against the particular events, processes, trends which typify the Church's life (rather than being their coded reformulation). And yet:

the drama only attains its full shape if we relate the sequence of images to the concrete communities addressed in the 'letters' and reflect on their situation as we find it in the images, magnified and projected onto an eschatological canvas.[12]

The images cannot be reduced to the situations; but they must nonetheless be led back to them. At the same time, on Balthasar's reading, so far from enmeshing the book in so determinate a historical period that it ceases to have a trans-historical message to utter, this proceeding enables us to identify the specificity of revelation's drama in its full dimensions for the first time. Revelation is theodramatic because it shows a God who is simultaneously 'superior to history and involved in it' – and this supreme dramatic fact finds a climactic expression in the 'law of proportionate polarization' which governs Balthasar's soteriology as a whole. In his own formulation, 'the more God intervenes [in this world, and its theatrical play], the more he elicits opposition to himself'.[13]

---

10 *TD* IV, p. 44.
11 Balthasar cites approvingly, at *TD* IV, p. 45, the judgment of Lucien Cerfaux that the 'Apocalypse is nothing other than a clear translation, in the light of the New Testament, of the prophecies of the Old', *Lectio Divina* 17, p. 89.
12 *TD* IV, pp. 50–51.
13 *TD* IV, p. 51.

The historical self-involvement of the sovereign God and its para-doxical effects, this will be, then, the *Leitmotif* of 'the Action' of salvation. The scenario remains profoundly Christ-centred for 'The Lamb is God's mode of involvement in, and commitment to, the world'.[14] This is no straightforward salvation-historical theology which pooh-poohs the customary high regard in which Catholicism has held philosophy. The Lamb of the Apocalypse, announced from the first as Alpha and Omega (1.8,17), Origin and Destiny of the world in God, constitutes in his relation with God the New Testament solution to the dilemma faced by all philosophy that bears on divine things. For God is not to be conceived as remote from history ('undramatic philosoph-ism') nor is he to be thought of as absorbed by history ('tragic mythology'). Balthasar draws his readers' attention to the way that, in the book of Revelation, the Invisible One hands over his divine prerogatives to the Lamb (5.12–13), including the Fatherly prerogative of giving gifts to his creation (3.21). Here the self-giving of Father to Son becomes the prototype of his self-giving in the Son to the world. The soteriological importance of this meditation on the theme of *traditio* ('handing over') is that it enables us to reconcile the Atonement-triumph of the Lamb with the ever increasing challenges to his reign which that same triumph releases. It is because the primordial handing-over of the Father, in the eternal generation of the Son, is beyond all challenge, not least in its constitution of the Son as ground of all creation, that the Son made man, and his disciples after him, can be betrayed into the hands of sinful men – as we say in the collect of the Paschal Triduum – without God's reign over the universe foundering in shipwreck. Or, in Balthasar's own terminology, with its play on the dual meaning of *traditio* (transmission and betrayal), this is how the saving eternal 'event' of the Lamb's slaying before the beginning of the world can embrace with such security 'all the endangered and costly *traditiones* flowing from it'.[15] God's loveable majesty can be adored even in such a world of bloody conflict as ours. Worship and slaughter, the aesthetic and the dramatic, *can* be Trinitarianly held together. The worshipper, accordingly, should always have the *unity* of God's action in his or her view.

God's love and his wrath, his reconciling work and his vengeance, are inseparably joined in the dramatic rhythm of the Atonement. The 'law of proportionate polarization' ensures that when the 'ever-greater' God is involved in the drama, the stakes for which the game is played will rise continually. The profile of Satan, the nature of Hell, the existence of the sin against the Holy Ghost – these things only become visible when the One who bears the Spirit without measure steps forth. Only Christ produces Anti-Christ. The final volume of *Theodramatik* will consider how it can thus be possible that 'he who encompasses all things, the Alpha and Omega, seems ultimately to be encircled by the final act'.[16]

If Pascal, in his memorial of his conversion, could call the biblical God 'fire', the same (literally) ardent metaphor concludes Balthasar's

14 *TD* IV, p. 52.
15 *TD* IV, p. 53.
16 *TD* IV, p. 58.

apocalyptic preface to his soteriology. The Pentateuch already knew Israel's God as a consuming fire, but, with the Incarnation, the drama is heightened as Jesus burns innerly with the fire of God. If an unwritten logion in the Jesus tradition maintains 'Whoever comes near me, comes near the fire', the canonical version of his sayings remembers his claim that his mission is to 'cast fire upon the earth' (Luke 12.49), and his wish that 'it be kindled'. Down the chasms which his saving action opens, the entire biblical revelation is seen (with the seer of the Apocalypse) as a blazing fire.

Before coming onto the main business of *Theodramatik* IV, Balthasar asks himself why a theological dramatic theory has emerged (through him!) at this particular juncture in the history of culture and Church.

He appears to have two answers – neither of them, perhaps, altogether credible. In the first place he believes that only in the late twentieth century has religion become a question of being for or against Jesus Christ – as the 'natural piety' which once sustained a metaphysical outlook on life disappears like the dew of morning. And in the second place, the attempt by a Godless world's most persuasive theology – liberationism – to incorporate the 'collapsing edifice' of Christendom into the city that positive humanism is building does nothing like full justice to the true scope of the biblical revelation. By way of the stark confrontation of the world with the gospel in the first, and the palpable insufficiency of the dominant attempt to mediate their relations in the second, the imperative need for a theodramatics makes itself heard.

The analysis is too *simpliste*[17] – but that is no reason not to be grateful for the soteriology which now unfolds, as Balthasar expounds three themes. And these are: first, human action – the acting of humanity both as individuals and as a corporate whole; secondly, divine action as God prepares the way for the coming in the flesh of the Christ who, as the Alpha of creation, was already presupposed in the making of Adam, bringing his involvement to its climax in the deeds of Jesus, above all in his Cross and Resurrection; and, thirdly, the continuing dramatic encounter of God and man in history, in what Balthasar calls, with an echo of the Apocalypse, the 'Battle of the Logos'.

---

17 Cf., however, *TD* IV, pp. 435–442, where the Christian 'polarization' of other religions, and the notion of a covert secularism using weapons foresworn by the Logos to build the divine Kingdom on earth are more satisfactorily described.

11

The Human Predicament

First, then, Balthasar must consider the parameters of human action, or, as he puts it, what it is like to be an actor on the stage of the world. In theo-drama, we are aware that the dramatic action takes place between heaven and earth – the action is first and foremost God's, yet not only his, for, as Balthasar remarks of the Lamb slain before the beginning of the world, 'Whence comes the Lamb's supratemporal wound, if not from his destiny on earth?'[1] Without the revelation which draws back the veil from the hidden divine action, however, what we are aware of is, rather, the horizontal (as distinct from vertical) time dimension, man's life in history. And straightaway that confronts us with a very basic question: Does humanity's historical existence have a meaning, or is man just a puzzle to himself? Is he, as Balthasar puts it, simply a 'living Sphinx'?

When Balthasar considers people's efforts to make sense of their activity the best word he can find to describe them is 'pathetic'. By this he does not mean of course that the human attempt to identify significance in man's own history is derisory, hardly worth a second glance. He means rather that the human creature fills us with pity and awe when we watch that creature trying to make of its life a whole when in reality it can only be a fragment. Human beings are congenitally incapable, it would seem, of abandoning the search for a complete meaning to their lives. And yet none of their actions brings such a total meaning within their reach. And alas, on the only occasion when a total and unconditionally valid meaning – what Balthasar calls an 'absolute' meaning – *did* pop up on the human horizon, in the Incarnation, men rejected it – which helps to explain why, in the Apocalypse, St John treats the 'pathos of the world stage' as not just terrible and pitiful but grotesque and demonic as well.

No philosophy, not even a religious philosophy, can solve this problem. The philosopher, certainly, can help in drawing out the implicit claim to absoluteness – to totality of meaning – which human beings invest in their actions. But in his concern with general or universal truths the philosopher can also be far from helpful: he has no time to linger over the individual things which are the bearers of the pathos of the world. For centuries such historical particulars have been regarded as beneath the

---

1 *TD* IV, p. 71.

philosopher's notice. Nor is even an explicitly *religious* philosophy – and here Balthasar is really thinking of Karl Rahner's 'transcendental theology' – any better placed. The redemption (as we shall see) was dramatically performed by God in utter freedom; it is wrong to say that man has always been somehow aware of its saving grace, even if only tacitly or obliquely, as in Rahner's theory of the human being as an 'anonymous Christian'. We cannot presume to say how God will enter our play and transform it. As Balthasar writes:

> True, man can stare spellbound at the point at which the finite, in its decline and demise, must – surely, he thinks – be joined and wedded to the infinite that comes to save it; but, in positing this point where the relative and the absolute conjoin, he is bound to go farther and farther astray, particularly if he is presumptuous enough to try to guess where this point might be or even aim for it.[2]

In other words, to assume that the answer to our dilemma – the baffling contradiction that we feel called to do things that carry ultimate value and yet are ourselves both finite and frail – must be a permanent relationship between God and man which anyone, be they Christian or not, could discover (were they fortunate enough) fails to take human freedom sufficiently into account (just as it *also* underplays *God's* freedom to act in our regard). And indeed, unless we have a strong dose of theodramatics added to our theology, the true dimensions of sin and grace – so Balthasar thinks – will always be sold short. As he writes:

> A theodramatic theory must relentlessly insist that, first of all, the pathos arising from the real world, a pathos full of obscurity and weakness, should be put fully before us before we go on to speak of God's free response ... If we fail to allow the world time and space to reveal itself as it is and keep interposing the divine response as something that was 'always there', we risk depriving the world/ God relationship of all dramatic tension. God's merciful *turning toward* a lost world, in Jesus Christ and, earlier, in the election of Israel – this fundamentally dramatic act of God in his freedom – becomes the undramatic, permanent, essential constitution of a God who, as in Plato and Plotinus, and later in Spinoza and the Enlightenment, is (and always has been) the eternally radiant 'Sun of Goodness' ...[3]

a God to whom, then, the phases of salvation history, as they develop, are fundamentally one and the same.

Before going on to consider the divine action, in other words, we need to look with clinical realism at what Balthasar calls the 'wounds of existence', which he numbers as fourfold. And they are: firstly, time, including death; secondly, freedom which so easily leads to, thirdly, the abuse of power; and fourthly, therefore, evil in all its forms. These wounds – death, freedom, power and evil – render the more painful an existence

---

2 *TD* IV, p. 75.
3 *TD* IV, p. 76.

already problematic thanks to finitude. More specifically, they give a pathological character to the way our finitude lays claim to meaning. As a result, it becomes extremely unlikely that any purely human would-be solution to life's riddle can count as a valid 'cypher' for redemption. Who could guess, after all, that God himself would have descended into this 'whole chaotic labyrinth of worldly existence'?[4]

Balthasar describes with care the negative features which render our activity so questionable – all with a view to showing that, while we cannot renounce the task of fashioning a complete meaning for our lives – individual or corporate – we cannot fulfil it either. We are not wrong in thinking that somehow our lives must relate to the absolute – we *are* open, by our reason, to the totality of being, truth and goodness, and must orient ourselves towards it. The problem is that we cannot see *how* to do it. In a hundred and twenty pages of description,[5] Balthasar brings our predicament before our eyes, presenting our pathology (the four wounds) in terms of three themes: in his own words, 'finite existence's claim to meaning and the problematical relationship between development and progress'; 'the multiple values attributable to the time dimension and to death'; 'the relationship between freedom, power and sin'.[6]

Meaning and progress

Thus, firstly, everyone feels some need to put their mark on fleeting time, whether it be to scratch their names on the bark of a tree or to change the direction of an empire. And this is itself a paradox: for it is a need to 'write the absolute upon the relative'.[7] This is not metaphysics: it is observation of everyday occurrences, of which metaphysics (and its surrogates) are attempted illuminations. Balthasar regards the idea of progress which can take many forms – from Bacon through the Enlightenment to the Victorian social prophets – as chief among these delusions. Seen anthropocentrically, the Old Testament people of God contributed to this development, since faced with the same problematic as everyone else (indeed, the notion that Hebrew man in his frail mortality can share a covenant with the absolutely Living One is a particularly perspicuous instance of the strange claim of finitude on the Unconditional), they hoped, in messianism and eschatology, that God's salvation would come to earth. When that religious hope fused with the *a*religious concept of technical progress it produced that deceiving theme on which the history of European thought has provided so many variations. But the true concept of progress, for Balthasar, is that of a *qualitative* progress inseparable from the (unpredictable) *spiritual* freedom of *persons*. Though there can be a Hogarthian Rake's Progress – a regress – in the lives of individuals, there can also be the Pilgrim's Progress charted by Bunyan, where what is dramatic

4 *TD* IV, p. 78.
5 In the English translation, *TD* IV, pp. 81–201.
6 *TD* IV, p. 79.
7 *TD* IV, p. 83.

is not only that a spiritual being, an identity, can learn from his past, enrich himself in his present and plan his future; [more,] at each successive 'now' he is able, through a free and responsible decision, to stamp the entirety of his finitude with a meaning that reflects, and is guaranteed by, the presence of the Absolute (through conversion, for instance). [Although] no man can estimate what this meaning is worth in the context of the Absolute (since no one can be his own judge), yet the drama enacted on the stage can allow us, as it were, to take a look at the Judge's cards.[8]

What, by contrast, is quite impracticable is the would-be extrapolation of such progress to the corporate realm of the historical process as a whole – for such collective progress can only be of a quantitative, measurable kind, and hence a technological progress which gradually, at the hands of such sociologists as Comte and Marx ends by swallowing the ethical and spiritual, acquiring in the process a spurious religious colouration of its own. Though Kant, at least, was well aware that a legally coerced curbing of selfishness, whatever its merits, did not equate with real moral behaviour, the tendency of nineteenth-century thought was to suppose with Hegel that our hope should lie with 'objective spirit', the potentially salvific force of social institutions. But this is not only a mirage; it is one peculiarly damaging to persons:

> If *per impossibile* a satisfactory final situation *could* be reached, it would rob all preceding historical present moments of their reality, reducing them to the level of purely instrumental preliminary stages, looking toward a future that cannot presently be envisaged; the individual would be cheated of the reward due to the efforts he had made and the suffering he had undergone. Belief in progress is a flight from time; it flees from everything that, in time, is eternal.[9]

Balthalsar's conclusion, from this survey of his first motif, is that we cannot unravel the 'paradox whereby man is forever trying to translate what is absolute into terms that are relative and transitory'.[10]

Time and death

But what of the second theme, time and death? The second theme, Balthasar shows, presents the first in a fresh perspective: for the issues of time and death exemplify how we find ourselves constrained to inscribe, once again, 'things of absolute validity' upon a 'time continuum that is running out'.[11]

The individual has his or her 'own' time, which fits into, but is not identical with, a neutral clock-time. My time for living is my own mode of existence, yet it is not under my control, as the incidence of dying proves so conclusively. As Augustine saw in the *Confessions*, my time is granted

8 *TD* IV, p. 88.
9 *TD* IV, pp. 93–94.
10 *TD* IV, p. 94.
11 *TD* IV, p. 100.

me in the very moment of its withdrawal from me, making the subject (myself) intrinsically historical. Though I cannot impart an overall shape to it by my own volition, I can, if I desire, dramatically shape each moment and – by supremely personal reformation – give new significance to both past and future. At any rate biological fulfilment does not correspond with dramatic or existential – as the foreshortened lives of many a youthful genius (Mozart, Schubert) or saint (Elizabeth of Hungary, Thérèse of Lisieux) make clear. This personal time is not, Balthasar stresses, hermetically sealed off from that of others; rather do our times communicate with each other. In fact, given Balthasar's view of the priority of receptivity in the constitution of the self (symbolised in the child's experience of identity-awakening by a mother's smile), both the 'I' and the community of persons share the same source: so neither Existentialism nor social philosophy, taken by themselves, can be the whole truth. The temporal continuum is, therefore, 'ours' – without in any way losing its character of being 'mine'. From this Balthasar draws the important conclusion that

> the individual's responsibility for his action and conduct in the face of death plays a part in the like responsibility of others ... Thus the individual becomes co-responsible for the common destiny of mankind, not only with regard to the time-span in which he lives but also for the generations who will live after him ...[12]

And since he or she can thus only work out their own salvation by contributing to that of all:

> If a God were ever to require him personally to give an account of his stewardship of his 'death-bound time', he would have to appear before the divine judgment seat together with all mankind.[13]

And here human freedom makes all plotting of curves on the graph of life wasted effort. As the analysis of progress has shown: even if, with Teilhard and Julian Huxley, one were to imagine humankind as seizing hold of natural evolution and continuing it on a new level, no guarantee can be forthcoming that evolution would continue to run in a law-governed way.

What we *can* provide, however, is an anticipatory sketch of the dramatic resources of that human freedom which deprives individual or corporate history of any clear grasp of destiny. We can, as Balthasar puts it:

> foresee the kind of gestures that will be made and the scenes that will be enacted on the world stage.[14]

In our temporal condition as beings bound for death we do indeed make 'gestures' that confront the concentrated energies of human existence. Balthasar speaks of those energies as media through which man tries to make absolute time – for instance by erotic love, which would make absolute a marriage partner, or by seeking a surrogate immortality in

12 *TD* IV, p. 100.
13 *TD* IV, p. 101.
14 *TD* IV, p. 104.

children, or by the self-affirmation of power-politics, or by creativity in art, music, and literature – and shows that in these examples too is no lasting city. As his Basle fellow-citizen, the historian of culture Jakob Burckhardt, pointed out, Who can guarantee that one day even the greatest literature may not cease to be intelligible?[15] By our principal 'gestures of existence' Balthasar has in mind such things as: taking responsibility, which he links with repentance in the widest sense; treating others with both justice and mercy; love, which is so ambiguous and always in need of purification; and hope or, in the best sense, resignation to our destiny – all these are shot through with pathos, with a (literally) dreadful feeling that we are never going to be able properly to fulfil them. For looking up to the norm while looking down to things of time is not an easy operation; doing what is both absolutely required and yet possible here and now is no 'push-over'. Nor is this in any way theologically surprising, interjects Balthasar, thus briefly abandoning the persona of phenomenologist, for, created as man was with a view to the Second Adam, the God-Man, we naturally cannot discover the equipoise between the Absolute and the relative, since it is only established in the Incarnation.

Human pathos comes to its climax in the phenomenon of death, on which Balthasar asks:

> How can a being that is able to recognize truth and has an obligation to do what is good be swallowed up by the law of the cosmic cycle?[16]

Perhaps it belongs to the very existence of such a creature that it should, with many religions and philosophies, look beyond its finite time to a sphere where, as Balthasar puts it, the 'unfinished business of life' is resolved – which could mean either protology, looking back towards a primeval Fall, or eschatology, looking forward towards a post-mortem survival or re-constitution. And of course Christian faith and its theology will eventually do that, and yet, as Balthasar points out, when the Apocalypse says of the victorious Crucified that he holds the 'keys of Death and Hades' (1.18) it evidently treats death with complete serious-ness as a reality – and so must we likewise, when observing the human condition.

Death, Balthasar points out, is both ordinarily run-of-the-mill and yet extraordinarily personal. Inasmuch as we are the product of the organic life of the cosmos, death is utterly everyday, almost banal. Yet at the same time (and here is where the distinctively human connexion between organic life and spiritual being comes into view) my death is something uniquely personal to me:

> the most lonely encounter with my I-that-is-no-longer, an encounter that sheds a light of absolute seriousness on everything I am still able to experience in the time that remains to me.[17]

---

15 J. Burckhardt, 'Die historische Grösse', in *Weltgeschichtliche Betrachtungen* (Stuttgart 1969), p. 221.
16 *TD* IV, p. 117.
17 *TD* IV, p. 122.

And here Balthasar can call to his side the Existentialist philosophers –
Kierkegaard, Heidegger and Jaspers, as well as one strand in the sensibility of the Old Testament. On reviewing more widely, however, the
history of both Israelite and pagan thought in ancient times, Balthasar
doubts whether antiquity *can* take us further forward: for while in Israel
it was above all the *nation* that was the principal subject of mortal man's
relation with the Absolute, the main option of the Greek and Roman
philosophers was to give the primacy to the eternal *universe* into which
the individual would be re-absorbed and from which (conceivably) he or
she could be reborn. And it is impossible for post-Christian man to return
to that

> comfortable security of being part of a chosen people (Judaism) or
> of an all-embracing, divine world of nature (as in paganism). Now
> the individual experiences himself not only merely as an individual
> but also as a person.[18]

After Christianity, the loneliness of *personal* dying cannot be palliated.
This does not stop secular society from treating death as a socio-medical
problem to be organised and manipulated, thereby throwing up the
idea of a 'natural' death which is in reality the most artificial. When
further medical probes or experimental treatment prove unrewarding,
the patient is 'left to die in a frighteningly inhuman way'. In the
technological society the dead are of no more account, their graves
neglected or trampled on. Balthasar finds it highly significant that *both*
materialism *and* Idealism concur in regarding the 'immortalisation' of
individuals as aspiration misplaced. The tension between my (personal)
death and our (general) death is collapsed unilaterally in favour of the
latter, thus intensifying the problem, for now the 'central paradox of
existence' (namely, the invitation to 'recognize and implement the
Absolute in the relative') understood, though not resolved, in all earlier
sacral societies, is simply pushed to one side. What Balthasar means by
modern suppressive or antiseptic attitudes making the problem worse
becomes plain when he asks:

> Are we not due an explanation for the stark contrast between the
> obscurity of man's beginning and ending (at the level of both the
> individual and the generality) and the clarity with which, at the
> height of his consciousness, man can distinguish between true and
> false?

And moreover:

> What of the equally stark contrast between the torpor and violence
> of nature that forms man's infrastructure and his irrefutably
> luminous awareness that good and evil are irreconcilable?[19]

True, man does not want to be just a surviving soul, nor does he, if he has
sense, require his present finitude to be infinitely prolonged, after the

18 *TD* IV, p. 125.
19 *TD* IV, p. 130.

fashion of much science fiction and some would-be science fact. What he is thoroughly justified in doing, however, is in postulating the need for a solution. Existence, which after all was *given* me – it is my givenness which calls for clarification – requires to be 'taken seriously in its finitude and justified ... from within, on the basis of its own substance ... in the face of the absolute'.[20] And here Balthasar looks ahead to the divine response to this demand of thought (and more than thought, of *life*). It turns out that

> God does not provide the answer from outside, from above – like the Spectator-Judge who sits in state above the Calderonesque world-drama – but comes on stage practically incognito and takes part in the action. He wants to share not only finitude, with all its happiness and sorrow, but also the human demise, human collapse and death.[21]

With the entry of the infinite into the finite, the latter cannot claim that its intrinsic significance has been overlooked. Yet something 'unimaginable' befalls:

> what is finite, as such, is drawn into what is ultimate and eternal; what is finite in its temporal extension, in each one of its moments and their interconnection, and not merely, for instance, in its final result ...[22]

The Jesus who was God's answer, adopting finitude's own gestures, succeeded, by his life, in living out our transitoriness in an ultimate and eternal way. Above all, his death, though in its uniqueness truly his (indeed, 'the most lonely anyone had ever undergone'), had the capacity to change our fortunes universally.

> Since he was the absolute answer, he could make it the most *communicable* death: all can share in it.[23]

And this is what the theology of the Atonement sets itself to explore. As a solution at once from above and yet immanent in finite existence this is the *only* possible resolution of our basic problem – the efficacious interrelating of Absolute and relative.

Freedom, power, sin

But before getting our teeth into that meat of the matter there remains Balthasar's *third* and last anthropological theme, the topic of 'freedom, power and evil'. The three terms stand in close association because, as human experience indicates, evil comes from freedom, and freedom uses whatever power is available, whether its own or someone else's. For Balthasar *sin* is revolt against our essential structure, so its depiction

20 *TD* IV, p. 131.
21 *TD* IV, p. 132.
22 *TD* IV, p. 132.
23 *TD* IV, p. 133 (italics original).

requires a reminder of what that structure may be. Following Kierkegaard, Balthasar sees created freedom as incapable of finding its own poise without a recognition of its own creatureliness, without in fact coming to rest in God. Now God, the absolute Subject, is, for Balthasar, spontaneously concluded to from the self's subjecthood – essential as this is for recognising the true and striving to implement the good. We are talking about a received subjecthood, dependent on awakening by others (parents, or whomever), and so contingent, calling out (logically) for its unconditioned Source. What the Paul of the Letter to the Romans calls 'the things that have been made' (1.20), by which God's power and deity make themselves manifest, are first and foremost, then, not cosmic realities but – on this view – spirits in their self-possession. Nonetheless it is still divine *power* which is at stake, though when we add to this thought the consideration that the absolute Subject – of all possible subjects! – must be capable of voluntary self-disclosure, the notion that freedom means power is tempered into the affirmation that true freedom is seen in self-giving.[24] This does not mean, however, that self-giving is *opposed* to power, for self-giving (pre-eminently) implies freedom, and freedom is the fundamental expression, for creatures, of their power which belongs, then, with the *goodness* of creation.

It is where the person engaged in the activity of choosing sets himself up as the standard of the good, subordinating goodness to his own exercise of power, that sin originally arises – the 'fontal sin', as the English churchman Thomas Ken calls it.[25] The separating out of power and goodness constitutes the primal temptation, for the individual first of all, but also for the *polis*, the State. Given the actual constitution of human society in a post-lapsarian world, the justice which the State's power structure protects can only be an *aspect* of the goodness typical of the divine self-giving. In the modern period, however, the State characteristically makes use of an instrumental rationality for which personal indebtedness to God and indeed goodness itself are irrelevant. Balthasar offers a Heideggerian reading of Descartes and Kant for which the philosophical meandering of the river of Western thought debouches in Nietzsche: those earlier philosophers' decision to base metaphysics (or its equivalent) on the self-conscious subject was a will to power without being aware of the fact. So must it ever be, once the 'supreme values' are no longer established by Being in its self-giving. What Nietzsche so shatteringly reveals, by his claim in *Wille zur Macht* that all grace comes from man in his autonomy, is our age's *inability to receive*.[26] Going beyond Heidegger, whom he has thus far followed, Balthasar locates the root of the malaise in the failure of that fundamental act which is *prayer*, and this brings him to the inescapable nexus which joins evil to the question of *God*.

On Balthasar's exegesis of the Fall in the Paradise garden, Adam and Eve in choosing pass from a pre-ethical to an ethical state but by the anti-

---

24 Balthasar leaves open the question as to how far the 'natural man' may proceed with such discovery; at any rate this is what a theologically tutored philosophy will say about the real.
25 In his fine Marian hymn 'Her Virgin Eyes'.
26 F. Nietzsche, *Wille zur Macht* XV, cited *TD* IV, p. 158.

God fashion in which they exercise autonomous choice do so in a non-necessarily negative way. Reminding his readers that, as *Theodramatik* II has shown, freedom is not only autonomy but also indebtedness and orientation to its own primal Ground, Balthasar explains:

> Insofar as the twin poles of finite freedom inseparably coinhere, autonomy cannot be conceived apart from the dynamism of its 'whence' and 'whither': it is this that makes it a real image and likeness of absolute freedom. As a result, when man exclusively opts for his own autonomy, this dynamism is attributed to the latter and, as it were, incorporated into it: he becomes his own origin and goal. But while man's autonomy is genuinely *given to him* in a fundamental and permanent sense, it is impossible to think of the Giver being absent; in fact, he is the One who, in the act of constant presence – both in his omnipotence and in his total goodness – communicates to the finite being something that is fundamentally his own. Thus, in attributing its own gift-quality to itself, finite freedom is alienating something that belongs to the absolute and is inseparable from it and attempting to put it at the disposal of finite freedom.[27]

But once autonomous freedom has been established as absolute, it can only regard itself as the norm of the good. Whereas for the Absolute the good *is* power, for the finite self the good can only be *in* its power. That self cannot reproduce the Absolute's aspect of self-giving within the category of autonomy, for it will not fit. But to *have the good within one's power* is a contradiction in terms: hence the unhappiness of finite freedom as we know it. This contradiction is then exported to any and every interpersonal relationship (thus Adam blaming Eve, and Eve the serpent); in place of loving solidarity come mutually antagonistic absolute entities. Owing to our primordial consciousness of the true (for our essential nature is not obliterated by the Fall, only its functioning), this makes of evil one continuous lie – something at its clearest, Balthasar thinks, in the frequently encountered assertion that only when human beings are liberated from heteronomy *vis-à-vis* the Absolute can the values of this world attain their full development. Now we begin to glimpse how only redemption can meet our need.

> Seeking 'liberation' through total autonomy, [man] is so fettered by it (for total autonomy belongs only to God) that release can only come from God.[28]

Resistance to this divine redemptive initiative leads the sinner to absolutise his self-righteousness, and so (just as in the Apocalypse of John, from which this volume of the theodramatics took its rise) evil becomes ever more entrenched precisely as God's power and goodness are the more generously displayed. This is why the

27 *TD* IV, p. 163.
28 *TD* IV, p. 165.

unity of power and goodness in God must show itself in the form of wrath, so that the power of his goodness can be seen as his mercy upon the sinner.[29]

God's self-disclosure is not everywhere met with the same intensity, or shared with the same clarity. In particular while 'all have sinned' (Romans 3.23), the nature and burden of sin is most directly manifested in Israel – precisely because in her God's light appeared at its most gracious and therefore most challenging. Revealing as it does the conditions under which humankind can live out covenant existence, grace and thus (in the way explained) sin increase in intensity until the final *dénouement* of the divine drama in Jesus Christ. God's love reacts 'violently' to the violence done it by men – so the language of the prophets bears witness: something to be explained by God's 'total investment of himself' in this relationship as well as by the 'utterly astonishing indifference, rejection and hardness of heart' to be found on the part of man. In his Passion Jesus the Christ will take upon himself the sin of the whole world, 'confessing' it in a fashion that is for the first time total and then, in his Resurrection, receiving an 'absolution' as wide as the whole world. (In this profound theology of the implications of the Death and Resurrection for sin and grace, Balthasar was in debt to the remarkable theology of the sacrament of Reconciliation produced by Adrienne von Speyr.)[30] Yet in the post-Easter Church, specifically in the Letters of John, the negative power of godlessness emerges in staggeringly concentrated form – as a resounding No to the Incarnation of the Father's Son. Owing to original sin, man's natural desire for God is crossed by a negative desire to be for himself. As a result of this distorted solidarity in which we now find ourselves in the first Adam, the form of the grace God offers is no longer based on the Son's mediatorship in creation. Rather is that grace's fashion as *agonal*, as much of a struggle, as fallen existence itself: it comes now through the Cross, so that only by dying to self with the Second Adam can fulfilment be. And this explains both the spirit of anti-Christ which can afflict human beings in the Cross's shadow, but also, at the same time, the Church's worshipping wonderment at the depths of the divine goodness: our 'common lack of an inner orientation toward God and his grace' has elicited from God a 'deeper and more painful form of his love'.[31]

Beyond even the sin of human origins there lies a further realm, relevant to Balthasar's conviction that the biblical theo-drama is not only world-historical but *cosmic* in its scope. Here looms (Balthasar has been recalling a reference to the sheer 'quantity and malice of evil *hic et nunc*' in Teilhard's *Phenomenon of Man*)[32]

the insoluble question of whether the 'excess' of suffering ascertained by the phenomenologist has not something to do, even at the level of the subhuman world, with the 'principalities and powers' of

---

29 *TD* IV, p. 167.
30 A. von Speyr, *Confession* (ET, San Francisco 1985), cited in *TD* IV, p. 180.
31 *TD* IV, pp. 190–191.
32 P. Teilhard de Chardin, *The Phenomenon of Man* (ET, London 1959), p. 341.

which Paul speaks. Has it not something to do with the 'god of this world', the 'prince' and 'ruler' of this world, whose original fall from God is responsible for the deep rent that goes from the bottom right up to the top, – where it emerges as mankind's tragic history.[33]

Balthasar will return to this question of the possible involvement of angelic evil in human affairs.

33 *TD* IV, pp. 197–198.

12

The Saving Deed

Enough has been said about the human pathos which strikes the spectator of the play of life. Balthasar must now turn to the centre of theo-drama, the pathos of *God*. But before presenting his 'dramatic soteriology', he furnishes us with some criteria for testing its adequacy in a concise history of soteriological thinking in the Catholic tradition as well as its pre-history in Israel.

Evangelical preparation

Harmonising with the picture already painted in the Old Testament volume of the theological aesthetics, Balthasar treats the time of Israel as the age of God's patience, when he endures sin in view of the coming redemption, an idea for which, in this new context, Balthasar is indebted to that intriguing document of the pre-Nicene age, the *Letter to Diognetus*. More generally, time before Christ (whether in its Israelite or in its pagan mode) is preparation not only for him but also for the inception of that 'one world' consciousness so marked today. The moment of the Incarnation is

> the moment at which the two universalisms or 'catholicisms', that is, that of Christianity and that of mankind, begin to enter into dramatic competition with each other.[1]

The struggle between the infant Church and the totalitarian claims of the Roman empire is its initial encapsulation, but, as Augustine saw, pagan Rome is but the transient concretion of a 'counterplan' fundamentally antithetical to the gospel, a counterplan which will throw up other forms in the course of history and, so Balthasar adds, with ever-increasing clarity once the 'programme' of the Kingdom has been set forth.

Israel's borrowings from her pagan neighbours show, however, that, even beyond her boundaries, there was positive as well as negative preparation for Christ. What remains, at the issue of Israel's history is:

1 *TD* IV, p. 210.

the dialectic of law: on the one hand, a genuine covenant faith and secret manifestations of divine possession (Merkabah mysticism, the Cabbala) and, on the other, self-justification, reaching its extreme of atheistic self-creation in the modern forms of secularized Judaism.[2]

Like the pagan religions, Israel, on Balthasar's view, is in the 'twilight'; what distinguishes her from them is that Israel's ambivalence is subject to prophetic critique, as, remorselessly, the gap between the covenant demands and the chosen people's practice is exposed. For Balthasar that is a 'divine barb', compelling Israel, alone of the nations, 'in the course of a genuine theodramatic history, to utter an ever-clearer Yes or No'.[3] But while the Suffering Servant of Deutero–Isaiah 'seems to gather into himself, in his mysterious destiny, all the counterforces that oppose' God's word of salvation, the prophecy of his vindication

> points beyond God's burning anger in the face of the broken covenant; it points to some event that is as yet indecipherable, which will unequivocally fulfill the covenant, not only for Israel but for the whole world.[4]

Pagan religion manifests the same culpability as Israel, but lacking that internal critique which divine inspiration provided for the chosen people, it also lacks by the same token Israel's possibility of opening to Christ. Over against Karl Rahner's more optimistic view that the world religions carry, or may carry, an implicit 'quest for Christology', Balthasar maintains that

> non-Christian religions do two things at the same time. They attempt to say what man is and why he exists, in relation to the world, on the one hand, and to be absolute, on the other. *Therefore* they also resist the answer that God, in sovereign freedom, provides in the person of Jesus Christ.[5]

Each puts forward a fragmentary solution, corresponding to some aspect of the splintered *imago Dei* in man; but each covertly or overtly claims to express the whole. Moreover, in striving to reach up to and enter the divine realm by a 'natural desire' that in fallen humanity is sin-infected, the created image becomes oblivious of the *distance* separating creature from Creator. Such religions

> may be *logoi spermatikoi*, but this 'seed' can only germinate in Christian soil, and only after a 'conversion' that involves far more than the mere supplying of a missing element; what is required is the death and new birth that the Bible calls *metanoia*. Only with the greatest reticence, therefore, should we speak of 'pre-Christian religions' exercising a positive salvific function. It would be better

2 *TD* IV, p. 216.
3 *TD* IV, p. 217.
4 *TD* IV, p. 218.
5 *TD* IV, p. 222 (italics added).

to locate them within the period of God's long patience, in which he 'overlooks' all prior perversity.[6]

Balthasar wants nothing to diminish, evidently, the dramatic force of the divine-human reconciliation worked in Christ's Atonement – in the light of which doctrine alone can we for the first time see theological persons playing their full parts on the stage.

The Cross and its mediations

An outline history of soteriology brings us up to Balthasar's own distinctive view: the *dramatic* theory of the Redemption. Christian soteriology begins with the Passion narratives of the four Gospels. In a remarkable exegesis of the Johannine Last Supper discourse, Balthasar calls Jesus' long-awaited 'hour':

the earthquake that is beginning to separate him from this world, lifting him up on the Cross as he returns to the Father. In this phase, he is both still in the world (17.13) and yet no longer in it (17.11); he asks for the restoration of the glory he had before the foundation of the world (17.1, 5), and yet he is already once more in possession of it (17.22, 24); he foresees that the disciples will fall away (13.38; 16.32), and yet looks beyond their fall to their final confirmation in faith (17.6–8, 25). Thus the last prayer of Jesus is not really a prayer before and with regard to the Passion; it is a prayer that expresses the total content of the 'hour'; both disaster (*Untergang*) and the new dawn (*Aufgang*), that is, it is the transition, the passing-over (*Übergang*). In this transition, his insight into his mission's universality attains its greatest breadth.[7]

Since the content of the Lord's 'hour' is a mystery resistant to all attempts to render it a system, Balthasar does not find it off-putting that the Passion narratives themselves, and the soteriologies countenanced in the later Church, should offer a plurality of perspectives for our contemplation. Though unconvinced by attempts to divide up the range of legitimate theologies of salvation into 'incarnationalist' (centred on Jesus' life) and 'staurological' (centred on the Cross), he holds that there is today a certain tendency to obscure the originality of the 'hour' *vis-à-vis* all that preceded it, such that we would do well to concentrate our attention on the Passion's 'inherent modalities'. (As for the Resurrection, it is 'the radiant side of the Cross, correctly understood'.)[8]

Thus for the *New Testament*:

1. the only Son gave himself up for us, both as Lamb obediently letting things happen, and as Priest deliberately acting by willing consent to this

---

6 *TD* IV, pp. 226–227, with an internal citation of K. Rahner, *Grundkurs des Glaubens* (Freiburg 1976), p. 307.
7 *TD* IV, pp. 236–237.
8 *TD* IV, p. 238.

2. this happened by exchange with us, when he substituted himself for us by 'expropriating' us into him in a reconciliation achieved (objectively) *before* any agreement by us to this changed state of affairs – though it falls to us to make it fruitful in our own lives

3. moreover, the fruit of the reconciliation worked on the Cross is not only negative, consisting in our liberation from sin and death, and the wrath to come; it is also

4. in the highest degree positive, for by means of it we are drawn into the Trinitarian life itself

5. finally, this entire process flows from God's gracious love.

The history of soteriology, so Balthasar judges, is the story of the attempt (not always successful) to keep all five of these balls in the air at the same time. To change the metaphor, it is at times a confused road whose signposts are not always consistent in the directions they give.

Among the *Church Fathers* it is the second of those five motifs, the 'exchange' theme, which predominates, and the reason for this is not far to seek.

> Its dominant position is explained by the urgent need – because of the Christological heresies – to assert the Covenant Mediator's full divinity and unabbreviated humanity.[9]

Balthasar does not intend that comment as an adverse criticism; the only question is whether the theme were so fully explored that all the remaining soteriological key motifs come into view. Did the Fathers manage, by means of exchange formulae, to 'unfold the whole dramatic potentiality of this central element of the theo-drama?'[10] The sheer wealth of their formulations, Greek and Latin, from Irenaeus to Augustine, enabled them to do so *to some extent*. What happens at the Annunciation is not a 'neutral' exchange of natures but one whereby the Son accepts a passible humanity, heading from the outset towards Passion and death, expressing his solidarity with humankind and achieving (with the sending of the Spirit) our redemption. The basic formula guards the unadulterated incarnational realism of the gospel as divine remedy for human sinfulness. But even when the historical narrative is taken further, to the great Dyothelite doctor St Maximus, Balthasar finds a certain restrictiveness in the way the Fathers speak of the identification of Jesus with our sinful situation. Relying on Père François-Marie Léthel's study of the Maximian theology of the Agony in the Garden, he holds that even here, at this high point of Neo-Chalcedonian affirmation of the humanity assumed by the Logos, Jesus takes on the consequences of sin, yes, but hardly sin itself.[11] But if so:

> the Redeemer acting on the world stage does not completely fill out his role of representing the sinner before God.[12]

9 *TD* IV, p. 245.
10 Ibid.
11 F.-M. Léthel, OCD, *Théologie de l'agonie du Christ: La liberté humaine du Fils de Dieu et son importance théologique mises en lumière par Maxime le Confesseur* (Paris 1979).
12 *TD* IV, p. 254.

What about the *mediaeval doctors*? For Anselm, the first systematic theologian of the Atonement, it is the third theme of the quintet – liberation by ransom (or satisfaction) that dominates, with the exchange aspect invoked in its service. The fact that Anselm ascribes the Atonement to the Father's mercy and the Son's self-surrender shows his sensitivity to what is first and last on Balthasar's list (the Son's *traditio*, and the Father's love, respectively). Balthasar will have no truck with those who would write off Anselm as hopelessly sunk in Latin legalism. Revelation under the Old Covenant teaches that by God's free grace, a two-sided standard of right conduct is established in shared life with God; the restoration of the imbalance on man's side is, for Anselm, the amazing feat of the mercy of God in Jesus Christ. Here the legal and the personal are one. At the antipodes from a tedious juridicism, Anselm's theology of salvation is filled with drama, and so must count as one of *Theodramatik*'s principal antecedents.

> He describes an action that takes place between God and the world; through the unity of 'freedom' (on God's side) and 'necessity', this action has the vibrancy of a closed dramatic action with an inner logic that comes, not from the necessity of fate that overwhelms freedom ... but from a necessity arising from the free character of the parties concerned ... Anselm was not afraid of taking great pains to show that, in God, freedom cannot be other than identical with 'rightness' (*rectitudo*), which contains not only absolute truth and goodness but also justice and mercy: they have a common source.[13]

The much deplored 'legalism' of the Canterbury archbishop is based on a misreading of the key terms *honor* and *ordo*. God's honour is his glory, and the order of his world is its beauty which must, in one way or another, be re-established. What Anselm did was to draw out the dramatic dimension enclosed hitherto in the theological aesthetics of his pre-decessors, and in so doing helped preserve the aesthetic itself – which is why Balthasar has already accorded him a substantial place in his constellation of 'clerical' theological aestheticians in *The Glory of the Lord*.[14] In a rare favourable aside on liberation theology, Balthasar calls Anselm's idea of Jesus' death as the final outcome of his lifelong commitment to God's righteousness a possible 'link' with what is commendable in that movement.[15] Balthasar is not without his criticisms of Anselm but they are far different from the customary – even less than in patristic soteriology is his Christ the Sin-bearer to the degree Balthasar would deem desirable. His Saviour is insufficiently representative of humankind, and the drama of his atoning work too straitly limited (here Balthasar finds Anselm Rahnerian *avant la lettre*!) to his death.

Thomas also makes 'satisfaction' central – but he is quite deliberately pluralistic in his theology of the Atonement, weaving together a variety of thematic threads in the explicit awareness that for so great a mystery

---

13 *TD* IV, p. 257.
14 See my *Word Has Been Abroad*, pp. 81–85.
15 *TD* IV, p. 259.

only the maximum number of convergent approaches will suffice.[16] His recovery of the Augustinian teaching that Christ's personal grace is also *gratia Capitis*, a grace meant to overflow from Head to members, restores the organic link between the New Adam and the rest of mankind left in shadow (at any rate in the context of a theology of Christ's death) by Anselm. Thomas pleases Balthasar by speaking of the way that by his satisfactory suffering Christ 'as it were ascribed [mankind's] sins to himself',[17] but what Thomas has in mind (Balthasar reluctantly concedes) is unlikely to be any different from the limited version of identification of sin and Sin-bearer in St Maximus and the other Greek Fathers who anticipated his vocabulary on the topic. Above all (and here Balthasar looks ahead to contrasting undesirable attenuations of the drama in some modern writers), the dramatic action on the Cross is (for Thomas) the real thing.

> It is more than a sign of God's constant and antecedent desire to be reconciled with the world; it is more than a sacramental sign that God *is* reconciled with the world and is applying the fruits of reconciliation to the world; it is in very truth the event *whereby* God's anger is turned away from the sinner, even if it remains the case that, from before all time, God has already specified Christ's Passion and satisfaction as the means whereby this is to be brought about.[18]

How do *contemporary* 'models' fare in comparison with those of the Fathers and the Latin Middle Ages? Balthasar finds that two are dominant, 'solidarity' and 'substitution'. Each has something to be said for it, yet the 'moderns' (whom he treats in effect as beginning with Luther) can find no way of combining their elements of truth. They are a whole's broken halves.

A 'solidarity' soteriology takes its cue from the Lord's humanity, and his public ministry, and, to be sure, the theme of a solidarity that goes the whole hog, *usque ad mortem*, as in *King Lear*, is a serious candidate in Passiology. A 'substitution' soteriology begins from Jesus' divinity; it takes up the 'wonderful exchange' motif of the Fathers in a radicalised fashion based ultimately on a reading of the Pauline letters, and insofar as it speaks of representative suffering has resonances in Euripides, Faulkner and Camus.

The problem with such soteriologies of solidarity and substitution is not simply, however, one of integration. For example, although the language of solidarity can be chosen for its greater vividness in expressing the incarnate Lord's communion with our sinful nature, thus Ferdinand Prat or Juan Alfaro[19] – it can also be selected by a dogmatically liberalising Christology that sees in the Cross no more than the ultimate consequence

---

16 See A. Nichols, OP, 'St Thomas Aquinas on the Passion of Christ', in idem., *Scribe of the Kingdom: Essays on Theology and Culture* (London 1994), I, pp. 192–204.
17 Thomas Aquinas, *Summa Theologiae* III a, q. 46, a. 6, c.
18 *TD* IV, p. 265.
19 F. Prat, *La Théologie de saint Paul* (Paris 1939[15]), II, p. 240; J. Alfaro, 'Die Heilsfunktionen Christi als Offenbarer, Herr und Priester', *Mysterium Salutis* III/1 (Einsiedeln-Zurich-Cologne 1966), pp. 649–708.

of Jesus' social solidarity with the marginalised of his time. For Hans Küng, Christian Duquoc and Edward Schillebeeckx, among others, 'the *commercium* no longer operates at the ontological plane but only at the social and psychological level'.[20] Karl Rahner's position, expounded by Balthasar in a densely argued ten-page excursus, lies somewhere in between the two, the drama of the wonderful exchange threatened by a Christological Antiochenism which sees in the incarnation a uniquely high 'instance' of the actualisation of the human essence.[21]

What of the soteriology of substitution? Unlike a solidarity Passiology reduced to sociology or psychology it is no thin gruel. Taking its cue from Luther's gospel of the exchange between the sinner and the divine Christ, it is very strong meat indeed. The absolutely holy Christ becomes sin while man becomes righteous by faith alone – on the Cross, in the Cross, respectively. The trouble is that here where Chalcedonian orthodoxy, though technically maintained, gives way to the 'obscurities and illogicalities' of Luther's version of the exchange doctrine:

> the high drama of Luther's reduction [of the exchange of natures to one of righteousness and sin] suppresses that *other* drama, which presupposes the existence of persons, with their prior being and constitution.[22]

The most celebrated – or notorious – aspect of Luther's substitution Passiology is the notion of Christ's *penal substitution* – the Father's diversion onto him of the wrath that should have struck ourselves. Balthasar plots the history of the concept of the Saviour's *vicarious punishment* – a related but not identical term – and shows its roots in Fathers and mediaevals, and its ubiquity in the Catholic tradition from Rupert of Deutz and Denys the Carthusian in the Middle Ages right up to the twentieth century. Though its possibilities have been exploited chiefly by the great Protestant dogmaticians of our day – Karl Barth, Wolfhart Pannenberg and Jürgen Moltmann,[23] one cannot be faithful to the Catholic theological tradition without allowing via the notion of vicarious punishment the concept of substitution to qualify that of solidarity, above all in the theology of the Cross. Balthasar cites with fullest approbation some words of the Belgian Jesuit Jean Galot:

> There is solidarity, it is true, but it extends as far as substitution: Christ's solidarity with us goes as far as taking our place and allowing the whole weight of human guilt to fall on him.[24]

20 H. Küng, *On Being a Christian* (ET, London and New York 1984); C. Duquoc, *Christologie* II (Paris 1972); E. Schillebeeckx, *Jesus: An Experiment in Christology* (ET, London 1979).

21 *TD* IV, p. 283, citing K. Rahner, *Foundations of Christian Faith* (ET, New York 1984), p. 218.

22 *TD* IV, pp. 288, 290.

23 K. Barth, *Church Dogmatics* IV/1 (ET, Edinburgh 1956, pp. 157–283; W. Pannenberg, *Jesus God and Man* (ET, London 1968); J. Moltmann, *The Crucified God* (ET, London 1974).

24 J. Galot, *La Rédemption, mystère d'alliance* (Paris–Bruges 1965), p. 268.

But there must be both identity *and difference* in the idea of penal suffering as applied to Christ and to sinners. That is why Balthasar rejects the penal substitution theorem, while accepting the vicarious punishment tradition. The Christologically determined anthropology of the contemporary French philosopher René Girard, whose interrelation of 'violence and the sacred'[25] Balthasar compliments, calling it 'the most dramatic project to be undertaken today in the field of soteriology and in theology generally',[26] has the misfortune to eliminate the concept of the justice of God, and so fails to recognise the factor of expiation common to Jesus' suffering and that of sinners. In contrast Girard's construal of the uniqueness of Jesus' suffering, which treats the Cross as the unmasking of ritual sacrifice as covert violence, misconceives what is different about Calvary. Here a useful corrective is supplied by a writer otherwise sympathetic to Girard's theories, the Jesuit Raymund Schwäger, who locates that crucial difference in the fact that, on Golgotha,

> God is at work … *enabling* the Smitten One freely to offer himself and by so doing to take upon himself the trespasses of others.[27]

This comes closer: it is sin, and not just the consequences of sin, that the Suffering Servant takes upon himself. The Russian Orthodox dogmatician Sergei Bulgakov and the French Catholic exegete André Feuillet enable Balthasar to edge nearer still to the most dramatic truth of all. In Bulgakov's *Agnets Bozhii*, the Christological volume of his so-called 'great trilogy',[28] the suffering of Christ on Calvary is in its supra-temporal intensity – a divine person undergoes it, albeit humanly – the 'equivalent' of that due to sinners. In Feuillet's *L'Agonie de Gethsémani*, the Gospel narratives are so handled as to emphasise how the innocent Victim was thrown to the ground by the impact of the eschatological chalice of the wrath of YHWH at an 'hour' identical with that of final judgment.[29] Here are building-blocks for a dramatic synthesis.

In his own 'dramatic soteriology' Balthasar tries to fill the lacunae left by his predecessors. He does not backtrack on his account of the elements essential to a theology of the Atonement he suggested by way of preface to his 'brief history'. Instead, and in the spirit of his general presentation of the merits of theo-drama in Volume I of this work, he tries to show that all five key features of the New Testament doctrine of salvation – the consenting self-surrender of the Son; his changing place representatively with sinners; man's consequent liberation *and* initiation into the Trinitarian life, which (finally) shows the whole of the foregoing to be a divine love-story – achieve satisfactory integration only when they are set

---

25 R. Girard, *La violence et le sacré* (Paris 1972); cf. idem., *Des choses cachées depuis la fondation du monde* (Paris 1978).

26 *TD* IV, p. 299. Certainly Girard makes considerable use of the Attic tragedians, seeing the theatre as signifying a 'crisis' in mythic presentation of a 'primal' event.

27 R. Schwäger, *Brauchen wir einen Sündenbock? Gewalt und Erlösung in den biblischen Schriften* (Munich 1978), pp. 140–141.

28 S. V. Bulgakov, *Agnets Bozhii* (Paris 1933); Balthasar cites the French translation, *Le Verbe incarné: Agnus Dei* (Paris 1943), and here at p. 296.

29 A. Feuillet, *L'Agonie de Gethsémani: Enquêtes exégétiques et théologiques* (Paris 1977), pp. 82–92.

within a *theodramatic* context. Just as the elements of (modern) theological method were like pieces of a jigsaw that only theological dramatics can fit together, so here the constituent themes of (New Testament) soteriology have never been interrelated with full coherence, owing to the absence of the key that would unite them – a *dramatic* doctrine of salvation. Balthasar asks:

> Are the systems hitherto attempted sufficiently dramatic? Or have they always failed to include or to give enough weight to one element or another that is essential to the complete dramatic plot?

And he comments on his own question:

> No element may be excluded here: God's entire world – drama is concentrated on and hinges on this scene. This is the theo-drama into which the world *and* God have their ultimate input; here absolute freedom enters into created freedom, interacts with created freedom and acts *as* created freedom. God cannot function here as a mere Spectator, allegedly immutable and not susceptible to influence; he is not an eternal, Platonic 'sun of goodness', looking down on a world that is seen as a gigantomachia, a 'vast perpetual scene of slaughter'. Nor, on the other hand, can man, guilty as he is in God's sight, lie passive and anaesthetized on the operating table while the cancer of his sin is cut out. How can all this be fitted together?[30]

As Balthasar presents things, all the topics of the classical theological treatises – from the *De Deo Uno* to the *De Ecclesia* – come together at this supreme nodal point. And similarly all the *loci theologici* – the sources of theology in Scripture and Tradition – as recognised by Catholic divinity – must here if anywhere be drawn on together. The climax of the whole theo-drama already contains the final act of the play. For Balthasar, as the apocalyptic opening chapter of Volume IV of *Theodramatik* – ostensibly on the Atonement, rather than the Last Things – makes glaringly apparent, soteriology and eschatology are separated more in notion than in reality.

In the first place, the doctrine of the *Trinity* is a *sine qua non* if we are to understand how the guilty ones (ourselves) and the Lamb who bears away their sin are to be related. It is the *triune* God who alone can explain, Balthasar would say, the first and the last motifs in that quintet of New Testament themes: the consenting self-surrender of the Son and the way the whole atoning event makes manifest the divine love for man. Behind the Cross, as its fundamental presupposition, there lies that 'primal divine drama' which consists in the Father's generation of the Son, his gift to him of equal and substantial divinity.

> This implies such an incomprehensible and unique 'separation' of God from himself that it *includes* and grounds every other separation – be it never so dark and bitter. This is the case even though this same communication is an action of absolute love, whose blessedness consists in bestowing, not only some thing, but itself.[31]

30 *TD* IV, p. 318.
31 *TD* IV, p. 325.

Avoiding at once the Scylla of a Rahnerian formalism in speaking of the eternal divine self-communication – stigmatised by Balthasar in the words 'hardly credible as the infinite prototype of God's "economic" self-squandering'[32] – and the Charybdis of a Moltmann-esque submersion of the immanent Trinity in the world in the style of Hegel or Whitehead – by means of what he calls a 'lumping together' of the internal divine processions and the salvation-historical process – Balthasar sets out his *via media* between these two pitfalls. He describes his theological passiology as

> employing a negative theology that excludes from God all intra-mundane experience and suffering, while at the same time presupposing that the possibility of such experience and suffering – up to and including its christological and trinitarian implications – is grounded in God.[33]

This is, he admits, to walk a knife-edge between orthodoxy and heresy, and yet so perilous a feat must be attempted. While rejecting as 'tragic mythology' all talk of the 'pain of God', Balthasar holds himself honour bound by the mystery of the Atonement to

> say that something happens in God that not only justifies the possibility and actual occurrence of all suffering in the world but also justifies God's sharing in the latter, in which he goes to the length of vicariously taking on man's Godlessness.[34]

Though Balthasar spurns Hegel's view that the Trinity *had* to pass through the contradictions of the world in order to cease to be 'abstract' and become 'concrete' instead, he certainly maintains that when the Trinity meets the world in Incarnation and Atonement there is drama. In a fascinating choice of emphasis he locates the heart of that drama in the clash between divine recklessness and human caution. The *passio Dei* of Calvary occurs only if and when

> the recklessness with which the Father gives away himself (and *all* that is his) encounters a freedom that, instead of responding to this kind of magnanimity, changes it into a calculating, cautious self-preservation. This contrasts with the essentially divine recklessness of the Son, who allows himself to be squandered, and of the Spirit who accompanies him.[35]

After the Holy Trinity, the second most important presupposition of all Atonement theology worth the name is, Balthasar tells us, that of *covenant*, of which the creation itself is the primary, and most universally telling, instance – though the historic covenants with Noah and Israel are needed in order to explicate that tacit covenant and give it greater

32 *TD* IV, p. 321.
33 *TD* IV, p. 324.
34 Ibid.
35 *TD* IV, p. 328.

specificity. Here Balthasar sums up all that he has said about the interrelation of infinite and finite freedom in Volume II of *Theodramatik* – but now from the perspective of the *death of Christ*.

In God's covenanted self-binding – his self-restriction in the kenosis of creation itself – man acquires the ability to say No to God as well as Yes. In its self-giving the Godhead observed no limits, thus revealing at one and the same time power and powerlessness. Given that our capacity to say No to God is itself the result of the share we were awarded, with our creation, in the divine autonomy, our refusal of the Creator

> reveals that abyss in the creature whereby it contradicts its own character as analogy and image, a character that arises necessarily from its position within the trinitarian relations.[36]

Reminding us of his claim to a special rôle for the divine Son in the creature's coming forth from God precisely as a *free* being, Balthasar calls that creature's pretension to owe its freedom to itself 'absurd', on the grounds that, implicitly:

> it tries to arrogate divine nature to itself without sharing in the Person [i.e. the Son] who is always endowing, receiving, pouring forth and giving thanks for that nature – and who embodies its self-giving.[37]

But just as the covenant allows us to grasp retrospectively the meaning of the creation so also for Balthasar does it point prospectively to the gift of the Eucharist which it makes possible.

> Given the plan to bring about creatures endowed with freedom, the ultimate form of this pouring-forth will be that of the Eucharist, which, as we know it, is intimately connected with the Passion, *pro nobis*.[38]

And if we ask why does Balthasar give so simple a thing as a sacrament (albeit the chief of sacraments) this high soteriological significance, the answer must be that the Son's being, not least in its human incarnation, is 'eucharistic': in other words, a thankful allowing oneself to be poured forth is what the Son's hypostatically distinctive possession of the divine Essence is like.

Not that this 'primal kenosis' in God himself should be taken as exclusively a Father–Son affair. The Spirit too is marked by self-expropriation: as various Johannine texts signalise (John 14.26; 16.13–15), he wants only to be the 'pure manifestation and communication of the love between Father and Son'.[39] However, the peculiar bond of the creature with the pre-existent Son in Balthasar's triadology means that the burden of emphasis will fall there – and how conveniently for a theology of the death and Resurrection of Christ! Eucharist illuminates

36 *TD* IV, pp. 328–329.
37 *TD* IV, pp. 328–329.
38 *TD* IV, p. 330.
39 *TD* IV, p. 331.

Cross, Cross covenant, covenant creation, and by following this phosphorescent trail we hit upon the truth that makes sense of them all: the everlasting *eucharistia* of the Son's being through which both human freedom and its abuse are exercised. Thus the stage is set for the events of the Passion, or what Balthasar calls the 'confrontation between ground-less divine love and ground-less human sin':[40] in the words of the Fourth Gospel

> It is to fulfil the word ... 'They hated me without a cause' (John 15.25).

All of this is vital if we are to attain a sufficient comprehension of the other three motifs in the soteriology not only of the New Testament but also of the tradition that flows from it: Christ's changing place repre-sentatively with sinners; his liberation of guilty humanity from thraldom; and the initiation of man into the Trinitarian life.

Balthasar proceeds to show how this is so. The kenosis to which the New Testament centrally attests is not the everlasting drama just described but that found in the self-identification of the Logos with the man Jesus. However, that primal drama enables us already to see the possibility of *Stellvertretung*, the substitution of the representative Saviour for guilty humankind:

> The Son, the 'light' and 'life' of the world, who enters into this 'darkness' of negation by becoming man, does not need to change his own 'place' when, shining in the darkness, he undertakes to 'represent' the world. He can do this on the basis of his *topos*, that is, of his absolute distinction, within the Trinity, from the Father who bestows Godhead.[41]

Appealing to the French philosopher-anthropologist René Girard's theory of a scapegoat mechanism at work in all human society where the accumulated tension of conflictual desire is offloaded, quasi-fortuitously, onto a common victim, Balthasar speaks of human beings piling the world's No to divine love onto Jesus, yet he also insists – here departing from Girard's account, theologically perfunctory as it is – that nothing could be achieved by this unless the One to whom sin is transferred were willing and able to bear it.[42] That this be so turns on the continuity of Jesus' mission with the Son's eternal procession – as Volume III of *Theodramatik* has shown.

The representative substitution, if it is really to deal with sin, requires

> an *inner* appropriation of what is ungodly and hostile to God, an identification with that darkness of alienation from God into which the sinner falls as a result of his No.[43]

---

40 *TD* IV, p. 332.
41 *TD* IV, p. 334.
42 See above, p. 000.
43 *TD* IV, pp. 334–335.

The Trinitarian decision to redeem human evil in this radical fashion can only be carried out by the Father's making known the divine will to the Word incarnate through the Holy Spirit. This may give the impression that the Father condemns the Son to his fate. But such an inference would be altogether misconceived. Balthasar makes his own Anselm's favourite adverb in these contexts, *sponte*: it was *of his own volition* that the Son desired only to do the Father's will, to fulfil his own mission.

Jesus experiences the dark night of the sinful state in a fashion wholly unique to himself – in the depths of the relations between the divine Persons inaccessible to mere creatures as those deep places are. The impossibility of aligning the experience of the Cross with any simply human experience accounts for Balthasar's otherwise baffling statement that what Jesus underwent can be called indifferently Hell's contrary or Hell's ultimate intensification. Though initiated in our time (because in our flesh) the Saviour's experience of his strange work is out of time: which is why, according to Balthasar, such mystics as St John of the Cross were able to glimpse the *noche oscura* for themselves.

Balthasar has made much use of the language of experience. He hesitates, by contrast, over that of penalty. With those who would have it that no innocent man can rightly be spoken of as 'punished', even if he be atoning for the guilty, Balthasar has no quarrel. If that is their stipulation for the use of terms, he will not object. But those who fight shy of penal language for the representatively substitutionary act of the Redeemer must take care not to introduce a distance between the Saviour and those who by rights should have borne the burden that he carried. Briefly, and taking up again the concept of experience, subjectively the Cross *was* punishment, though objectively it could never be.

Balthasar's unwillingness to abandon the harsh language of much of Scripture and Tradition – unpalatable though this be to an age for which 'goodness' is anodyne, not terrible – comes over clearly enough in his lengthy disquisition on the 'cup of wrath'. With Lactantius – whom, he says, modern Catholic theologians, and Protestant ones too since Schleiermacher, would do well to read – a God who 'only loved and did not hate evil would contradict himself'.[44] The 'cup' which Jesus fain would let pass by, were it the Father's will, on the Mount of Olives, is the Old Testament cup of divine wrath, for the New Testament does not contradict Israel's expectation that the 'Day of the Lord' will reveal wrath as well as mercy. The righteous anger shown by Jesus, for example, is for Balthasar the manifestation of a strictly divine attribute; and it covers, on his view, numerous aspects of Jesus' speech and behaviour – towards the demons and towards sickness, towards the hardheartedness of Pharisees, the venality of the desecrators of the Temple. Now in the Passion, the Lamb diverts onto himself the divine anger – God's offended love – at the world's infidelity. Whereas in his ministry Jesus disclosed both God's love and his wrath, in his ordeal the wrath of God is poured out upon him.

Balthasar integrates the 'theology of pathos' of the Jewish student of the prophets Abraham Heschel, as well as the relevant contributions of

44 *TD* IV, p. 339.

Barth's *Church Dogmatics*, into his own highly distinctive presentation. Following Heschel, he remarks of the divine affect:

> It is not an irrational emotion but, on the contrary, identical with God's ethos, which can never be detached from his free involvement that is controlled by love and righteousness.[45]

Where as a Jew Heschel cannot follow Balthasar is when the latter adds that in *Jesus'* case the wrath of God – his indignation at man's scorning of his love – descends on one who is more than a prophet, since he is the Mediator. Here Barth comes to his aid instead, since, for the former,

> the reason why the No spoken on Good Friday is so terrible, but why there is already concealed in it the Eastertide Yes of God's righteousness, is that he who on the Cross took upon himself and suffered the wrath of God was none other than God's own Son, and therefore the eternal God himself in the unity with human nature that he freely accepted in his transcendent mercy.[46]

These pieces from earlier writers are fitted into a mosaic of Balthasar's designing. The distinctive Balthasarian touch is evident in the recourse had to the Holy Eucharist for the purpose of explaining the Atonement:

> God's anger strikes him instead of the countless sinners, shattering him as by lightning and distributing him among them; thus God the Father, in the Holy Spirit, creates the Son's Eucharist.[47]

Or again, we glimpse this particular theological artist's style in the interpretation of the Son's sin-bearing as a divine refusal of the human refusal of God.

> The Son bears sinners within himself, together with the hopeless impenetrability of their sin, which prevents the divine light of love from registering in them. In himself, therefore, he experiences, not their sin, but the hopelessness of their resistance to God and the graceless No of divine grace to this resistance.[48]

And, as the culmination of a series of puns in theological German (these also are characteristic), Balthasar concludes by observing that 'at the end of absolute futility (*Vergeblichkeit*) comes forgiveness (*Vergebung*).'

In going so far as to say that, with the Atonement, the divine wrath becomes literally objectless, Balthasar raises, evidently, the spectre of universalism. His solution draws on the distinction between the guilty sinner *tout court* and a creature that identifies itself with its refusal.

---

45 *TD* IV, p. 334; cf. A. Heschel, *The Prophets* (New York and Evanston 1955).
46 K. Barth, *Church Dogmatics* II/1 (ET, Edinburgh 1957), p. 396.
47 *TD* IV, p. 348.
48 *TD* IV, p. 349.

'It is a terrible thing to fall into the hands of the living God' (Hebrews 10.31). These words apply, not to just any sinners, but to those who resist the triune work of atonement with full consciousness and realization.[49]

And if so far Balthasar has profited from the insights of Jew and Evangelical, he concludes by synthesising with them those of a Lutheran as well. In *Persons in Christ* Balthasar has already said that the *Stellvertreter*, the substitutionary Representative, must have, in his saving death, an effect both forensic and ontic – external and internal – on those human persons involved in theo-drama in whose place he stands. Now with assistance from Paul Althaus, a leading theologian of inter-war German Protestantism, he gives greater precision to these two facets of objective redemption.

Insofar as Jesus does what we cannot do, his action is primarily exclusive; but insofar as, on the Cross, he vouches for us in God's presence – and vouches for us effectively – his action becomes inclusive.[50]

---

49 *TD* IV, p. 350.
50 *TD* IV, p. 351.

13

Fruitful Consequences

There remains the question, however, of how this redemption, at once inner and outer as it is, may be mediated to those who are to become free with the freedom of the children of God.

Marian reception at the Cross

For Balthasar that question cannot be answered without reference to *Mary*. The faith of the covenant humanity of Abraham and his seed is present and active at the Cross in the person of Mary whose standing-by-Jesus amounts to a consent which reiterates her *fiat* at Nazareth. Referring to the delicate debates among maximalists and minimalists in Catholic Mariology over such titles as 'co-redemptrix', Balthasar concedes that it is not easy to describe aright Mary's theodramatic rôle in a soteriology based on Christ's Cross. Avoiding the conventional ways in which all this is described, Balthasar defines the crux of the dilemma like this:

> It is to mediate between Yahweh's faithless covenant-partners, who have adopted Gentile ways ('We have no king but Caesar', John 19.15), and the future covenant-partners, who will come to faith through the grace of the 'Lamb as though it were slain'.[1]

Here are the elements of his resolution of the difficulty:

1. Though there is no need to present Mary as consenting to the Atonement on humanity's behalf – for that is done by Jesus himself, nevertheless, to the extent that Mary's consent at the Annunciation was a precondition of the Incarnation it cannot (at the Cross) simply be engulfed by the human 'Yes' of Jesus.
2. Moreover, Mary's 'Yes' included not only the coming Saviour but all who stand in need of the 'redemption of Israel'. Precisely as the Immaculate, she is in complete solidarity with sinners, endlessly at their disposal. In a surprising twist of thought, Balthasar places under this rubric the 'relegation' of Mary during the public ministry (for her solidarity meant she must take a back seat – her privilege is

1 *TD* IV, pp. 352–353, with an internal citation of Apocalypse 5.6.

at the opposite extreme from that of heroine), and also the committal of her from the Cross to the care of John.

> Hidden behind the multitude of sinners, embracing them all, she is objectively closest to him: she makes his suffering possible and guarantees its goal. Now, however, he can only see her as the farthest from him; this is how he *must* see her. He is forsaken *absolutely*, and the only way of fellowship with him is to take leave of him and plunge into forsakenness. He must withdraw from his mother just as his Father has withdrawn from him: 'Woman, behold your Son'.[2]

3. That the Son is accompanied by a witness to God's atoning action means that the Trinity cannot be expounded, as Moltmann would wish to do, on the basis of the Crucified alone (Balthasar says, the Cross alone). Moreover, Mary's witnessing is also – and this concept is, we have seen, quintessentially Balthasarian – *fruitful receptivity*. She alone in her 'open' poverty, behind sinners and with them, can receive the measureless 'Eucharistic' outpouring of the Son on the Cross – and this makes her the Bride of the Lamb and the Womb of the Church – a 'nuptial relationship that begins in the utter forsakenness and darkness they both experience'.[3]

The upshot is, then, that the language of 'co-redemption' *may* be used, but only on the condition that we keep firm hold of the *paradox* it contains. At the Cross, Mary's 'Yes' is to her own helplessness, and (consigned to John) she is despatched to apparent uselessness. Yet in this sterility – this fruitless virginity – she remains nevertheless a 'womb' for the seed of the dying incarnate Word.

> Here, finally falling silent, the Word is empowered to make his whole body into God's seed; thus the Word finally and definitively becomes flesh in the Virgin-Mother, Mary-Ecclesia. And the latter's physico-spiritual answer is more fruitful than all the attempts on the part of the sinful world to fructify itself – attempts that are doomed to sterility.[4]

Sacramental reception in the Spirit of Easter

So far we have spoken of Good Friday: but what of Easter? It is the return of the Son to the glory he had before the world was made; but not that alone, for it is incremental as well. Something is *added*. Only through this dramatic Trinitarian act of his Resurrection does his humanity come to share the glory of the pre-existent divinity – and manifest that glory in the self-giving of the Eucharist and the self-spending of the opened Sacred Heart. Somewhat in the manner of Odo Casel, Balthasar speaks of the perduring, constantly actual character of this drama – on the grounds

2 *TD* IV, p. 356, with an internal citation of John 19.26.
3 *TD* IV, p. 358.
4 *TD* IV, p. 361.

that, experienced as it is by the economic Trinity, it engages in that fashion the immanent Trinity, who is the Ground of all creation. And in any case the drama of the Passion (including the Eucharist) 'embraces all past and future points of world time'.[5] And just as sin, continuing with the world's history, provides ever fresh occasions for this revolutionary Passover to be pertinent (or 'concrete', as Balthasar himself puts it), so the Mass, continually celebrated in the Church's history, enables that definitive event to be 'implanted' in all succeeding time.

With the Resurrection, moreover, what Balthasar has termed the 'Trinitarian inversion', whereby economically, during the time of his ministry and Passion, the Son is led by the Father through the Spirit, is brought to an end, for now the Son-made-man sends the Spirit of the Father forth. In a beautiful orchestration of themes from (chiefly) Paul's Corinthian correspondence, Balthasar writes:

> The Exalted One can grant his friends a share in his Spirit, for now he possesses the Spirit in himself – and 'where the Lord is, there is the Spirit' – and he can give them a share in the Spirit's freedom, the Spirit's direct access to God: 'Where the Spirit of the Lord is, there is freedom' (II Corinthians 3.17). Such direct access liberates man from the mediation of the law (Galatians 3.12ff.; Acts 7.38); the Father's bosom, which, in infinite generation, brought forth the Son, is henceforth the only law for those who have been endowed with the Spirit, the milieu of love's absolute freedom. From this wide perspective of the 'Spirit of God', 'the spiritual man judges all things, but is himself to be judged by no one' (I Corinthians 2.15).[6]

The consequences of the glorification of the crucified Jesus are spelt out by Balthasar in terms of three themes: beginning with Baptism and ending with the Eucharist with, in between them, a meditation on the effect of Easter on that primordial concern of theo-drama, the question of freedom.

On Baptism he writes:

> The Son, totally buried in the baptism of sin, rises again to the Father's bosom (which in Trinitarian terms, he never left), taking with him those he has saved from the tide of sin, who are 'destined to be his sons' (Ephesians 1.5). That is why, in Baptism, Christians are essentially 'baptized into Christ's death', 'buried with him', under the waters that submerged him.[7]

And this means, secondly, the soteriological liberation of finite freedom from its sinful constraints into a condition of transfiguration – the third and fourth of Balthasar's quintet of New Testament motifs in the matter of salvation. On the question of the 'personal being of some extra-human evil' implicated in our will's subordination to fallen powers, Balthasar comments tartly: 'the reality will not go away just because we refuse to

---

5 *TD* IV, p. 363.
6 *TD* IV, pp. 364–365.
7 *TD* IV, p. 366.

entertain the idea'.[8] Here demythologisation is beyond us. Balthasar reiterates the view expressed at the outset of *Theo-Drama*'s fourth volume: though the Devil's power is broken in principle with the Atonement, in practice it takes on, until the eschaton, a hitherto unknown intensity. More consoling, therefore, are his remarks about the positive aspect of finite freedom's liberation: Balthasar's account does not simply resume the version of finite freedom's relation to infinite freedom provided in *Theodramatik* II but deepens it and, of most importance in the present context, furnishes it with new content deriving from his Atonement theology.

What is new? First, Balthasar gives depth to his account of finite freedom by drawing in the distinctively Przywaran mystical under-standing of the analogy of being so as to throw light on what grace 'adds' to nature – but in a specifically theodramatic setting.[9] He writes:

> How can God freely communicate himself to the creature he has endowed with freedom? The only way to envisage such self-com-munication is this: it must mysteriously heighten and fulfill the law of 'natural' philosophy that says that God is completely immanent in his complete transcendence ... The free creature ... must be understood to be *in* [God], in his own infinite realms of freedom, sustained, accompanied and totally permeated by God; and so the creature's *being-over-against God* grows in proportion to its being-in-God.[10]

Accordingly, a straightforward personalism which would see God as purely and simply 'Thou' to my 'I' will not do – least of all at the level of grace. By the gift of spiritual nature, the creature was endowed with freedom and thus made the image of God (as Pelagius rightly saw), and yet this is but the precondition of our inner participation in the essence of God – in the 'vibrant, divine love-life of the Trinity' (so Augustine is right too, as Balthasar concludes after a much more nuanced discussion of the debate between the doctor of Hippo and Pelagius – and his radical disciples – than he had offered earlier).[11] The creature, however, has no way of translating the divine offer that its finite freedom should enter God's infinite freedom into the proper terms of its own finitude. The attempt to do so leads to Gnosticism. Only the Incarnation and atoning work of the Son of God can account for it, for God has descended not simply into the form of his creature (the stress of the Fathers with their cry, *O admirabile commercium!*) but into the sinner's alienation from God (the characteristic Balthasarian emphasis) – all with the purpose in view

8 TD IV, p. 369.
9 '[This] basic formula of the *analogia entis* is also the ultimate foundation of our Christian theological dramatic theory, just as it has its concrete center in the Chalcedonian "unconfused and indivisible" with regard to the two natures in Christ.' Ibid., p. 380.
10 *TD* IV, p. 373.
11 He made much use in *Theo-Drama* IV of Gisbert Greshake's study *Gnade der konkreten Freiheit: Eine Untersuchung zur Gnadenlehre des Pelagius* (Mainz 1972) – while, as he himself remarks, rejecting Greshake's central thesis that Augustine's differentiation of grace from nature was the *real* innovation in the Pelagian controversy.

that human beings should become 'divine'. This is how Balthasar understands Ephesians 4.9–10.

> In saying, 'He ascended', what does it mean but that he had also descended into the lower parts of the earth? He who descended is he who also ascended far above all the heavens, that he might fill all things.

Balthasar approaches his *third* theme in evoking what the glorification of Christ might mean for us – namely, the Eucharist, by way of a meditation on the Christian's discipleship, but specifically in its inner dynamic of dying-and-rising with Christ. Here Balthasar's chief point is that the Holy Spirit, as the Spirit of Christ's mission breathed out onto a mankind redeemed by the Passion (the Church) when the Son in dying gives that Spirit back to the Father, is simultaneously the *Spirit of both Cross and Resurrection*. As the Spirit of the entire economy – not only of the Father in his giving the Son but also of the Son himself in his sacrifice and glorification, the Spirit enfolds within him both the movement toward the Cross (i.e. the Incarnation and historic ministry) and the movement from the Cross (i.e. into the Resurrection). Nor, Balthasar adds, should we regard such insistence on the unity of the Christ-event as estranging us from the Jesus of history for whom all of these happenings took place one after the other. Even for the pre-Easter Jesus there *was* a unity of a kind:

> The Spirit of his mission was complete at every moment, since he was ready for the Father's 'hour' at all times during his earthly life – indeed, as the Transfiguration scene shows, he had the potential for Resurrection life within him always, by way of anticipation – but he did not wish to pre-empt it.[12]

At every moment Jesus was the 'synthesis' of his own mission. In his public life he mirrored the paradox of subsequent discipleship – simultaneously revered and even fêted and yet misunderstood and rejected. For the Christian knows both Resurrection and Cross (though the former only proleptically, by way of anticipation), and his 'in-Christness' includes a defining reference both to the Jesus of history and the risen Lord of faith. As Balthasar puts it – drawing, surely, on his knowledge of both the history and, in Adrienne von Speyr, the reality of mysticism:

> Whether these phases of darkness and light, distress and consolation (II Corinthians 1.4–7) are synchronous or diachronous for the individual Christian is a secondary matter; where the Spirit of the Lord is involved, there is nothing against these phases being simultaneous, even if particular forms of inner distress and darkness exclude a concomitant experience of consolation. The Christian is both crucified with the Lord and risen with him: both these *existentiales* stamp his existence simultaneously and inseparably.[13]

12 *TD* IV, p. 385.
13 *TD* IV, p. 386.

That is brought home by the sacrament of Penance, which is at once Good Friday judgment and Easter Sunday absolution. And that thought of the relation between the Redeemer and the Church (for it is *ecclesial* penance which is in question) brings Balthasar to the culminating section of his writing on the fruits of the Resurrection.

The Eucharist is, evidently, a drama related to the Paschal dramatic action. By its very existence, this sacrament, then, raises the question of the relation of *the Redeemer and the Church*. In the Mass, the Church both recalls and offers – and this duo of verbs displays the truth of that wider relationship. 'Recalls': that term bears witness to the absolute initiative, the fundamental priority of Christ in the saving drama, the *pro nobis* of Incarnation and Passion. 'Offers': this complementary word demonstrates that we, the Church, are to be included, and in no irresponsible fashion, in Christ's act of *Hingabe*, his self-surrender. The Passion, for its part, remains abidingly actual because, in the first place,

> what takes place in the 'economic' Trinity is cherished and embraced by the 'immanent' Trinity and, in particular, by the Holy Spirit, who, as the Spirit of Jesus' entire temporal existence and pre-eminently of his Passion and Resurrection, is poured out upon the Church and the world.[14]

But this would not happen without, secondly, the 'continual representation of Christ', as given up for us in his body. The divine Liturgy both makes Christ present and, in so doing, relates the faithful to the supra-temporal presence of his saving mystery. And here, no matter how much we emphasise the far-reaching biblical resonances of recalling, *anamnêsis*, what is involved far exceeds any commemoration, never mind how efficacious. It is Balthasar's account of the Eucharistic Sacrifice which leads him to explore most deeply the Church's dramatic link-up with her Lord.

Augustine's well-known discussion of 'the Church's sacrifice' in Book X of the *City of God* leaves open the question, so Balthasar notices, whether the Church is *already* the Body of Christ when she offers her sacrifice, or whether she does not become such *until* she carries out this action. Is she offering the sacrifice of one who is simply other than herself, or does she 'already enjoy an intimate harmony with Christ's self-sacrifice, in such a way that her offering is part of it'?[15] Though nothing may detract from the priority of Christ (it is only because his sacrifice on the Cross included us 'passively' that the question of our [subsequent] active collaboration can be raised at all), that such a thing as active, consenting co-operation *exists* is clear, to Balthasar's mind, from the place of Mary on Calvary. Just as the Incarnation required Mary's fiat, so at the Passion Jesus is 'sustained by consent of the feminine Church, suffering with him'.[16]

> Insofar as the Woman plays the part allotted to her in this drama, she can be drawn in the most intimate way into the Man's fruitful

14 *TD* IV, p. 390.
15 *TD* IV, p. 394.
16 *TD* IV, p. 397.

activity; she can be fructified by him. Thus (and only thus) can we say that, in the Eucharist, the community is drawn into Christ's sacrifice, offering to God that perfect sacrifice of Head and members of which Augustine spoke in celebrated terms. Within this perspective, the 'general priesthood' of the faithful, with Mary as matrix and archetype, forms the background on the ministerial priesthood; it is the condition that makes the latter possible.[17]

Playing once again on the theme of *traditio* – the Latin term for the Lord's *betrayal*, for his *handing over by the Father*, and for the *tradition of the Church* which flows from these human and divine actions during the twenty-four hours that saved the world, Balthasar speaks of Jesus *giving himself into the hands of the apostles* at the Last Supper with its Eucharistic command to 'do this', to renew his sacrificial offering – something that would be unthinkable, blasphemous, without the explicit, empowering mandate of the Victim himself.

> For, if the Church can never attain the existential perfection of Mary's Yes (which must always be the Church's pre-condition), the feminine Yes of consent can never take the place of the official offering in the name of Jesus himself.[18]

Though the Mass is Eucharist, thanksgiving, a sacrifice of praise, it is not (as the Council of Trent insisted by an anathema) *only* that. Those baptised into the death of the Lord are to ratify that saving sacrifice in a personal way, and this must mean, in the first instance, *letting it be* in its own inherent power to affect their lives. But – and here comes Balthasar's second move – baptismal faith cannot be thus *Marian* unless it have some relation to that 'gesture' whereby Mary gave her Son to the Father in the Holy Spirit on Calvary: the climax of her Annunciation fiat. Her act of 'giving back and surrendering' her Son is reproduced by the liturgical gestures of the celebrating priest, in the name of all the baptised, at Mass. And just as, by committing the infant Church, in the person of the beloved disciple, to Mary, and Mary to John, the crucified Saviour 'inserted Mary and all men' into his work of 'do[-ing] everything the Father wills', so the Eucharistic Sacrifice offered by the Church, in crowning the faith of Baptism, shows itself to rest on the prior initiative of Christ who willed to save us uniquely – yet not without our active collaboration. Here we see Balthasar attempting to unify the Tridentine doctrine of a sacrificing priesthood and therefore Church with the *soli Deo gloria* which joins Calvin, and so Barth, to Ignatius Loyola.

Reception by the saints

The principles he puts forward in his discussion of the Eucharistic Sacrifice are eminently applicable, as he now shows, to a wider domain as well, that of the doctrine of the communion of saints. For, seen theo-dramatically, the heart of our personal *being* is our personal *mission*. But

17 *TD* IV, p. 398.
18 *TD* IV, p. 399.

this, our supreme *inmost* engagement, can be nothing other than a 'participation in the once-for-all, all-embracing mission of Christ'.[19] By sharing in that latter mission, our freedom is graciously employed at the service of all the redeemed.

Balthasar's account of the 'dramatic dimension' of the *communio sanctorum* draws on not only such recognised theological sources as Paul, Augustine, Thomas and the writers of the Second Scholastic but also (prose-)poets like Bloy, Péguy and Claudel, in order to establish his basic claim that the inclusion of personal mission within the economy of the Son (itself at once 'pneumatic', in the Spirit, and 'somatic', in our flesh)

> signals an unimaginable expansion, in the order of creation, of the individual's sphere of influence.[20]

In the mystical Body of the Second Adam unexpectedly dramatic possibilities open up for us: only in this realm of salvific goodness, the solidarity of the communion of saints, can we have interior influence on the inner reality of other persons – consequential intercession for others, action on behalf of others, even the winning of the grace of conversion for those sunk hopelessly in sin.

This is to be explained Christologically, by reference to the way in which (as Cajetan argued at the time of Trent)

> Christ's fruitfulness 'overflows' onto the members of his Body, so that the latter are enabled to bring forth fruit for eternal life on the basis of a power that is their own yet comes to them in a secondary way, from Christ.

The Saviour, as Cajetan's disciple Nazarius has it, is not only a 'physical person' but also the 'personal bearer of all the members of his mystical Body'.[21] Such effective solidarity cannot be understood on the basis of, simply, our common sharing in fallen Adam, for the unity of humankind was only fully actual when recapitulated in Christ, while as to 'honour among thieves', evil is essentially fissiparous and isolating: only the good creates unity, so there can be no *civitas diaboli*, no *communio maleficorum*. And if the secret exchange of influence which Bloy compared, in his *Méditation d'un solitaire*, to 'those modest flowers of the field whose seeds the wind carries far away in all directions to land and germinate on God knows what mountain, in God knows what valley',[22] is not to be explained by anthropology, much less can it be founded simply on 'cosmic sympathy' – the temptation to which Claudel's generously meant blurring of the boundaries between universe and Church exposed him. Here, not for the first time in Balthasar's work, *Péguy* provides the solution.

> He too, like Claudel, regards the 'osmosis' between the realm of nature and that of grace as central; for him, there can be no Christianity without the ancient world and Judaism. However, he

---

19 *TD* IV, p. 406.
20 *TD* IV, p. 407.
21 *TD* IV, p. 411.
22 L. Bloy, *Méditation d'un solitaire* (Paris 1909), p. 140, cited *TD* IV, p. 413.

sees this osmosis coming from a 'mysterious, fleshly spiritual effluence, whereby the kingdom of grace overflows into the kingdom of genius [that is, antiquity]'. And when, in *Eve*, he describes the gigantic triumphal procession of the historical civilizations, this whole procession moves in homage toward the crib of Bethlehem; only in this perspective is it clear why the whole *epos* can be dedicated to Eve, the primal Mother.[23]

Balthasar's account of what the Anglican lay theologian (and poet and novelist) Charles Williams called 'the co-inherence' is wonderfully evangelical. Owing to the very nature of charity as the energy of *koinônia*, even so apparently individual, even private, a thing as the reception of a sacrament or the achievement and preservation of a good disposition, can never be without helpful consequence for others. The celebration of Mass 'for a particular intention', can never be *reserved*, after all, to that alone.

Resistance to reception

But faithful to the opening leitmotif of 'The Action', Balthasar does not wish to end his theology of the Atonement on this reassuring note. For the chief consequence of the victory of the Cross is, as we noted, not pacification but, paradoxically, a disturbing intensification of struggle. Here Balthasar prepares us for the final volume of *Theodramatik* by showing how the crucial action leads into the consummation of the drama. Gathering his flock to God, the crucified and risen Logos brings peace; but calling for decision, he brings a sword (cf. John 14.27, with Matthew 10.34–36).

> So it comes about that his peace-bringing action ... introduces more division in the world than any other; not through fanaticism but because of an inherent logic: the very One who has come 'not to judge, but to save' utters that 'word' that judges those who reject it ... This yawning abyss is inevitable, however, if in Jesus God wished to provoke his freed creature to the highest degree of responsibility.[24]

Polarisation for or against the gospel affects all subsequent world history (and not just the story of fidelity and infidelity in the Church). It changes the character of the pre-existing religions and even those (like Islam) not yet born, and renders atheism sharper and more negative. It provokes the attempt by secularists (declared or covert) to construct a perfect kingdom on earth, using the means and methods of worldly power. An arrogant Enlightenment, or self-illuminated humanism, take over elements in the message of Jesus and 'stage' them as if man were their creator. Balthasar does not hesitate to speak of the masks of Anti-Christ, and the consequently perennial need of the Church for the counter-testimony of the martyrs.

23 *TD* IV, p. 418.
24 *TD* IV, p. 435.

The polarisation wrought by the gospel also enters the Church, where schism and heresy have been from the beginning, flowing as they do, on Balthasar's view, not from some internal necessity whereby the primal innocence of the apostolic understanding had to unfold through the stimuli of error and division, but from a sin and guilt whose effect is to obscure the person and mission of Christ himself. Ecumenical benevolence cannot suffice to reverse this maleficent splintering in Church history.

> In concrete terms, Christ only exists together with the community of saints united in the *Immaculata*, together with the communion of the ministerial office visibly united in Peter and his successors and together with the living, ongoing tradition united in the great councils and declarations of the Church. Where these elements of integration are rejected in principle, it is impossible to return to unity, however much good will is displayed by the partners.[25]

And in the meantime, a second front has opened in the inner-ecclesial battle of the Logos: as with the tussle between Irenaeus and the Gnostics in the ancient Church, this is a struggle with the theological rationalism that would substitute for the articles of faith a 'new and essentially reduced content that relies on anthropological plausibility'.[26] More drama ensues.

> This is no mere battle of words and ideas between human beings: here mankind is drawn into the theodramatic war that has broken out between God, in his Logos, and hell's anti-logos. That is why the combatants need 'the sword of the Spirit, which is the word of God' if they are to 'stand' ... that is, not to 'advance' but to 'stand fast, eye to eye'.[27]

But where is Christian hope and joy in such a bleakly agonistic portrayal? For Balthasar it lies in the saints, who are the Church's living powers of regeneration. They alone can re-animate the dead and render the desert fruitful.

> 'My kingdom is not of this world' (John 18.36). This remains true despite all the possibilities of sowing the seeds of the non-worldly in this world and seeing them sprout and blossom. It remains true despite our efforts to make what is worldly serviceable for the kingdom of the Logos, as it were, to transpose it from the sphere of the old Adam into that of the New. These things are possible because even the strictly worldly has the Logos as its origin and goal. But such transposition can only take place through a 'dying with' the Logos and a 'rising with' him.[28]

In the *analogia libertatis*, 'the analogy of liberty' (ours, as regenerated in Baptism, with Christ's, founded on the hypostatic union as that is), we, like Jesus, are to work in the world not so much to perfect it as to imprint upon it the signs of the transcendent Kingdom.

25 *TD* IV, p. 456.
26 *TD* IV, p. 459.
27 *TD* IV, p. 463, with an internal citation of Ephesians 6.17 and 13.
28 *TD* IV, p. 475.

THE LAST ACT

14

Preamble to the Last Act

New Testament foundations

Naturally, in a theodramatics, *ta eschata*, 'the last things', the subject of the traditional Latin theological treatise *De novissimis*, become 'the last *act*'. Balthasar's introduction – on the very concept of Christian eschatology – sturdily maintains in the context of this 'final act' as elsewhere that, if theology is truly to be Christian, it must have Jesus Christ as its 'determining center'. Nonetheless, this is both the most thoroughly *triadological* volume of the theological dramatics, and also – of all Balthasar's works – the one most saturated by the thinking of Adrienne von Speyr, as abundant citations and footnotes attest.[1]

Balthasar reiterates his basic idea of Christian eschatology as a unity of dogmatic and exegetical considerations,[2] all turning on the destiny of Jesus Christ with his unique experience – as the One sent for us by the Father – of the time of salvation. The fate of Church and world, as that of Israel, is determined through him – not the other way round. The categories of Jewish apocalyptic – those closest to hand for the portrayal of salvific realities whose meaning, stored up in heaven, was now to be released on earth – were in part serviceable for the expression of this novel eschatology. But only in part. They constituted a providential preparation for his mission, yet at the same time distracted his hearers from the question which really decided Israel's destiny – her recognition (or otherwise) of Jesus as Messiah and divine Son. The same is true – *a fortiori* – of the Scripture-reading Church of early (or any) times. As Balthasar has sufficiently shown by his remarks on Christian discipleship and the Redeemer–Church relationship in *Theo-drama* IV, ecclesial existence is determined by Jesus' eschatological fate as the Crucified and Risen One. Here the still potent images of Jewish apocalyptic could mislead. That is not to say, however, that the editors of the various versions of the so-called 'Little Apocalypse' (ostensibly delivered by Jesus himself) were mistaken. For Balthasar the rejection of the Son, the last prophet, by Israel/Jerusalem meant necessarily that 'God's progressive salvific revelation

---

1 Balthasar remarks as much himself in his Preface, *Theo-Drama: Theological Dramatic Theory*. V. *The Last Act* (ET, San Francisco 1998), p. 13. Cited below as *TD* V.
2 *TD* V, p. 20.

within history had come to an irrevocable end'.[3] And if Jesus were conscious of the certainty of his own coming baptism of fire in his atoning death, he was equally convinced of this concomitant tragedy as well: the end of Jerusalem and the end of the world will have appeared together in his optic.

As a theologian with a particular *attrait* to Johannine thought, Balthasar lets us hear the 'accents' of St John's eschatology before reproducing those of the Synoptics. And he defends this order of exposition in specifically exegetical terms. Following the German Lutheran exegete Ethelbert Stauffer: just as we rightly regard John as in some respects more reliable *in Christologicis* than the Synoptics for he portrays more faithfully the chronology of the ministry, so also we should trust him *in Eschatologicis* – Stauffer's terminology in his contribution to the *Festschrift* for the English Congregationalist New Testament scholar C. H. Dodd.[4]

> For John, the Christ-event, which is always seen in its totality, is the vertical irruption of the fulfillment into horizontal time; such irruption does not leave this time – with its present, past and future – unchanged, but draws it into itself and thereby gives it a new character.[5]

And the 'I AM' sayings of Jesus in John show the Old Testament as brought to its consummation in him: where he is, all the presence, action, promises of the Old Testament Lord are likewise.[6] Past, present, future of saving time come together in his person. Johannine realised eschatology does not constitute an option *over against* futurist eschatology, but draws the latter into that eschatology which alone is central, because Christ-determined. Witness the (Johannine) Letters to the Seven Churches where the judgment of the glorified Son of Man is *now*, the light of life and love shining already in the darkness. And yet, as the law of proportionate polarisation studied at the outset of *Theo-Drama*'s penultimate tome would lead us to predict, the rest of the Apocalypse of John testifies to the way that light intensifies as the surrounding darkness grows deeper.

More and more, as *Theodramatik* draws to its climax, we shall have to reckon with the fact that the meaning-bearing and form-giving principle (*das sinn- und formgebende Prinzip*) not only of the Judaeo-Christian revelation-in-history but also of the course of nature in its unfolding will come *from above*. It is in the final act alone that the *theo*dramatic quality of this play becomes all-determinative. Balthasar stresses – over against Bultmann and the early Barth – that this is no mere *Unzeit*, 'non-time', cancelling out time altogether, but rather an *Überzeit*, a 'super-time'. In the Fourth Gospel, Jesus warns the disciples that he will leave them for a 'little time' (16.17–19), but not so short that they will not weep and lament, while the world will rejoice. His comparison with a woman in labour would surely have insinuated into their minds the Jewish concept of the times of messianic suffering. In Jesus' own unique mode of time, the

---

3 *TD* V, p. 23.
4 E. Stauffer, '*Agnostos Christos*', in W. D. Davies and D. Daube (eds), *The Background of the New Testament and Its Eschatology* (Cambridge 1956), p. 286.
5 *TD* V, p. 25.

essential caesura between all other time and the time of his absence is that of his Crucifixion and Descent into Hell. Whether *for the disciples* this time of departure will last until the Parousia, or only till the Resurrection, is a more open, and less essential, question.

The super-time which will break into the world, so Jesus predicts, is characterised above all by the mission of the Spirit. Via the time of the Church, the Spirit will deepen the disciples' understanding of the work of Christ, and amplify its construction. Yet this can also be described as a 'calling to mind' of all that Jesus had already said to them. In other words:

> This means that everything not yet uttered, every apparently new interpretation and understanding, was always there in the 'utter-ance' that Jesus is – and here we must think first and foremost of his whole existence as Word of the Father rather than as the word uttered in human terms.[7]

This future extension, then, the time of the Church, is the 'space' the Christ-event needs in order to deploy itself in its fullness. But *that* it is not in any Christomonistic way, for it belongs to the entire economic Trinity, which sent the Son and the Spirit, and thus to the whole immanent Trinity, with its duly ordered processions.

Johannine realised eschatology does not drive out futurist – Balthasar points here to the importance of the little word *ean*, 'if', so often high-lighted in the Johannine version of the sayings of Jesus. *If* you abide in me, *if* you keep my commandments, *if* you do what I say . . . This future conditional plays the same rôle in the Fourth Gospel as does the command to keep alert for the Son of Man in the Synoptics. It also shows, incidentally, contrary to what is sometimes alleged about the 'Gnosticising' tendencies of that Gospel, John's resolute affirmation of human freedom over against a Gnostic-type determinism.

Moreover, when studying the Synoptic discourse on the End for its own sake, Balthasar argues strongly that its dissonance from the Johannine 'accent' has been greatly exaggerated. The most striking thing about the Little Apocalypse, if we leave aside the material on the fall of Jerusalem, is its Christological character – its focus on the 'direct effect of the presence of Jesus in the world'.

> If we concentrate on this clear, central thrust of the Synoptic apocalypses, we can say that, in formal terms, they do not differ from the Johannine view: statements and warnings attributed to Jesus regarding the historical future all focus on the fact that he is and has been here in historical reality. Thus his 'word' (which signifies his entire existence, his life, death and Resurrection) embraces the whole of world history: accordingly, it is present in and governs, all temporal futures: 'Heaven and earth will pass away, but my words will not pass'.[8]

---

6 Here Balthasar draws once again on Stauffer in: idem., *Jesus: Gestalt und Geschichte* (Bern 1957), p. 145.
7 *TD* V, p. 31.
8 *TD* V, p. 35, with an internal citation of Matthew 24.35 (and parallels).

Such themes as the uniqueness of the authentic Messiah, the division of minds for or against him, the increasing sharpness of that decision, the prediction of persecution for his hearers precisely as his disciples, the preaching of the gospel to all the nations before the End comes, these sustain Balthasar's thesis of the Little Apocalypse's Christological 'nucleus'. The cosmic apocalyptic signs, part and parcel of the props for the End's setting in Jewish thought, are, moreover, re-interpreted as signs of the Parousia of the Son though Balthasar admits that some of the images resist Christological 'assimilation'.

But what of the motif of an expected 'final' judgment, when for St John the judgment is *now* (cf. 12.31). For Balthasar this is no discrepancy but solely a matter of the 'diastasis' separating the inauguration of judgment by the Son made man from its (equally Christological) conclusion. Characteristic of the New Testament and, when compared with the main bloc of the apocryphal literature of the time, differentiatingly so, is a strange indifference to the time-distinction between General Judgment (at the resurrection of the dead) and particular judgment (at the moment of the individual's dying), and indeed between the individual's death and – beyond the intermediate state, hinted at by a number of New Testament passages and later developed as the doctrine of Purgatory – their final being with Christ. Yet this will not surprise us if we grasp the fact that both the 'linear' eschatology of Judaism and its 'vertical' apocalyptic have now been re-located as axes of the event of Christ, within whose ambit all aspects of the 'day of the Lord' are now contained. Each moment of time, in so far as it is 'Christologically significant' is

> directly related to the exalted Lord, who has taken the entire content of all history – life, death and resurrection – with him into the supra-temporal realm.[9]

As a result, both Jewish and pagan speculation about the End, meta-history, are fulfilled and transcended in integrative style: they undergo an *'erfüllende Überhöhung'*. Through the happenings, both temporal and more than temporal, which link the Cross of Christ to his return to the Father, the linear scheme of approach to the End is fractured, as all history now comes under the dominion of the ascended Lord who henceforth, as the Letter to the Ephesians portrays matters, disposes of its elements. *Vis-à-vis* the Jewish expectation, the Christian must say that nothing further in the way of theological novelty can be expected in history. Only the further interpretation and continuing impact of the Christ-event is left. And yet this of its nature is, in more and more heightened form, the 'incentive and the theme' of inner-historical dramatics. So far as paganism is concerned, and here Balthasar really has pagan Gnosis in view, the gospel 'takes up' and 'goes further' by refusing to exclude from the cavalcade, whereby all things leave the One and return to him, matter, the body, history. Over against the clamantly anti-matter dramatics of the Gnostic mythico-speculative systems stands the 'soberly historical experience of the Resurrection of Christ, in its

9 *TD* V, p. 48.

retrospective illumination of the truth and meaning of his Cross and entire Incarnation'.[10] Not that Balthasar denies all value to the Gnostic images (else there would be no question of a 'transcendent fulfillment' by the gospel). Mythopoeic images grant us a 'pre-understanding' of what salvation might mean: the newness of Christianity inheres in its proclamation that what the myths dreamed of has become flesh in the Jesus of the Transfiguration and the Ascension.[11]

Balthasar's enquiry into the specifics of Christian eschatology is meant to prepare our expectations of his final volume. He states its 'thematic' concisely. The previous tome, on 'The Action', has already given away to the alerted reader the ultimate secret of humankind's history with God, which was the ever-increasing magnitude of worldly resistance to the ever-greater love of God and his incarnate Son. Yet a 'mass of questions' remains. And notably: Can the divine freedom, even when it is the freedom of love, simply 'trump' created liberty? If it be persuasive simply, what guarantee is there that it will attain its end? Shall we not have to reckon with the eventuality of a human rejection of the divine refusal to accept man's rejection? And, more widely, in what sense can a *theologia viatorum* – a theology written by and for those still on pilgrimage – encompass the final End at all? Prescinding from the question of the *ultimate* destiny of created freedom, Balthasar thinks that the route traversed so far by *Theo-Drama* can show us a way.

Creation from the Trinity

Scanning the list of dramatis personae, we found an original interplay of infinite and divine freedom where at first God appeared simply as 'the One'. Only when there was Christological cause to bring on stage the figure of the God-Man, did we first begin to reckon with the Trinity. In the context of the world's alienation from God, Christology became soteriology, whereupon, in the Cross and Resurrection, the Trinity was further displayed. It is clear enough, then, that the mystery of the Three-in-One is the ultimate framework both of divine revelation and of the human good. *To eschaton* can only mean, in the truly final analysis, the Trinity itself.

It follows that, for Balthasar, eschatology must mean, in the first place, a theology of the *imago Trinitatis* in the creature, for it is the development of that image – be it just, be it perverted – which will decide a man's last end. But because – as our brief survey of New Testament eschatology led us to conclude – all human time has now been assumed by Jesus Christ into the divine form of abiding (*Dauer*), the 'time' of the ever-greater God must be the measuring rod and principal orientation for the future, past and present not only of the human creature at large but, and especially so, of the redeemed creature in particular. The true Omega of history is the triune life as opened to us in Jesus Christ. But the Omega must embrace

10 *TD* V, p. 52, translation slightly altered.
11 Here Balthasar is much indebted to Heinrich Schlier's essay, 'Das Neue Testament und der Mythus', to be found in idem., *Besinnung auf das Neue Testament* (Freiburg 1964), pp. 83–96.

the Alpha, the start of the story, the presupposition of our destiny. And here is where Balthasar will begin – with a Trinitarian protology, or, in the title of a rightly acclaimed study, 'the creative Trinity'.[12]

The world comes *from* the Trinity. Balthasar shows how it is an axiom of High Scholasticism that 'a non-Trinitarian God could not be the Creator'.[13] For Thomas, while the entire Trinity are active in the creation, they are so according to their hypostatic properties, which must mean that their own processions are invested in the very structure of creatures themselves.[14] As with his older contemporaries Albert and Bonaventure, the making of a commentary on Peter Lombard's *Sentences* gave Thomas a great opportunity to expound this doctrine. As he explains, in the *exitus* of creatures from God the divine nature in its plenary perfection serves as the model for whatever perfections the creature may itself possess, while the latter are granted to the creature owing entirely to the unnecessitated liberality of the divine will. In the first regard, the creature's 'procession' from the Creator is founded on the Father's generation of the Son; in the second respect, too, the creature's existence must be 'led back' to a principle equally foundational – that, namely, of free communication, which, in God, must mean the Holy Spirit who is 'spirated' on the basis of love alone. Furthermore, since in generating the Son the Father expresses not only himself but also his whole creative power – everything he can create (for this is entailed in calling the Son the divine Logos), so also the Spirit has to be seen as not only the Father's love for the Son but also his love for creatures – from the moment when he determines to communicate to them, in creating, something of his own perfection.[15] Once the divine creative act is posed, then the intra-divine processions and the extra-divine missions are really one and the same thing.[16]

But what of *reditus*, the 'return' of creatures to God? Naturally, it must take place via those same missions of Son and Spirit. Whether visibly, in the Son, or invisibly in the Spirit, those divine persons arouse in us knowledge and love for God himself.

Bonaventure adds two nuances which Balthasar makes his own. Following the consensus of the Fathers it is the divine Word, the Son, who is the three-personed God's model in creating. So for Bonaventure's commentary on the six-day work of Genesis, the Word expresses not only himself and the Father but the Spirit also: this no doubt attracts Balthasar as validation of the Christological focus of Triadology.[17] And Balthasar further approves the way Bonaventure moves the concept of *expression* into central place in these issues. The processions manifest – *express* – first

---

12 G. Emery, *La Trinité créatrice: Trinité et création dans les Commentaires aux Sentences de Thomas d'Aquin et de ses prédécesseurs Albert le Grand et Bonaventure* (Paris 1995).
13 A. Gerken, *Theologie des Wortes* (Düsseldorf 1963), cited *TD* V, p. 61.
14 See, for example, *De Potentia*, q. 2, a. 6, ad iii. It is often forgotten that Thomas speaks of a knowledge of the divine persons as necessary not only for an understanding of human salvation but also of the 'creation of things', *Summa Theologiae* Ia., q. 32, a. 1, ad iii.
15 *In Libros Sententiarum* I, dist. 10, q. 1, a. 1, sol.; ibid., dist. 14, q. 1, a. 1, sol.
16 For St Thomas's doctrine at large, see G. Marengo, *Trinità e creazione: Indagine sulla teologia di Tommaso d'Aquino* (Rome 1990).
17 Bonaventure, *In Hexaemeron*, IX.2, cf. *TD* V, p. 65.

and foremost the sheer interior vitality (*Lebendigkeit*) and fertility (*Fruchtbarkeit*) of the inner-Trinitarian life. What could bring home more forcefully the fact that the mystery of being is not self-enclosed but, as Balthasar has steadfastly maintained since the publication of *Wahrheit*, the first volume of the theological logic, in 1947, a mystery of *voluntary self-disclosure*? To discover being as expressive of a mystery yet only by way of free donation, this tells us that logic itself, the analysis of being, participates (analogically!) in the absolute Logos who points at one and the same time 'behind' himself to his Source in the Father, and onwards, 'ahead' of himself, to the freely flowing Spirit of love.

But as with his general ontology, so here. It is not enough simply to repeat the dicta of the Scholastics, however true and fair. Our very admiration for the *philosophia perennis* should move us to add to its resources. So Balthasar now enquires after a specifically modern reconstruction, in the High Scholastics' footsteps, of the Trinitarian being of the world.

First of all, however, Balthasar furnishes the reader with a little summary of Trinitarian doctrine to guide his or her reflections. It is in orientation strongly 'personalist', though not to the exclusion of concern with God's Essence. Since each divine person is identical with the divine Essence itself, that Essence can be no fourth quantity, alongside the three of Father, Son and Spirit, for it is identical with the 'event' (*Geschehen*) of the eternal coming-to-be of the Trinity. And furthermore, the properties of the Essence – the divine attributes – cannot rightly be thought of in abstraction from the inner-divine processions – for they are properties of, precisely, the Trinitarian event. Thus, in Balthasar's own example, the divine omnipotence should not be described without reference to the kenotic fashion in which the Father, in generating and spirating, continually transfers power to what is other than himself. Only when that power is re-envisaged as the absolute Trinitarian love can it be seen for what it truly is. While not ascribing to God a genuine becoming (*Werden*) which would enmesh him in the toils of temporality and so finitude, Balthasar nonetheless considers that the 'mobility' (*Bewegtheit*) of the inner-Trinitarian life requires from our side the language of *event* for its evocation, and that the 'eventfulness' of the triune God founds the possibility of the becoming (in the common-or-garden sense) that typifies the world. As he writes:

> All earthly becoming (*Werden*) is a reflection of the eternal 'happening' (*Geschehen*) in God which ... is per se identical with the eternal Being or essence.[18]

But *how* is it such a reflection? In a way that can resolve the greatest enigma, the supreme *aporia*, of all philosophy. It has been well said of Aristotle's 'aporetic ontology':

> It is difficult to resist the conclusion that Aristotle hoped that the classification of things from empirical investigation, and the demonstration of properties from the intuition of essence (but

18 *TD* V, p. 67.

supported by the strictest logic), could be so brought together that there would be an *epistêmê* [knowledge] which would grasp things in their universality and individuality at the same time. But the demonstration of properties entailed the grouping of individuals in units or wholes ... so that they could be treated together and then subdivided. Yet how could this be done if the individual substance had a primary existence as *ousia* [being]?[19]

And while, as the study from which these words are taken shows, this key issue taxed the minds of post-Aristotelian thinkers in the late antique and mediaeval worlds, Balthasar casts his net even more widely in identifying as *the* metaphysical problem *par excellence*

the distinction between the unity of all existing beings that share in being and the unity of each individual being in the uniqueness and incommunicability of its particular being.[20]

Now at one level the discomfort generated by this 'difficulty' can be eased by metaphysics itself. Balthasar finds enlightenment in Thomas's celebrated 'real' distinction between essence and existence, whereby each and every finite essence shares in reality – the 'act' of existence, as Aquinas calls it, but none is identical with that act of being and all finite essences in their totality fail to exhaust it. But this mystery implicit in the composition of creatures also has something to do with the *divine* difference between the common Essence, identical with each Person as this is, and the differentiating hypostatic properties. Though in God essence and existence are identical, there is not simply a One, nor is there purely a Three.

Balthasar now evaluates a trio of attempts at a Trinitarian metaphysic *of the creation*, which seek light in the great mystery, God, for the lesser mystery, the world. And these are: Clemens Kaliba's *The World as Parable of the Triune God*,[21] Wilhelm Moock's *Letters on the Holy Trinity*[22] and Klaus Hemmerle's *Theses for a Trinitarian Ontology*.[23] Kaliba, a disciple of Heidegger, who drew heavily on the metaphysical essays of Gustav Siewerth – a Catholic philosopher much admired by Balthasar,[24] produced a scheme both complex and, from the viewpoint of Trinitarian doctrine, slightly disconcerting. The being which God communicates to the creation reflects his own nature in that it goes beyond the finite, and yet is the quintessence of each finite existent. Actualising itself at all levels of the real, the received ('non-subsistent') being of the world already furnishes us with a faint outline of the Holy Trinity. For those degrees of being are essentially *threefold*: the realm of existence as such; that of consciousness, where existence is presupposed; and, founded on both of

19 E. Booth, OP, *Aristotelian Aporetic Ontology in Islamic and Christian Thinkers* (Cambridge 1983), pp. 4–5.
20 *TD* V, pp. 67–68.
21 C. Kaliba, *Die Welt als Gleichnis des dreieinigen Gottes* (Salzburg 1952).
22 W. Moock, *Briefe über die Heilige Dreifaltigkeit* (Dülmen 1940).
23 K. Hemmerle, *Thesen zu einer trinitarischen Ontologie* (Einsiedeln 1976).
24 See especially his tribute 'Abschied von Gustav Siewerth', *Hochland* 56 (1963), pp. 182–184.

these yet going beyond them, *Ichheit*, the being of the 'I' which is the root of all knowledge. It is in considering the powers of that 'I', Augustine-like, tutored by revelation, that Kaliba sees a fuller adumbration of the Trinitarian mystery. Three powers are united both by succession or sequence and yet circumincession or simultaneous co-inherence. For despite the inevitable limitedness which attends all beings that 'happen to' exist, the *will* poses itself in freedom as the basic foundation of the person; that foundation, moreover, expresses itself in *reason*, seen as the self-comprehension of the person and their grasp of being at large; while from these two there issues that fundamental feeling of the self for its own flavour, its affirmation of the goodness of its own distinctive inwardness. But because the latter is, of its essence, open to the *infinite* Good, so far from being morally solipsistic it is, rather, restless *desiderium*. Self-possession, Kaliba goes on to comment, is, then, freedom, but freedom via a will that can only understand itself as such through reason, and yet will and reason are unthinkable without that self-familiar 'I'. However, this 'trinal' structure of the created 'I' would seem to derive as much from its finitude as from anything else. In God, certainly, these distinctions could only be 'virtual' (real to our analysis) rather than 'real' (real in themselves), and so could not found the reality of Trinitarian persons. By contrast with ourselves, God in his *Ichsein* already has the mastery of his *Dasein* – his being is eternally at the disposition of his 'I'. Yet his existence could not be identical with his rational will were it not the case that, equally primordial with his 'I', will and reason in the blessed self-penetration of spirit everlastingly formed that 'I'. In Kaliba's Trinitarian vision, then, the Deity is *Sichsetzen* – 'self-positing', but only as self-knowing and self-feeling – and this is the Father; *Sichwissen* – 'self-knowing', but only as self-positing and self-feeling – and this is the Son; and *Sichfühlen* – 'self-feeling', but only as self-positing and self-knowing – and this is the Holy Spirit.[25] Crucial to Kaliba's approach is the claim that no origin of any one of these is possible (whether this be in the sense of *conditions* of possibility or in that of efficacious causal bringing into being) without reference to the origins of the other two. The Logos and the Spirit are the a priori origin of the Father, just as the Father with the Son is the genetic origin of the Spirit.[26] Balthasar does not go on to expound Kaliba's Trinitarian analysis of the created order or his account of the creation's raising up from a state of reflecting the Trinity to one of sharing, by grace, in the Trinitarian Archetype. And the reason is that he cannot think that such a doctrine of the originatedness (in the sense explained) of the *Father* (of all persons!) is conformable with Sacred Scripture – and so, by implication, with Church teaching. Moreover, Kaliba's exclusion (which might, by contrast, seem ultra-orthodox) of any analogy for *becoming* in the generation of the Son and the spiration of the Spirit also sits uneasily with what Balthasar has affirmed of the Holy Trinity so far – as well as, he would add, with Jesus' self-description.[27]

25 C. Kaliba, *Die Welt als Gleichnis des dreieinigen Gottes* p. 134.
26 Ibid., p. 163.
27 *TD* V, p. 71.

Balthasar finds Wilhelm Moock's wartime study much more sympathetic; indeed, it 'confirms the course we are taking in our entire endeavor'.[28] To Moock's eyes the mystery of the Trinity is implicated in the ontological constitution of all creatures, for whose understanding the concepts of unity, form and rhythm are key. In its unity the world's being has, so to speak, a Father-like relation with any individual formation within the world, while any particular being finds its reality and goodness only in the context of an ordered (compare the Son) yet mobile (compare the Holy Spirit) relation to that same universal unity in return. The beauty of existence is a matter of the give-and-take between form and the unity that both precedes and beckons it. As Balthasar reads him, Moock's Trinitarian ontology points to the selfsame Christological, paterological and pneumatological conclusions to which Balthasar was led by his own investigation of the gospel record with the aid of the interpretative techniques of theological aesthetics and theological dramatics. The form (of Jesus Christ) is true and splendid only in revealing its own origin in the Father's unity and returning to him in the Holy Spirit. And that is enacted in a drama which displays, in the order of the world's redemption, the *Überbewegtheit*, 'supermobility', of the eternal Trinity itself. Here then is a unique confirmation of Moock's own revelation-derived metaphysic of the signs in creaturely being of the Trinitarian origin and destiny of the world. Especially important for theo-drama's final act is Moock's insistence that the divine fullness of the movement of 'return' does not put an end to eventfulness but achieves its eternalisation.

Klaus Hemmerle's *Thesen* on the same subject appeal to Balthasar by adding a reference to the ontological significance of charity, that central New Testament concept for the divine. Somewhat in the manner of, at the beginning of this century, the court philosopher of French Modernism Lucien Laberthonnière, but avoiding the latter's unhelpful anti-Hellenism, Hemmerle pleads for a more distinctively Christian ontology where the charity-idea will transform the interpretation of being. Though accepting that the Word of God presupposes the validity of philosophical reason for its own understanding by humankind, Hemmerle proposed a re-working of the substance-accident ontology of the *philosophia perennis* through a recognition of the primacy of charity. In the beginning is not so much the substantive noun as the transitive verb. For the evangelical doctrine of God, the divine self-giving *is* the maintenance of the divine identity; its outpouring *is* its preservation.[29] And since the a priori need of theology for philosophy implies in turn the possibility that finite reason can register the divine language, this breath-taking metaphysical discovery *in divinis* ought to find reflection in a renewed ontology of being at large. Substance exists in view of communion, for it is modelled on that all-founding Trinitarian self-giving (the Father), self-opening (the Word), self-recovery (the Holy Spirit).

From his soundings in these essays Balthasar draws some wide-ranging conclusions. First and foremost, if, as patristic and mediaeval tradition, basing itself on the New Testament's Christological hymns, stoutly

28 *TD* V, p. 72.
29 Hemmerle, *Thesen zu einer trinitarischen Ontologie*, p. 62.

maintains, all things find their creative 'idea' in the person of the Logos, then every ideal essence – everything in its kind – must have an impulse to go beyond itself (as does the Logos) towards its own ultimate ground in the Father, and find its ultimate self-determination (as the Logos does) in the call to its own self-gift in the Holy Spirit.

> Essence receives this ultimate determination from the being in which it is founded, for its ground (the Father) is not only self-expressive power but precisely in and through that the power of self-giving – just as, within the Trinity, the Son acquires the will (in the sense of will as nature) to breathe forth the Spirit in the moment of his own self-reception at the Father's hands.[30]

The will to self-surrender, which leads to the Spirit's co-spiration, is already present in the Son's generation by the Father. In God each divine person is itself inasmuch as it lets the others be (and here *sein-lassen* is deliberately ambiguous – each hypostasis *allows* to be, and *makes* to be, the hypostatic distinctiveness of the other two), and that in an infinity of affirmation and thanksgiving (a point to which Balthasar will return) for both its own being and its inseparable co-being.

This illuminates from a Trinitarian perspective the celebrated Thomistic 'real distinction' to whose mast Balthasar has already nailed his colours. Among creatures no individual thing is either identical with its own participation in being or deducible from being, but holds its unity from within itself (in Thomas's words, *per seipsam, non propter esse suum*),[31] while at the same time it is never outside being, since outside being is only nothing. A creature's essence, in other words, cannot guarantee its reality, nor can its share in being guarantee its essence. This, for Thomas, is the tell-tale sign of its non-divinity: its essence is not its existence (and vice versa). And yet – and here comes Balthasar's original contribution – even this fundamental determination of what it is to be a creature, over against God, must have some sort of foundation in God the Creator! The *origin* of the real distinction is the marking of the creature's being with a *Trinitarian* stamp.

> Just as the Divine Persons are *themselves* only insofar as they go out to the Others (who are always Other), the created essences too are *themselves* only insofar as they go beyond themselves and indicate their primal ground (whence being in its totality shines forth) and their vocation of self-surrender. They are to surrender themselves for their neighbor (whoever he may be); thus, concretely, they offer their self-surrender through every particular instance to Being in its totality.[32]

When created being thanks Uncreated, its Maker, it gives thanks to the entire Trinity whose works *ad extra* are common, but more especially it gives thanks to the Logos for its determinate essence, to the Father for its

30 *TD* V, p. 75. Translation author's own.
31 Thomas, *De Veritate* q. 21, a. 5, ad 8.
32 *TD* V, p. 76.

participation in endless being, and for its destiny in self-giving to the Holy Spirit.

Balthasar's second main conclusion from his brisk canter through the fields of Trinitarian ontology concerns the issues of immutability and change. How can we see becoming as itself founded in absolute being – in the *Trinitas Creator*? The idea of the perennial vitality of the Trinitarian 'event' serves to mediate between the idea of the creature in its perpetual mobility and absolute being in its permanent abidingness. The personal processions and the exchange between the persons in their relations of communion are everlasting, and this means (for Balthasar) that God is not only – as Przywara had seen – the *Je-mehr*, or 'Ever-greater One' in relation to his creation. He is also such *in relation to himself*. Leaning on Adrienne von Speyr's authority, Balthasar does not hesitate to speak of their persons as continually re-finding each other, maintaining that, otherwise, the divine Essence could not be absolute freedom. Most daringly of all, he finds in the eternal Love which is God, and more especially in its 'livingness and freedom', the archetype of the finest human love, not least in *das belebende Moment der Überraschung*, 'the stimulating moment of surprise'.[33]

Balthasar returns from harvesting these fruits of theological speculation with a conviction that he has thrown light on the basic affirmation of the Pauline letters to the effect that all creaturely being and becoming is directed to, as surely as it is en route to, the divine Son who is himself at once eternal and incarnate (cf. Ephesians 1.10; Colossians 1.16). Since the word whereby God spoke out the creation is contained within the Word he speaks eternally in his Son, the created world cannot be alien to the Only-begotten. In the incarnate Son, being begotten and being created form a unity which draws the created world into the eternal generative act. The *procession* in which creation is enclosed is fulfilled in the *mission* of Christ, its own extension.

Otherness and potentiality

The doctrine of the Trinity teaches us the positive value of otherness and potentiality – two themes which ever since Parmenides have given the philosophical tradition enormous trouble. On the first, 'alterity', it enlightens us by its demonstration of the truth of the following axiom: 'The fact that "the Other" exists is *absolutely good*'.[34] If God is Love, he cannot only be intransitive, but being divine the transitiveness of *this* love must be unconditional self-surrender of a kind unthinkable for ourselves, since we cannot dispose of our being and being a subject, in the way that God can. And what way is that?

> This self-giving cannot be motivated by anything other than itself; hence it is a boundless love where freedom and necessity coincide and where identity and otherness are one: identity, since the Lover gives all that he is and nothing else, and otherness, since otherwise the Lover would love only himself.

33 *TD* V, p. 79. Translation author's.
34 *TD* V, p. 81.

And yet that difference cannot be the absolutely final word: identity and alterity, without being removed, are nonetheless transcended in a reciprocal surrender whereby a new identity of love given and love received takes its rise, and appears to the two who love as the 'miracle, ever new, of their mutual love' itself.[35]

Because divine begetting means the definitive setting free of the Begotten to share in the divine freedom for ever, the 'return of thanks' (the phrase is deliberately ambiguous) of the Son for his generation is equally eternal – all of which means that, during his earthly mission, the Son's egress from the Father and return to him are not two successive phases. And that implies for the creature (given the analogy between Trinitarian life and its own) that – whatever some mysticisms may say – going to God does not abrogate one's own alterity *vis-à-vis* God. Of itself, otherness is not alienating from God; only sin is that. Nor does Balthasar omit to point out that in the kenotic self-gift of the triune persons to each other there is a kind of *Über-Tod*, 'super-death', the archetype of an inescapable aspect of human love in all its reaches – from the self-forgetfulness implied in any love worth the name to that highest love which lays down its life for its friends.

Which brings him to the topic of 'letting be' or potentiality. When the creature/Creator relation is considered in temporary abstraction from its Trinitarian aspect, potentiality is the sheerest symptom of creatureliness, over against the *actus purus* of the Godhead. Yet viewed triadologically, one can speak of a 'passivity' of the persons when faced with each other's activity – and Balthasar can cite passages of Bonaventure to this effect about both Son and Spirit. The everlasting being-in-accord (*Je-schon-einverstanden-Sein*) of the Son with his generation from the Father, of the Spirit with his spiration from Father and Son, is an *actio passiva* which conditions the *actio activa* whereby the Father consigns all that he has to the Son, and with the Son to the Spirit, and yet finds in that act his very being. Moreover, in generation the Father *receives* a Son, in spiration Father and Son their Spirit. Receiving and letting be are as vital to the absolute Love as is giving itself. One must remember that the processions are eternally ongoing: Son and Spirit never cease to place themselves at the disposal of another for their own continuing origination – though the divine life eventuates, of course, not in time but in a supra-temporality. In this dialectic of active and passive agency Balthasar would find the uncreated source of such creaturely realities as act and potency, action and contemplation, and even the difference between genders, in the human world.

So far one might be forgiven for thinking that Balthasar has overplayed his hand in stressing so unilaterally the divine freedom in the constitution of the Trinity (and here as elsewhere in modern Germanophone Catholic thought the emphasis on God as freedom reveals the influence of Schelling). But now he countermands such a conclusion by insisting that the free acts of generation and spiration correspond to a 'will of nature' or even 'will of necessity' in God; they simply 'recapitulate' in the divine freedom what is in any case an irreversible order (Father to Son, Father

---

35 *TD* V, p. 83.

and Son to Spirit). And this in turn tells us that for the creation, whose archetype is God the Trinity, freedom is always inscribed within an order, inside a hierarchy. It can and should re-appropriate value with a spontaneity all its own. It does not for all that *invent* value.

But this is not his last word on the topic. For the Father allows the Son to petition him for the doing of his will (for instance, to save the world by his Cross), so as to lose his own (Fatherly) priority in this free con-validation of what the divine nature requires. In this perspective, the Spirit embodies the *common* rediscovery, by Father and Son, of that convali-dation but in such fashion as to add to reciprocal decision the element of 'surprise' and (Balthasar would say, apropos of the *specificum* of the Spirit) 'exuberance' which belongs so intimately with the nature of God as the *Je-mehr*, the one who is 'always more'.

In the light of Balthasar's Trinitarian theology, as here set forth, we can see why he regards the doctrine of the triune God as a supreme manifestation of the significance of potentiality. The creature's *becoming*, downgraded in the Parmenidean strain in metaphysics, here emerges as the 'highest possible approximation to [the] ... unattainable vitality' of God.[36] Indeed, Balthasar can speak of passivity as thoroughly active, for true receptivity engages the subject fully, while, complementarily, agency presupposes a space in which action can unfold. Similarly, the unity of action and contemplation lies in the more primordial union of doing and letting be in God himself, where the 'distance' between the Trinitarian persons – at once 'ever greater' and yet perfectly bridged in the way Balthasar has expounded – is the foundation of both labour and repose among the creatures who are made to their likeness. Finally, the same rhythm of making be and letting be, with its consequent fruitfulness in the Holy Ghost, is the light whose shadow, once cast on human soil, is the differentiation of the sexes.

Space, time, eternity

Even more speculatively audacious is Balthasar's claim that the Trinitarian relations also found this-worldly *space* and *time* in, again, their positive value and meaning. Space and time are metaphysically co-ordinate: space gives to what exists room for the play of events, but, conversely, needs time for its own measuring and mastery. The eternal present (*Gegenwart*) in which the Son meets the Father is really an *ereignisvoll (Ent-)Gegen-wart* – an event-filled movement towards the Father. In his ever-fulfilled expectation of the Father, the being of the Son constitutes the foundation for past, present and future in the time of the world made through him. In a similar way, Balthasar takes the hierarchical distance which distinguishes the Trinitarian processions to be the archetype of space. The originating foundation of space is that *Raumlassen*, 'leaving room', whereby the Father as giver bestows freedom on the recipient of his self-gift – not, however, in the Cabbalistic sense of a 'self-retraction', for the Father can never be so much as thought without Son and Spirit. Such 'distance' is in no way contrary to that intimacy which the Trinitarian

36 *TD* V, p. 90.

circumincession requires, for it precisely establishes the singularity of the persons.

In the Trinity, the more differentiated persons are the more closely are they united – something which has the faintest of reflections in the attraction of difference in human love. The mutual alterity yet coincidence of will which reigns in the triune God is the archetype of 'worship', *Anbetung* – than which, in an adage of von Speyr's, quoted by Balthasar, nothing is more divinely grounded.[37] If faith can be called a continual *disponibilité*, 'eine stete Bereitschaft', then the archetype not only of love but of faith itself is in the Trinity, and indeed such divine 'faith' is the basis of the Trinitarian interpersonal love. (All of which discussion makes it clear how little 'Nestorianising' is Balthasar's ascription of a *kind* of faith to Christ.)

Though Balthasar will not attempt to answer the question *why* God created the relative, temporal-spatial multiplicity of the world until he reaches the end of *Theodramatik*, we can already say that were God so to create, the world he would make would be formed according to the *Urbild* of the love-life of the Trinity, and formed, moreover

> not as an after-image sundered from the archetype and shut up in itself but – since God consists interiorly in communication – in an openness to the archetype and participation within it of a kind that presupposes an *exchange*.[38]

But since the world projected from the inner-Trinitarian life enjoys in the persons of the members of its pre-eminent species (humans) the gift of *freedom*, we have to add that, should negativity enter the picture from the side of the world, it can be encountered by what is most interiorly positive in the triune life. And in that case – citing von Speyr's *Die Schöpfung* – 'the Cross becomes the dominant form of the entire creation'.[39] After all, the Word of the creation expresses the perfect readiness of the Son to go forth from the Father.

If time is not only from but for eternity, then essence and nature must point on beyond themselves, and the world be caught up in a dialogue or contrapuntal exchange with God. As the reverberation of the eternal event of the divine being, the world's becoming can only be ordered to the Trinity. Precisely the positivity of otherness in God's Trinitarian nature ensures that the finite is not thereby swallowed up by the infinite; indeed nothing which bears an image of God can attain its definitive form save by sharing in the triune life. There is a certain correspondence, then, between our time and the eternity of the Trinity which allows eternity to inhabit our time and our time to be assumed by eternity through the mediation (as Balthasar will shortly show) of the time of Christ.

---

37 A. von Speyr, *Die Welt des Gebetes* (Einsiedeln 1987²), p. 48.
38 *TD* V, p. 99. Translation author's own.
39 A. von Speyr, *Die Schöpfung* (Einsiedeln 1972), p. 31.

Free exchange

A world fashioned by God the Holy Trinity, in whom each person transcends himself towards the other two, and where the divine Essence (the divine totality) possesses therefore the property of 'ever-more' for each divine person, can only be a self-transcending world where each created thing moves by inner tendency upwards and outwards, beyond itself. But this means that the creature only attains its own final significance when it reaches absolute Being – and this it cannot do without that Being's grace. Balthasar accords this grace 'ontological primacy'.[40] He considers that the interplay between self-transcending nature and the grace which alone can give nature fulfilment mirrors the way that, in the Trinity, the Father is always greater (in his hypostatic origin) than the Son in whom creatures are made, yet, through the free communication to him by the Father of a share in the spiration of the Spirit, the Son receives even that power of Trinitarian origination which is the Father's own. Just so in Mary the process that leads from her conceiving her Son on earth at the Annunciation to the Son at the Assumption receiving her in heaven involves a 'circulation' (*Kreislauf*) of nature and grace, yet it is the grace Mary is given at the beginning as the *Immaculata* which holds the primacy in her becoming the *Coronata* at the end.

It is on that note of circulating exchange that Balthasar ends his account of the world as a world which is from and for the Trinity. And here Christ remains central.

> If God's idea of the world is to bring heaven and earth together in Jesus Christ in the fullness of time, so that we may be 'holy and blameless before him', it follows that this incorporation of all created beings into the Begotten is, in Trinitarian terms, the most intimate manner of union with God. For it implies that the creaturely 'other-than-God' is plunged into the uncreated 'Other-in-God' *while maintaining* that fundamental 'distance' which alone makes love possible.[41]

It is for this that the Son receives dominion over all things. Only on the basis of the Word can the creature make a valid response to its existence – fulfilling that essential responsiveness which Balthasar ascribed to it, following Barth's footsteps, in his theology of the *imago Dei* in *Herrlichkeit*. Only thus, in the words of Jesus to the Samaritan Woman in St John's Gospel, can we obtain that living water which wells up to life eternal. The trajectory of the human being who comes forth from God in creation and returns to him in eternity is possible only because of the course the Word incarnate took from birth to death, and that mission of the Word is itself enabled by his origination and termination in the Father. Only a Trinitarian God can guarantee that man will not, in his union with God, be deprived of *Selbstständigkeit*, 'independence' in the sense of a place of his own wherein to stand, for his true End is exchange (*Tausch*), the mutual inhabitation of the earth of man and the heaven of God.

---

40 *TD* V, p. 104.
41 *TD* V, p. 105, with an internal citation of Ephesians 1.4, 10.

15

Expecting the End

The Christological centre

How then will earth reach heaven? Or, to put it less imagistically, what is the form of the human hope? These will be Balthasar's next questions. Now 'no one has ascended into heaven but he who descended from heaven, the Son of man, who is in heaven' (John 3.13). Hence it is Jesus who not only brings about the exchange between heaven and earth but actually *is* it. The location of believers is to be defined christologically as a simultaneous dwelling in heaven as citizens and continuing existence as pilgrims on earth – and this is especially clearly seen in Christian death, which joins something purely earthly – the decision for God in the faith that sees not (without which decision no one can become a sharer in absolute Freedom) – and the wholly realised freedom of the creature *in* that of God.

The formal structure of the world must be described, then, as filled with content only through the Word incarnate, the Christ who deals with the alienation of a sinful world on that Cross which is always 'the Cross of the Trinity', and then, in dependence on the Word made crucified flesh, through that continuation of the Incarnation which is the Church. Human life on earth was always meant to be inserted into eternal, heavenly life: in the language of the Fathers, the 'image of God' in man to be fulfilled by the 'divine likeness' in him. Accordingly, the partial aims we pursue on earth must tend towards the ultimate goal of life eternal, given us as our mission. Projecting the future as eternal life is done on the foundation of the immanence of eternity in the present through the reality of grace.

Balthasar stresses, in company with von Speyr, the way 'heaven' keeps provoking 'earth' into actualising the capacity for self-transcendence heaven has given it. The saints apply themselves to things of earth – that is their mission; yet they also suggest how those things can have a 'form of existence' in heaven. If this seems to the unbeliever a phantasmagorical conception, to the believer it is very reality, verified in the mediator between Trinity and creation, Jesus Christ. The new heavens and new earth have come to be in the unity of his divine-human person, incarnate and risen; the creation's final form can be surveyed only from there. He is the presence of the eternal in time, not just inasmuch as the Son's mission represents the Trinitarian God in the world, but also because the risen

201

Christ exists in heaven as the 'completed creature', the 'head of the
heavenly and the earthly Church'.[1] By transposing onto the level of
creaturely time his own eternal relation with the Father, the Son can bring
to completion the sense in which (as already examined under the heading
of 'Trinitarian ontology') creaturely becoming has its archetype in the
everlasting Trinitarian 'event'. And here the Son's obedience – which
binds together his eternal attitude as Logos and his temporal as man – is
critical. The Saviour always knew himself to be the Father's unique Son,
yet in his permanent hold on the vision of God sought only the Father's
will – which opens the possibility that his experience of that vision might
have had a quality at times analogous to ours by faith.[2] But that obedience
was (supremely) fruitful obedience, bringing our time into its own true
fatherland, that eternity which is (once again) time's not only source but
magnet.

> In his Resurrection, Jesus has already taken the whole of transitory
> time (including life and death) with him into that eternal life
> which was the source of his constant obedience to the Father's
> commission.[3]

And this incomparably fulfilled time of his Christ places at the disposition of Christians in his Church so that our mortality can shake off
the atmosphere of hopelessness and lostness once its own. Through the
Parousia which Jesus' past guarantees, eternal 'time' will take the time
of this world into itself and our creaturely becoming have a share,
accordingly, in the 'supra-becoming' of the divine being.

Because the Church continues Christ's being and work in the world,
her institutions and sacraments (her 'objective' life), her saints and in
principle all her members (her 'subjective' life) draw sustenance from the
exchange between heaven and earth. In the risen Lord, the idea of the
'world in God' has become concrete reality and the Church which as
Christus-Gemeinschaft is Christ's organ shares in this heavenly–earthly
duality in unity. 'For the Christian saint heaven is not, as in the Old
Testament, in the future',[4] even though one (say Peter) may live more
from earth to heaven, another (John perhaps) from heaven to earth. This,
'eternal life' in which ecclesial life participates in, for instance, the sacred
Liturgy, in prayer, and the Beatitudes ethos of the devout faithful cannot
be something different, moreover, from the Trinitarian life, for in the *Von-
her, Zu-hin* quality of his Sonship – its being *from* the Father, and *to* the
Father, and in both directions in the Holy Spirit – the Word incarnate, like
the pre-existent Word, is always a Trinitarian reality, and that he is as
both God and man.

> [The Son's] 'economic' movement is not solely restricted by historical
> time but stretches beyond it, since his historical return to the Father

---

1 *TD* V, p. 118.
2 Cf. Balthasar, '*Fides Christi*: An Essay on the Consciousness of Christ', in idem.,
   Spouse of the Word: Explorations in Theology II (ET, San Francisco 1991), pp. 43–79.
3 *TD* V, p. 128.
4 *TD* V, p. 133.

takes the form of an ever-new (eucharistic) coming to his Church (and through the Church to the world).[5]

The nature of Christian hope

Balthasar has so stressed the presence of the content of faith within the act of faith that perhaps his readers are wondering (he says) whether he has left any space for the virtue of theological hope at all! But in fact there *is* a Christian hope, a better hope than that of pagans who, at best, in the Platonic tradition, looked to an immortality paid for by the loss of man's bodily being, and a better hope, too, than that of Judaism, for which – even when certain ambivalences in the Old Testament canon are ignored – the object of hope is so entirely future that hope can become, as with so secularised a Jewish thinker as Ernst Bloch, simply a 'principle' – call it prophetic or messianic – in history. Christian hope, whose object and efficacious ground is the risen Christ, concerns the whole man, soul and body, and has its first-fruits in that living personality. However, we are speaking about *theological* hope, hope that binds to God, and so theocentric hope – not, then, a kind of infinitely extended egotism but a hope in the God who will give the disciple of the risen One that form of identity which in his loving-kindness pleases him. And this means that what finalises the creation as the ultimate object of its hope is also that through which the world is 'saved' (Romans 8.24) already. In fact, for Balthasar, hope is underpinned by the divine Trinity for 'in those who exercise hope the Spirit addresses the Father "with sighs too deep for words", that the Son's redemption may be fulfilled in the world'.[6] Leaning on Adrienne's *Sieg der Liebe* (her commentary on Romans 8), Balthasar points out that, while what the Son has shown us authorises hope, it does not indicate how hope is fulfilled.

We can, however, say that Christian hope must be primarily 'vertical' in character, for the Christ-event which founds it is now 'above'.

> Hope is not the result of a yearning or a postulate, but a gift that comes from the goal of our hoping.[7]

'Christ in you, the hope of glory' (Colossians 1.27), already discussed by Balthasar in the context of theological aesthetics, is also, as the theological dramatics will now insist, 'the hope stored up for you in heaven' (Colossians 1.5). The anchor, that ancient Christian symbol of hope, descends vertically to take hold of the sea-floor. Before moving on to consider whether we can *in addition* speak of a 'horizontal' dimension to Christian hoping, Balthasar notes that the co-presence of suffering with hope (and the characteristic linguistic product of these two is the vocabulary of patience) does not, in the New Testament, call hope's validity in question. While for the 'average' Jewish sensibility and for a demythologised paganism suffering is a sign of the absence of God, in the Apocalypse the glorified Lamb stands with his throat opened. He who

---

5 *TD* V, p. 139.
6 *TD* V, p. 146, with an internal citation of Romans 8.26.
7 *TD* V, p. 148.

has been taken up into the 'all-time' of God is glorified even in his 'supratemporal' suffering, for

> what John brings together in his concept of [the] exaltation and glorification [of Christ] is not so contradictory that it cannot be undergirded by the absolute stance of Trinitarian self-surrender and – albeit in a way that remains mysterious – thus reconciled.[8]

The Lamb slain defines the 'space' in which the Church's – and finally the world's – time makes its passage.

But what if anything can horizontal movement to the future – biological in evolution, technological in applied-scientific progress – have to do with such a hope? Balthasar feels he must consider two schemes which, albeit cautiously, would find a connexion. Despite his collaboration with Teilhard in the interwar years and the often respectful references to that poet-scientist's attempt to reintroduce the cosmic aspect of Christianity to centre-stage which punctuate Balthasar's writing, his account of the Teilhardian version of an 'earth open to heaven' is pretty negative. Teilhard's aim was to integrate with a Christian mysticism of transcendence as 'above' us a 'neo-humanist mysticism' of transcendence 'ahead' of us, transcendence as future. Anticipating de Lubac's discovery in *Surnaturel* that the world – which must include, therefore, its 'ascending', material aspect – has only one ultimate goal and that a supernatural one, Teilhard hoped to find in the Pauline–Johannine theology of the cosmic Christ, developed by the Greek Fathers in their Logos speculation, a truly evangelical way of including the evolutionary *Weltanschauung* in Catholicism's total picture of reality. Though toying in his earliest writings with the notion of an *anima mundi* as the natural intermediary between nature and God, in the 1918 essay '*Forma Christi*' he rejected any idea of a 'determinate natural final end' in favour of the thesis that the true goal of evolution can be given it only from above, with the 'Omega', Jesus Christ, without whom the universe is but a flock without a shepherd. Nonetheless, thanks to the Incarnation, the Word has of course his purely natural reality as well. Granted the cosmic necessity of the evolutionary ascent which his Incarnation presupposed, Teilhard spoke of the Incarnation as co-extensive with the history of the universe, and of the cosmos as Christ's third 'nature', neither human nor divine but both natural and supernatural at once. Evolution moves towards a Person, and the anxieties generated by its 'complexification' in human development can only be pacified by the 'amorisation' of the world, its transformation by the love of Christ, who in the power of his resurrection draws the entire evolutionary process efficaciously to himself. Treating the Cross more as a symbol of the 'hard labour' which evolution demands than as the expiation of sin, Teilhard is not, however, a Pelagian activist, since the Logos on the Cross carries a message about renunciation and the fruitfulness of letting go into the arms of God.

Yet Balthasar finds Teilhard's eschatology an ambiguous affair. The highest synthesis of all evolution is the ingathering (*Einbergung*) of human

---

8 *TD* V, p. 152.

'monads' in Christ.[9] (That terminology for human 'selves' is not accidental: Balthasar believed Teilhard to have been much influenced by Maurice Blondel, and not least by the most cosmological of Blondel's writings, his study of the monadology of Leibniz.) But Teilhard could not make up his mind whether matter, 'centred' in the case of the human organism on spirit, and now finding in the Omega-Christ the Centre of all centres is, as a result, glorified or, by extreme contrast, volatilised – for the Jesuit writer, no rigorous metaphysician, sometimes speaks of matter as imperfectly realised spirit. And if such a vision of the ultimate future is hardly reconcilable with the doctrine of the resurrection of the flesh, Teilhard's ambiguities on the subject arise, Balthasar believes, from his (very un-Goethean!) estimate of the 'myriad variety of forms in the organic and animal kingdom' as only side-roads if not indeed cul-de-sacs of the evolutionary highway.[10] Although Teilhard knew of the 'principle of the Eternal Feminine' and its realisation in the Church of Mary, and Balthasar praises his devotion to the Mother of Christ as the true Demeter – nature in man become maternally gracious for the purposes of God, the idea of the nuptiality of the human body does not really figure in his account of evolution and the Logos.

Will a German Lutheran do better where a French Catholic has not done so well? Jürgen Moltmann was influenced not only by the Old Testament prophecy of a total future realisation of *shalom* – the well-being of the world of man within the world as a whole (something he shared with Latin American liberation theology) – but also by the atheistic messianism of Ernst Bloch. For Bloch reality *is* 'hope' in the sense that

> from the alpha of nothing, by way of the self-transcendence of becoming, turning the Utopian into reality as this does, actuality travels towards the omega of being; in that sense the project of an absolute God is itself a Utopia which becomes real through the 'incarnation' of this 'God' in self-absolutising man ...[11]

Prescinding entirely, in his *Theologie der Hoffnung*, from the Gospel of John, Moltmann points out that the Old Testament hope for the future remains as 'actual' as ever – for the Resurrection of Jesus is rather the annunciation of his definitive Lordship over history than its realisation, the latter being still to come. Moreover, in the Cross and Resurrection of Christ the triune God has himself become historical by engaging himself in the world's history: here, at the price of acquiring a family resemblance to process theology Moltmann underlines the all-importance of the Easter event which otherwise his futurist eschatology might seem to have taken away. The risen Christ is for Moltmann a principle of utopian hope as a programme of action – defined over against both a purely 'vertical' trans-cendence and any merely passive expectation of final divine intervention to extend Christ's Lordship to being as a whole. For Balthasar, the redeeming grace (literally!) of Moltmann's theology of hope – and a point

9 *TD* V, p. 164.
10 *TD* V, p. 166.
11 *TD* V, p. 169. Translation author's own.

on which it merits, in comparison with the liberation theology which it otherwise resembles, a 'preferential option' of its own – is the way it unites eschatology and Cross. It is when believers take up the Cross, itself the sign of the total evacuation of inner-worldly hope, that they anticipate the redemptive future.

But *what* is hoped for in this theology, and *for whom*? Owing to Moltmann's refusal to practise a Trinitarian theology of creation save from the departure point of the Cross (here his Lutheran origins declare themselves), he cannot speak of the Trinitarian archetypes inscribed in beings and calling out for their full realisation through both providence and grace. And if the desire to take both Hegel and Bloch into the forecourt of Christian theology prevents Moltmann from developing a Trinitarian ontology which could help answer the question, *What* is hoped for?, no more does he answer the question, *Who* does God 'hope' for? though speaking of the 'certainty' which attaches to the divine promise. With regard to the first enquiry: Moltmann has failed to distinguish the theological virtue of hope whose object is God himself, if also, secondarily, according to Thomas, the divine provision to us of means to this ultimate End, from *spes communis* – that common-or-garden hoping which, though it may well be virtuous in various circumstances, is, more fundamentally, a *passio animae*, one of the soul's motions. For Balthasar, Moltmann is right to think of hope as social, since what Christians hope for is the re-direction of the world to God, but wrong to give the impression that the object of this social hope could be another disposition of the things of earth. Of course nothing prevents Christians from having human hope as well – but, Balthasar is saying, nothing can be gained theologically from adding these two unlikes together, since the Church's mission rests wholly on *spes theologica*, not *spes communis*.

But then, secondly, for whom does God hope? If Balthasar ascribes to Moltmann an at least tacit notion of divine hoping (linking the theology of hope to that theologoumenon of Origen, taken up in the patristic age by Ambrose and in the mediaeval period by Gerhoh of Reichersberg and Pope John XXII, whereby Christ and the saints await expectantly the conversion of the world), he himself will prefer Péguy – rather than either Teilhard or Moltmann – as a guide. If Teilhard's eschatology is weak on Trinitarianism, and Moltmann's, despite its strongly Trinitarian character, cannot escape from the domination of Bloch, Péguy, with fewer ideological debts to pay, can do more justice to the hope of Father and Spirit for the Son's mission and to God's hope that, through the mission of the Son, man will be saved. In *Le Porche du mystère de la deuxième vertu*, the importance of which Balthasar had already signalled in *Herrlichkeit*, Péguy presents hope as the key figure in the trio whose other members are faith and charity. What not only sustains but actively helps to realise a hope for all history, symbolised in the poem by the woodcutter meditating in the frozen forest on the fragile continuity of things, is the heavenly Jerusalem; to this end *le spirituel* and *le charnel* must work in tandem, and the conversion of what is at once spiritual and fleshly is precisely that for which the Father and the Son anxiously wait, though at the same time all depends on grace.

Here the 'hope principle' has become Christian: what is at stake is the attainment or the loss of eternal life on the part of man (who is both body and soul) through God's grace and through penance, within and through the communion of saints. Here, in this present reality that is vertically open to God, are the last things, here is the Last Act, and not in some end time at the close of a horizontal future.

Only theological hope changes the uniformity endemic to horizontal time into inexhaustible novelty: 'the earthly future is inserted into an ever-new "now" that is a gift of divine grace'.[12]

Hope and the tragic

Balthasar's task is, then, to consider the *content* of the theological hope of which this is the *form*. Is the final act – as would seem from a first reading of the New Testament to be the case – basically a *tragedy*, or is the tragic outcome of salvation history – in an intensifying bifurcation of response and rejection to God – itself underpinned by a deeper reality still, called by Balthasar the 'Trinitarian drama'?

Both Balthasar's theology of creation as image of the inner-Trinitarian life, an image directed toward its own realisation in the archetype, and his theology of the Resurrection as the proleptic achievement of that destiny, exceeding the hopes of Jews and Gentiles alike, might seem, he admits, excessively optimistic. Has he weighed enough the reality of sin, the possibility of the human No? Wanting, as he says, nothing to do with any superficial justification of a theory of final apocatastasis such as is entertained by those for whom mortal sin requires titanic immoral abilities to commit, he will look now at the New Testament evidence for the radical – and even ineradicable – nature of evil. Thus in Paul, while the atoning work of Christ means the triumph of the free gift of God's righteousness to those who had fallen short of the glory of God, there still remains a coming day when each individual will present himself before the tribunal of God, or of Christ, there to give an account of his works. Are we to suppose so massive an incoherence in Paul's teaching that he could espouse at once a doctrine of maximally universal salvation (for Pauline reprobation, on Balthasar's reading of the Letters, is economically directed towards a wider extension of saving grace) *and* an Old Testament theory of justiciable individuals as well? No, it suffices to be aware that for Paul faith subsists only in union with efficacious love – and so with heavy responsibilities in life and mission. In the Synoptic Gospels – though here, consonant with his attempt to press upon his readers a Péguyesque universalistic hope, Balthasar stresses the pre-paschal character of much of their material – nothing could be clearer than the division at the judgment between sheep and goats. In John, the Light, come into the world, has the effect of convincing the darkness of its preference for itself, not only revealing the essence of that darkness but arousing it, and making it deeper. The non-acceptance by the darkness of the 'absolute and groundless love revealed in the Son', allows us to see that darkness as

12 *TD* V, p. 187.

equally 'abyssal' – without determining reason other than itself, a reference to the Fourth Evangelist's citation (John 15.25) of a psalm verse, 'They
hated me without a cause'. The abyss of the Father's saving love,
manifested in the Son's mission, brings out of its hiding-hole *das ernstlich
Gegengöttliche*, the 'seriously counterdivine' diabolic power, what (in
Graham Harrison's fine translation of this work) is 'implacably hostile to
God'.[13]

While Balthasar himself tends to define the diabolic as essentially hate
– which is the exact antithesis of the love that typifies God in his
Trinitarian and economic self-gift, the way he has introduced the subject
of directly counter-divine evil (as well as his enormous respect for the
theologian concerned) makes his discussion in large part an exchange of
views with Karl Barth. For Barth brings diabolic evil under the heading of
das Nichtige – not just a mere absence of something, or simple creaturely
defect, nor the 'shadow-side' of the good creation, and certainly not, as
Schelling had imagined, a reality rooted in the last analysis in the being of
God, but a third fundamental form of existence, besides those of the
Uncreated God himself and his creatures. What saves Barth's ontology of
evil from dualism is his clear assertion that evil exists only as (divinely)
'rejected and overcome'.[14] Man, however, neither can nor wants to share
in this overcoming – which is why God becomes man in Jesus Christ,
permitting *das Nichtige* to show its true colours on the Cross. The Cross is
at once, therefore, the revelation of evil's nature and man's opportunity
to participate in its definitive defeat by God. Balthasar cannot follow
Barth's theology of evil save in one important point, and that is his
'Christological concentration' of the divine encounter with evil. In terms
drawn from Adrienne von Speyr: the Cross is the sign of the devil's fall
from heaven; the dragon has no power over the 'Marianly-immaculate'
Church. Otherwise, Balthasar would reinstate a classical angelology (and
hence diabology) while admitting, however, that the demonic has no
'univocal structure'. The biblical figures of serpent, Devil, dragon, imply
the multiple forms that angelic evil can take, just as the 'seven heads' of
the beast of the Apocalypse express its varied register of sin-filled expression in 'accumulating arguments against man'.[15] Balthasar emphasises
chiefly, however, the paradox with which he opened *Endspiel*: Christ's
triumph over the powers triggers the intensification of their action, or, as
he now puts it:

> The satanic 'great power' whose rage comes from the fact that in-
> wardly it knows it is beaten, fights against the Christian powerless-
> ness of the Cross, which inwardly knows that it is victorious.[16]

Though the victory of Calvary cannot be reversed, evil loses whatever it
had of 'pagan innocence': after the public combat of the Cross, ill is done
and even celebrated for its own sake, and fascinates like the snake-

---

13 *TD* V, p. 203.
14 *TD* V, p. 206.
15 *TD* V, p. 209. Translation author's own.
16 *TD* V, p. 210.

engirded head of Medusa. If the Synoptic Jesus wonders aloud whether, when the Son of Man comes, he will still find faith on earth, the Johannine Jesus warns that, on those who will not obey the Son the divine wrath shall rest.

And all of this seems to justify the language of eschatological tragedy. The divine plan will, it seems, fail in part, even or especially at the End. God must suffer the immuring of a part of his creation in absurdity. And indeed, recent theology, chiefly Protestant it is true but found on a worldwide basis from Germany to Japan, has not scrupled to speak of the 'suffering of God', thus taking insuperable tragedy into the very divine nature itself. It might be thought, after all he has said about 'receptivity' and 'letting be' as enjoying archetypal existence in the inner-Trinitarian being of God, that Balthasar might well be sympathetic to this movement of thought, but despite the presence of the language of divine vulnerability in biblical and rabbinic tradition he expresses misgivings. In the age of the Fathers even heretical theologies – Monarchian, Apollinarian, Mono-physite – though allowing a direct divine appropriation of emotion 'did not seriously propose to subordinate the divine essence to the suffering of the world'.[17] However, Balthasar believes the patristic idea of divine immutability to be less rigorist than that of the Scholastics which succeeded it: the Fathers' horror at the notion of God as subject of *pathê* ('passions') derived in large part from the connotations both of in-voluntariness and sinfulness which that word frequently bore. Balthasar inclines to the thesis that the divine 'livingness' – expressed in God's compassion and patience – includes *analogues* of human *pathê* though without the latter's mutability (and without too our emotions' frequently involuntary, and – *a fortiori!* – sometimes sinful character). The Swiss theologian is not encouraged to go further in the direction of modern theopaschitism by the all too manifest debt of the relevant writers to Hegel for whom the world's finitude – and thus suffering and death – must be a real moment in God. Quite apart from the historical question as to whether Hegel set up a smokescreen to conceal the atheism of his philosophy of religion for reasons of political self-defence, seen philosophically Hegel's account of Trinity and Passion may be internal, simply, to his general ontology – and not an account of 'event', divine or human, at all. Com-menting chiefly on relevant works by the 'Lutheran Hegelians' Jürgen Moltmann and Gerhard Koch,[18] Balthasar writes:

> This 'Lutheran Hegelianism' stands on a knife-edge: it deliberately submerges the life of God (including his death) in the world's coming to be and passing away, while wishing to distinguish it, *within* this immanence, from living and dying as the world knows them. Materially this achieves a certain distance from Hegel, but formally his 'ambivalence' remains.[19]

17 *TD* V, p. 218. Translation author's own.
18 J. Moltmann, *Crucified God*; idem., *The Future of Creation* (ET, London 1979); idem., *The Trinity and the Kingdom of God* (ET, London 1981); G. Koch, *Die Zukunft des toten Gottes* (Hamburg 1978).
19 *TD* V, p. 231.

Placing pain and death in God so that God can suffer and die outside himself in the world is a tactic suspiciously resembling the recreation of mythology. The post-war Japanese theologian Kazo Kitamori, adding the influence of the Kyoto school of Buddhism to that of Luther, similarly fails to do justice to the divine freedom *vis-à-vis* the world (an inevitable weakness when Luther's insistence that all theology must be done from the standpoint of the Cross is taken *ad litteram*) – and also sins by locating the ultimate divine basis of the Son's Passion in the Essence (not, as Balthasar would say the inner-Trinitarian communion) of God.[20]

And if Balthasar does not get much help from the attractively entitled study *The Suffering of the Impassible God* by the little known Scottish Episcopalian B. R. Brasnett,[21] or from the relevant sections, nuanced though these are, of Barth's *Church Dogmatics*, he finds what he is looking for with the help of the Belgian Jesuit Jean Galot who led him to a remarkable essay by the influential French Neo-Thomistic lay-philosopher Jacques Maritain. All the apparently negative experiences– '*les renonciations*' – which incarnate, crucified Love accepted in the work of our salvation, have their source and archetype, so Galot argued in his *Dieu, souffre-t-il?*, in the mutual outgoingness of the Trinitarian persons – what he called the 'inner-Trinitarian ecstasy'.[22] In other words, as between Father, Son and Holy Spirit in eternity there is already a constant renunciation of self – and precisely this is the condition of possibility for a suffering *divine*-human Saviour. This intuition of Galot's was confirmed for Balthasar by Maritain's essay where, writing virtually at the end of his long life, Maritain proposed that, like all creaturely perfections, that wonderful quality of some human beings whereby they accept pain in a really generous and even triumphant, as distinct from either resigned, or resentful, or masochistic, spirit and are ennobled by that victorious acceptance, must have its source in God. Maritain found here an essential attribute of God, though one for which we have no obvious single word. Insisting that, unlike our suffering, this quality involves no imperfection in God, he treated it as an integral aspect of God's bliss, his beatitude.[23]

Balthasar takes this intuition of Maritain's and extends it by applying it to God's specifically *Trinitarian* livingness or vitality. The selflessness, *Selbstlosigkeit*, and even recklessness, *Vorsichtslosigkeit*, with which Father and Son surrender themselves to each other in the Holy Spirit from everlasting to everlasting enables in time the atoning suffering of Christ.

---

20 Balthasar made use of the German translation of the Japanese original of 1946, namely *Theologie des Schmerzes Gottes* (Göttingen 1972), as well as the comments found in B. Oguro-Opitz, *Analyse und Auseinandersetzung mit der Theologie des Schmerzes Gottes von Kazoh Kitamori* (Frankfurt–Berne–Cirencester 1980).

21 London 1928.

22 J. Galot, *Dieu, souffre-t-il?* (Paris 1976), pp. 175–176. As Balthasar points out this thesis is not in fact given pride of place in Galot's own theology of these matters which emphasises above all the idea that the Father is the primal sacrificer on Calvary, so that the Son's rôle of offering the world to the Father through himself is consequent on his more primordial mission of revealing the Father's grief.

23 J. Maritain, 'Quelques réflexions sur le Savoir théologique', *Revue Thomiste* 77 (1969), pp. 5–27.

There are no inbuilt securities or guarantees in the absolute self-giving of Father to Son, of Son to Father, and of both to the Spirit.[24]

The Trinitarian persons, accordingly, are at one and the same time utterly impassible and yet absolutely defenceless. Or, as one student of Balthasar has put it:

In their transparency to each other as subsistent relations, they are selves without self-protection[25]

– a metaphor of the glass walls of the Trinitarian personhood more delicate, if also less memorable, than Balthasar's own somewhat brutal statement that mutual 'bloodletting' (*Verbluten*) is God's 'circulation' (*Blutkreislauf*).[26] And what this leads Balthasar to believe is that, in a Christian context, the term 'tragedy', though not deprived of all validity, must be surpassed. The all-embracing reality within which tragedy makes its appearance is eternal bliss.

A God beyond tragedy?

Balthasar proposes to show this in a series of stages. He begins from the statement that when the Son enters the world of time he does not abandon the eternal life he enjoys as God – for the Father created the world not outside the Son but for him, and in this sense within the divine life. The Son's human life expresses his eternal 'behaviour' (*Verhaltung*) towards the Father. As the Word of God in human words he practises to perfection the art of representing the Eternal in time. His being in the world of itself changes the Father's relation to creatures since that being *is* the presence in time of Eternity itself.

Now the Trinitarian mission which the Son brings from heaven to earth is a reconciling mission carried out in a flesh like ours in view of sin (thus Paul in Romans 8.3) and so is inescapably a mission in death, death as sin has made it. His task will be to assume the death of sin into the death of donation, since when death is seen (prelapsarianly) as the loving surrender of life, it can be said to have its archetype in God – not *qua* death, but *qua* donation. In this sense the death of Jesus, even in its bitterness and abandoned quality, is the expression of his Trinitarian livingness.

And this tells us that his extremest suffering 'follows from and actually expresses his eternal triune joy'.[27] Just so the woman in travail in the metaphor of the Fourth Gospel forgets her pains in the joy that a child is born to the world; joy and suffering will go together in the apostolic letters, too, and in the Eucharist the Church will receive Cross and Resurrection rolled into one.

It is by no means suggested that, while he bears sin, the Son can actually feel this glory, this joy; but it does not alter the fact that joy

24 *TD* V, p. 245.
25 J. Saward, *The Mysteries of March: Hans Urs von Balthasar on the Incarnation and Easter* (London 1990), p. 14.
26 *TD* V, p. 245. Translation author's own.
27 *TD* V, p. 252.

is the consistent presupposition for all experience of forsakenness. On the Cross, the lived reality of death, objectively, is life; so extreme suffering, objectively, is joy.[28]

Citing von Speyr's *Der Mensch vor Gott*: the Father can make no response to the Son's cry of abandonment on Calvary, since he 'wants to give the Son perfect joy'.[29] We forget too readily that the bliss of the Trinity lies in *Hingabe*, self-donation. The eternal life which the Son carries into the world ruptures the 'autorelationality' of the egoistic 'I', and proves in the Resurrection that perfect giving *is* inexhaustibly flowing life.

By a paradox now comprehensible as only apparent, therefore, separation is here identical with union. To manifest the completeness of his union with the Father, the Son not only assumes the lot of mortals but descends below them, beyond 'all possible distance from God and alienation from him'.

> Such distance is possible . . . only within the economic Trinity, which transposes the absolute distinction of the Persons in the Godhead from one another into the dimensions of salvation history, involving man's sinful distance from God and its atonement.[30]

The Son's abandonment in the Passion is a mode of his conjunction with Father and Spirit, just as his death is a mode of his livingness, his suffering of his bliss. Not especially happy is the metaphor of *Hinterlegung*, the 'depositing' of his divine power and glory with the Father, which Balthasar, conceding its strongly anthropomorphic coloration, borrows at this juncture (with so much else in this section of *Theodramatik*) from Adrienne von Speyr. The Son can 'deposit' everything with the Father – except his obedience. The Cross reveals *both* the difference of the persons, manifest in the abandonment, *and* the unity of essence in God, apparent in the unity of the plan of salvation of which the death and descent are the centre.

But the Cross is also the revelation of sin, and as the concentration of sin on the person of the Son it is the locus of God's judgment on that sin which the Son embodies. And yet the casting out of the prince of this world in that atoning *passio*, 'undergoing' for our sake, is not an external divine decision; only the insertion of *Gottverlassenheit*, divine abandonment, into the Trinitarian love-relationship renders it possible at all.

> The Son 'takes the estrangement into himself and creates proximity': nearness between God and man on the basis of the union between Father and Son that is held fast through every darkness and forsakenness.[31]

The Spirit, as *vinculum unitatis*, the unifying bond, in the Trinity, sustains both conjunction and separation, in virtue of whose unity the Son's

---

28 *TD* V, p. 254.
29 A. von Speyr, *Der Mensch von Gott* (Einsiedeln 1966), p. 82.
30 *TD* V, p. 257.
31 *TD* V, p. 261, with an internal citation of Adrienne von Speyr, *Der Epheserbrief* (Einsiedeln 1983), p. 92.

death-cry is the supreme statement in the knowledge of God, the proof of God's triune love for the world. Balthasar takes the opportunity to mark off his own position (and that of von Speyr) from Moltmannianism: there is no question of the Trinity 'arriving' via its history in the world at its own fullness: nothing in the Economy can go further than the absolute self-surrender which characterises the triune life from all eternity.

And this is so even if the Cross, as judgment on sin, reveals in the first place the wrath of God, which Balthasar interprets in a patchwork of references from Adrienne, as response to the invasion of the infinite spaciousness of divine love by the violence of human presumption in sin. Good Friday enables God to pronounce his utter 'No' against the sin borne by the vicariously self-substituting Redeemer, while at the same time saying 'Yes' to sinners. On Holy Saturday before turning to the world at Easter the Father turns to the Son-made-man so as to initiate him, as the Incarnate One precisely, into this 'reserved' secret; from now on there is no longer wrath but love alone. Since what the Son experienced on the Cross in the form of wrath was the Father's love, his suffering cannot be without fruit, and no news can be better news than this.

And so, Balthasar concludes, there is no tragedy in the God of Christians. The 'Trinitarian depth' of the work of reconciliation relativises, seemingly, all possible rejection of that work by its prior embrace (*Unterfassung*) of those who would say 'No'. But does that mean, then, that the supporters, ancient or modern, of *apokatastasis* have theological right on their side, and that all *will* be saved? Certainly we must take full account of the fact that, with the 'turn of the ages', the symmetry whereby the Old Testament Lord gave weal to the faithful and woe to the unfaithful is replaced by an 'asymmetry' characteristic of the Cross where the Judge is the Saviour. The ethos flowing from the Cross forbids the new people of God from handing out declarations of damnation. All sins, themselves only finite, are underpinned – the connotations of (Trinitarian) holding and (substitutionary) limiting in Balthasar's key term *Unterfassen* are, I hope, suggested in this English quasi-equivalent – by the infinite love shown in the Crucified. Fortunately:

> men's freedom is not infinite: 'they are free within the greater freedom of God'.[32]

But Balthasar now pulls himself up in his tracks. Is this not to go too fast, to simplify excessively? God may indeed offer all men their true identity in the redeeming Christ, but notwithstanding his greater, uncreated freedom must he not respect their albeit limited and created freedom, even if, rejecting his offer of salvation, finite freedom turns against its own human bearers likewise? In considering this possibility of *Selbstverweigerung*, 'self-refusal', we come up against what the New Testament calls the 'mystery of iniquity'. The rejection of the world's reconciliation in the precious blood of Christ is more serious than any previous infringement of the Law; hence the way the contrast between

---

32 *TD* V, p. 284, with an internal citation of Adrienne von Speyr, *Johannes*, II, *Die Streitreden. Betrachtungen über das Johannesevangelium, Kapitel 6–12* (Einsiedeln 1949), p. 143.

eternal bliss and eternal perdition is *sharpened*, not moderated, when it
makes a New Testament appearance. And has not Balthasar himself
already shown, in *Theodramatik*'s last volume, how the ever-fuller
epiphany of the divine love provokes an ever-more lethal outburst of
the world's hatred? 'There is sin which is mortal' writes the apostle John
(I John 5.16) – and no one can suppose, in view of the earlier teaching of
that epistle, that this warning is made in ignorance of the love revealed
on the Cross of Christ. Before the judgment-seat of Christ where the
disclosure to us existentially of that love once shown to all historically
will not only bless but burn (for it demands a congruent response), who
can say with certainty that he or she *must* be saved?

In the light streaming from the face of Christ we shall, in being judged,
essentially judge ourselves: Balthasar brings forth from Fathers and
mediaevals a host of citations to support this view. This is self-judgment,
however, where Christ is our measure – hence that 'fear and trembling' of
which Søren Kierkegaard spoke, and even that 'descent into the hell of
self-consciousness' which exercised Jakob Georg Hamann.

> Talk of hell and damnation arises from the fact that the ideal of
> eternal blessedness, which is glimpsed in the illumination accom-
> panying the Judgment and which constitutes man's sole further
> possibility, totally surpasses the ideal of pleasurable satisfaction that
> was the sinner's goal here below; it is alien and actually contrary to
> it. The 'reality principle' (if we may adopt Freudian terminology) is
> so contrary to the 'pleasure principle' that as far as the sinner can
> see there is no question of accommodating the latter to the former.
> He is asked to give up his idea of 'self-realization' (using his neighbor
> – and even God, if necessary – as a means to this end) and actually
> to lose his self; thus he may gain what, in the real and concrete God,
> is blessedness. And this blessedness is a Hypostasis who is himself
> precisely by surrendering to the Other. That is what blessedness
> consists in. Christians may find Mohammed's vision of coarsely
> sensual paradisal joys simply naïve; but how far removed is its hope
> of blessedness from that real blessedness of God and of the man
> Jesus Christ that is presented to Christians in the Judgment![33]

But the portrayal in art of human life reckoned in the moment of death on
a set of scales of which an angel holds the balance suggests the complementary truth that, however much the absolute freedom of God may
respect the self-judgment which finite liberty decrees, it cannot regard
itself as unconditionally bound thereby. While admitting that a sheerly
vicarious salvation without internal resonance in the being of the guilty
would leave the (hypothetically) absolved person in a state of contradiction, Balthasar recalls how

> the One who judges us is also the One who came, not to judge but to
> save (John 12.47). He will therefore take every available path to bring
> back the person whose sins he has borne, even if this person rejects

33 *TD* V, pp. 293–294.

him and, if this proves impossible, he will not positively thrust him from him ... but will negatively leave the sinner to his blinded will.[34]

Though it is never salutary for the individual Christian to presume on divine forbearance, Balthasar (famously – or notoriously!) holds that, in pursuance of revelation's own teaching on God's universally salvific will we can – hypothetically – consider the chance that 'all may be saved'.

Even for those students of Christian divinity whose reading of the sources of Scripture and Tradition makes them unsympathetic to Balthasar's 'hypothetical universalism', his account of 'approximations to hell' is illuminating. As he explains, finite liberty is always transcendentally ordered towards the absolute good. At the same time, that good is in fact the absolute freedom which is God – and so created freedom's egoistic treatment of self as the good's true centre involves it in a contradiction which, when thought through definitively, gives us the concept (and not only the concept!) of Hell. It follows from this analysis that, as one of Balthasar's masters in theological aesthetics, Matthias Joseph Scheeben, saw, the fire that burns in Hell is God himself while with equal truth it may be said that Hell is 'in' the human person. Against this, however, we must set the countervailing consideration that the person, being *imago trinitatis* can only find him- or herself in relation to others – an adumbration on the level of nature of vocation in grace. It follows from the human creature's making in the Word that, willy nilly, that creature finds itself involved in dialogue with God. Appealing once again to von Speyr's curious metaphor of *Hinterlegung*, the essence of human freedom is always 'deposited' with God and Christ. More intelligibly, the trajectory (*die Kurve*) of human life which starts in God and with death begins like a boomerang to return to him, is only possible because of the more foundational space-time track of the incarnate Son in his *exitus* from and *reditus* to the Father.

> The attempt of a human being to exclude themselves from the Christically world-involving Trinitarian life so as to be Hell in their own person is always environed (*umfangen*) by the 'curve' of Christ and to that extent determined thereby in its essence and significance, which consists in imparting the freedom of the absolute Good to the world.[35]

Limits must be assigned, Balthasar concludes, to any idea of an unlimited option by man against God.

A second consideration which mitigates the force of traditional eschatology, on Balthasar's view, is that though the New Testament uses for the eternity of damnation the same adjective (*aiônios*) that it applies to the eternal bliss, the tradition has sometimes treated the concept of the eternal as analogically differentiated in its qualifying respectively Heaven and Hell. The eternity of Hell is not for St Thomas, for instance, precisely that of the everlasting contemplation of God which *includes all time*.

---

34 *TD* V, p. 299.
35 *TD* V, pp. 303–304. Translation author's own.

Balthasar interprets this to mean that Hell's eternity is exclusive of such inclusiveness, to the point of being as it were temporally dimensionless, characterised by the subtraction of all that in time gives positivity to duration. In *The Great Divorce*, C. S. Lewis expressed this in spatial imagery when he called Hell minuscule in relation to Heaven. Again, Franz von Baader, that mighty figure of the Catholic Revival in nineteenth-century Germany, distinguished between the *finite* duration of Purgatory, the *infinite* duration of Heaven and the *indefinite* duration of Hell. Since God can only punish by love, he takes a soul which insists on its self-damnation 'outside of' time. Balthasar himself, however, prefers to draw attention to a third (analogous) form of eternity or timelessness, that of the Son on the Cross who, in 'measuring' what the loss of the Father entails experienced a timelessness (in the sense just explained) even more radically infernal than that of the damned. Something of this has been tasted, Balthasar thinks, by a number of the Christian mystics in the phenomenon of the 'dark night'.

Balthasar (with von Speyr) finds a relation between the timelessness of the Godforsaken damned and that of the Father-forsaken (but as we have seen, in the Spirit, supremely Father-conjoined) Son. The man who has turned his back on God to walk in the opposite direction finds that, with the Son's death and descent to be 'lower' (as the measure of all sinful distance) than the damned, he is *actually moving towards One who is divine*. The sinner desirous of being perfectly abandoned in order to demonstrate the absoluteness of his freedom before God encounters one who is 'even "more absolutely" forsaken than himself'.[36] Just so, in Dostoevsky's *Crime and Punishment* Sonia melts the heart of Raskolnikov. In 'Notre Dame auxiliatrice' which closes the first part of his poem cycle *Corona benignitatis anni Dei*, Claudel wrote: 'There is no sure friend for a poor man, unless he find someone poorer than himself . . . / Look to her who is there, without complaint, without hope, / As a poor man finds one more poor still, and the two gaze on each other in silence.'[37] These references from Christian imaginative literature compose, in Balthasar's eyes:

> remote metaphors for the unimaginable process whereby man, timelessly closed in upon himself, is opened up by the ineluct-able presence of Another, who stands beside him, equally timelessly, and calls into question his apparent, pretended inaccessibility.[38]

The shell of the damnable person, Balthasar suggests, will not prove hard enough, for (as we have noted) it is made out of contradiction.

What on this hypothesis – and we must recall the less than fully committed character of Balthasar's proposals – would remain in Hell? Sin would remain there, but without sinners. Damnable actions will be like the amputated limbs of Jesus' own paraenesis (Mark 9.43, and parallels) – cut off from sinners through the redemptive work of Christ to burn for ever in the Gehenna fire. In the victorious aspect of the Descent into Hell Christ as martial Lord surveys these trophies as he passes by.

36 *TD* V, p. 312.
37 P. Claudel, *Oeuvre poétique* (Paris 1967), p. 408.
38 *TD* V, p. 313.

Naturally, the question arises as to whether such hypostatisation of sinful actions is plausible. Can there be memories without rememberers? (Some interpreters of para-psychic phenomena have thought so.)

Balthasar's view is that the New Testament Scriptures are open to this interpretation – just as they are to its alternative, the doctrine of a twofold outcome (*doppelte Ausgang*) of final judgment. He insinuates that, had not Origen and his disciples claimed to *know* of ultimate universal reconciliation, the mind of the Church would not, in reaction, have tended to the other side of the debate. And yet, we can ask, is not the *tending* of the *sensus Ecclesiae*, the *ekklêsiastikon phronêma*, precisely the index of doctrinal truth in disputed questions? Apart from a handful of women mystics of the Middle Ages (Hildegard, the two Mechthilds, Julian of Norwich) and one or two Greek Fathers still under Origen's influence in certain respects (Gregory of Nyssa and, with less assurance, Maximus the Confessor), the witnesses Balthasar cites are either Protestant or stand in a somewhat uncertain relation to the mainstream Catholic tradition (as with Eriugena or the father of *Reformkatholizismus*, Herman Schell). Balthasar admits that the catalogue is not encouraging, for the motivation of these writers – with the notable exception of Barth – derives from somewhat murky theological and philosophical springs which have little or nothing to do with the Trinitarian and Christological reservoirs on which his own thinking draws. Balthasar finds consolation in recollecting a more sparkling source, the little Teresa, with her remark in the *Histoire d'une âme*, 'One can never expect too much from God ...'.[39] And does not the *Dies Irae*, Thomas of Celano's fearful yet tender poem on the Last Judgment, a work that can hardly be accused of facile optimism, include the words, *Mihi quoque spem dedisti*? It is hope, not theological asseveration, with which Balthasar is concerned.

---

39 Cited *TD* V, p. 320, from Thérèse de L'Enfant Jésus, *Histoire d'une âme* (Lisieux 1923), p. 246.

16

Final Scenario

What, then, might the Last Things look like for a man who has been 'underpinned' by the sovereign mercy of God in Jesus Christ? Here we must remember that, as with all the best contemporary eschatology, the final realities are not simply posterior to Christian experience but have already entered time. Balthasar, then, will not discuss simply death, judgment, Purgatory and Heaven (Hell has already been 'dealt with') but the presence of the divine reality to which these terms refer in Christian existence now.

Death

Before discussing how Christ's life-giving death 'underpins' our own dying, therefore, he turns his mind to how it embraces our living likewise. Of course living and dying are intimately connected: here Balthasar makes his own Heidegger's dictum in *Sein und Zeit* that death is the highest possibility existence affords, since only in relation to death can we decide the overall bearing of our life. In this sense, finitude is a precondition of moral meaning. From being lost in everydayness we can in death stamp existence with the mark of self-renunciation – and it is by a relation, then, to our dying that moral acts in life possess their force. The preciousness of a human individual derives in part from their transience, but it also comes from the fact that their mortality is 'the dwelling place of a higher and wider consciousness of the Whole'.[1] Thus, if in a prelapsarian universe the union of personality and biological species (with its finitude) might in natural fashion have escaped tragedy, in the postlapsarian world where humans now exist this is no longer so. The positive and negative aspects of death are too intimately conjoined to suffer disentanglement. Liberation from death's tragic quality can only come from 'the fact that the human destiny of death is undergirded by the death of Jesus Christ'.[2] His life lived for that 'hour' (Heidegger could hardly be more satisfied than by this Johannine locution!), his whole existence shaped by its 'format', he nonetheless guarded himself from knowledge of its moment, thus rendering possible his obedience as man to the Father. But in moving, via

1 *TD* V, p. 324.
2 *TD* V, p. 325.

these most human conditions, to a death which, in its sealing of the New Covenant in his blood (and Godforsakenness), was his whole life's 'own-most' possibility, Jesus embodied – so the dogmatician would have it – not that general 'thrownness into existence' of which the agnostic Heidegger speaks, but the kenosis of his divine form, undertaken as an act of obedience by the Son as God to his eternal Father. This twofold surrender – the Father's in sending the Son, the Son's in allowing himself to be sent even (and especially) unto death, is the 'expression of absolute love'. But its purpose is

> to undergird and embrace the concrete 'end' of all those who were unable to understand this end in terms of love ...[3]

– unable so to understand it either because their finitude was rudely broken off, or because they found life just a burden, or, again, because they had not wanted to let go of their 'being for themselves' or, finally, on the contrary, had hurled it from them as something unbearable in the act of suicide. But the Son goes to the absolute end, bearing up these deaths in their darkness and overcoming this darkness as he gives himself in that same darkness to the hands of the Father who sent him. In so doing, as the *Stellvertreter*, the substitutionary Representative, he changes the meaning of all the impotence and Godforsakenness which people have hitherto experienced in dying, giving the deaths of sinners new value by identifying them with his own uniquely valid end. He also reveals the Trinitarian love itself, for in dying the person of the Son does not cease to be eternally generated by the Father and indeed gives his Sonship its highest temporal expression. The dying Son, so far from being sundered thereby from his eternal life, has in that action made it known. Indeed:

> In itself the Son's death is so much a consummation of the redeeming love of God that it already bears the Resurrection within it, albeit in a hidden manner.[4]

The mystery of the Son's death is redemptive inasmuch as it opens up the 'ultimate horizon of meaning which is God's all-embracing Trinitarian love'.[5]

When therefore we find St Ambrose distinguishing three sorts of dying – the death of sin (bad), biological death (neutral) and 'mystical' or sacramental dying with Christ in Baptism and Eucharist so as to live again with him (good and very good) – Balthasar would have us understand the last of these as founded on something more primordial than the sacraments, namely the death of the Lord himself *in its underpinning of all human dying*. Only on the foundation of this indica-tively mooded statement, 'One has died for all' (II Corinthians 5.14), does Paul make his imperative statement that all are to live for him – sacramentally, and of course, existentially. The re-definition involved entails an *Entselbstung*, a disappropriation of self, which is, however, not to be understood in a Buddhistic way, as a simple denial of personal

3 *TD* V, p. 326.
4 *TD* V, p. 330.
5 *TD* V, p. 331.

substance-hood, but rather as a making space for Christ and that Spirit of his who confirms that we are children of the Father and therefore 'sharing a relation through the Son to the Spirit, so that the *imago trinitatis* is fulfilled in us'.[6] And the order of the day here is, as with Christ, first death, then resurrection. Suffering and death have a temporal priority in our lives over joy and resurrection not just for the reason given by Heidegger but more deeply still, because Christ came only through his death to his Resurrection – which does not exclude, however, that joy be now to hand (whether we feel it or not), for Balthasar has already explained its presence in the Passion. Indeed, the super-measure of his Cross explains the overflowing quality of the gospel's consolation. The 'impregnation' of our life by the Lord's death makes it intelligible that Christians, and some very great ones – Paul, Ignatius of Antioch – have desired to be with Christ by death, though at times, through philosophical influences of a Stoic or Neo-Platonist kind, this nostalgia for eternity has lacked the counter-consideration that mission on earth is more urgent still. (Balthasar praises the other Ignatius, Ignatius Loyola, for his 'energetic' re-establishment of the just equilibrium.) The true mark left by the God-forsaken death of Christ is not so much the love-ecstasy of the *mors mystica* as the daily carrying of one's cross. (At this point we can no doubt hear the sound of dripping as Balthasar pours cold water on his more exalted *dirigés*.) Not that this sober reality is banal: it is struggle against the anti-divine power where self-renunciation means the growth of Christ's kingdom on earth. It is fruitfulness for others, and substitutionary co-inherence – here Balthasar invokes the prose dramas on the deaths of nuns in the French Revolution by Bernanos (*Dialogues des Carmélites*) and Gertrud von Le Fort (*Die Letzte am Schafott*).

But of course we too shall actually die. Without Christ death is experienced as fearful: sinful man comes up against the limit to his being which signals the unconditional power of God. The unselving of the sinner (itself objectively a new possibility of self-disposition towards the living God) is *with Christ* underpinned by his more radical disappropriation of self and by that latter is turned towards the Saviour God has sent (equally objectively, for 'If we die, we die to the Lord', Romans 14.8). Yet death does not entirely lose its character as punishment: Christ did not come, remarks Adrienne von Speyr, 'to abolish the work and measures of the Father but to justify them from out of the trinitarian love'.[7] The Resurrection shows how the Father can transform punishment into highest reward; to profit therefrom we must learn that counterpart of self-renunciation in living which is refusing to die to ourselves alone, to *dispose* of our own death, in taking leave of life. The hand that Jesus stretched out in Galilee or Judaea to Jairus' daughter or to Lazarus anticipates the hand given now through the Church – the Church at once of office and *communio sanctorum* – in a person's last agony, but the eternal risen life thus mediated is given 'in the condition that gave it birth: his own death'.[8]

6 *TD* V, p. 334.
7 A. von Speyr, *Das Geheimnis des Todes* (Einsiedeln 1953), p. 46, cited *TD* V, p. 342.
8 *TD* V, p. 344.

With the sacraments comes the whole Church in her objective and subjective holiness and so all saints, but above all the Mother of the Lord who represented their communion at the Cross, and the conclusion of whose salutation (the *Holy Mary*: 'pray for us sinners now and at the hour of our death') remains, Balthasar says, 'unconditionally important for everyone, be their death harsh or gentle'.[9]

Judgment

After death comes judgment. Balthasar insists on the unity of the individual (or personal) and general (or universal) judgments. The Grand Assize of Matthew 25 is absolutely universal yet utterly particular. The post-mortem judgment of a soul and the great and general judgment are two aspects of the same event, with the judgment after death as proleptic realisation of a final judgment which 'the great Greek Fathers' (and notably Chrysostom) were 'much inclined to portray as a strictly personal affair'.[10] In this doctrine, Israel's conviction that she awaited corporately a great and terrible 'day of the Lord' and her developing belief that individuals within the covenant community might stand differently in respect of that 'day' are satisfied together.

The ambiguities of Jewish eschatology in (especially) the inter-Testamental period (Is there to be a – partial or general – resurrection of the dead in 'horizontally' future historical time, or, by contrast, are certain privileged souls, perhaps amounting, however, to all the just, 'vertically' caught up to God in death?) are also clarified in relation to Christ. The Resurrection confirms the truth of the 'horizontal' hope, while bringing that future into the present, and yet the New Testament also describes Christ's destiny as exaltation to heaven. And just as Balthasar is willing to credit that the 'sleeping saints' of Matthew's Passion narrative, brought from their tombs at the moment of the Lord's death, were in point of fact co-raised with Jesus, so (with rather fuller New Testament backing) the believer in Christ, even if he or she die in intramundane time (cf. John 11.25) will not die for ever, but be with him in eternal life. And citing Joseph Ratzinger's *Eschatology*, Balthasar reproduces the Bavarian theologian's comment that, since for the Fourth Gospel Jesus *is* the Resurrection, then faith, which comprises real contact with him, already crosses the frontier of death.[11] It was therefore not surprising if the question of the 'intermediate state' – Purgatory – remained for long unasked.

Insisting on the unity of personal and general judgment, Balthasar feels dissatisfied with the way modern Catholic dogmatics, accepting an inherited view of their differentiation, would relate them. Thus for Karl Rahner, the temporal history of the world, producing as it does in the deaths of persons subjects for divine judgment according to the works of each, makes cumulatively possible a 'sum of the particular judgments of individual men and women', leaving to the great and universal judgment

---

9 *TD* V, p. 346. Translation author's.
10 *TD* V, p. 351.
11 J. Ratzinger, *Eschatology: Death and Eternal Life* (ET, Washington 1988), p. 117.

the rôle of vindicating the plan of God for history as a whole.[12] But the latter, Balthasar comments, is not judgment in the relevant sense at all. Or again, for the Indian theologian Raimundo Pannikar what the general judgment adds to the particular is disclosure of the causal nexus (compared by him with the Hindu notion of karma) which binds human destinies together as one man influences another.[13] But, Balthasar asks, can this mean that the person is brought a second time before the judgment-seat of God? And if, by rejection of these proposals, Balthasar tends to the view that post-mortem judgment is the individual's entry on the general judgment, it is not surprising if he also toys with the idea that many more people than Church tradition suspects may have entered in Christ upon the resurrection of the dead – and not solely his blessed mother. Here we are rather surprised to find Balthasar lapsing into the mode of speech of the 'Why not?' school of theology.[14] Though human ignorance of the mode of the heavenly *Überzeit* ('super-time') induces a certain restraint, Balthasar's final thought seems to be of the general resurrection realising itself by a *process* in the world to come, just as does, by way of post-mortem judgment, the universal judgment likewise. And at least that creates an open area which the dogmatic tradition of the Church on Purgatory can make its habitation: there is still *some* room, after all, for the intermediate state.

Purgatory

After a brief précis of the history of the doctrine, Balthasar treats Purgatory in terms drawn largely from von Speyr's *Objektive Mystik*. The Saviour brings the 'new mercy' of the Cross into the realm of the lost and Purgatory takes its rise on Holy Saturday as he passes through. Totally exposed to the fire of the Father on Calvary, the Son can now bring that fire to the 'justly lost' as a fire of love. For the souls who enter Purgatory now, the time of judgment is extended to enable the fire which is the Lord himself to take effect throughout their being. Though noting the increasing accentuation in Church tradition of the corporate nature of Purgatory, the 'expectant Church', Balthasar makes his own von Speyr's contrary emphasis on the absolute solitude of the soul under purgation, though, to be sure, this exclusive preoccupation of the holy souls with God's relation to each of them is meant to prepare the way for a new, definitive communion. The grace of Purgatory is to learn to see sin, and above all one's own sin, no longer anthropocentrically but in relation to God and the Cross of God which are – in a vocabulary drawn directly from the theological aesthetics – sin's true measure. Purgatory draws to a close for

---

12 K. Rahner, 'The Intermediate State', *Theological Investigations* XVII (ET, London 1981), pp. 114–124, and here at p. 115.

13 R. Pannikar, 'La loi du karman et la dimension historique de l'homme', in E. Castelli (ed.), *Herméneutique et eschatologie* (Paris 1972), pp. 205–230.

14 *TD* V, p. 359; Balthasar can cite testimonies in favour of St John the Divine in this respect (Cosmas Vestitor in the East, Fulbert of Chartres, Mechthild of Magdeburg and Giotto's fresco at Santa Croce, Florence). But these are based, evidently, on the prophecy of John's exceptional case recorded at 21.21–23 of his Gospel.

me once I apprehend the *Umfang*, the real dimensions, of the sin of the world, and mine within it, by reference to the redeeming Tree, and from that vantage point consider how much heavier man's punishment ought to have been. Yet this vision is tolerable for the soul since, once again, the sinner's anguish is underpinned by that of One who was personally divine.

Heaven

Balthasar's treatment of Heaven, under the title 'world in God', is much ampler than his account of Hell or Purgatory or any of the other Last Things. For this is the goal to which the entire drama of saving history moves. How should a theology of Heaven unfold? For Balthasar it will begin with a salutary self-reminder that *theologia viatorum*, theology made by travellers, can never be *theologia comprehensorum*, theology for those who have arrived. But substantively it will base itself on

> the Resurrection of the Crucified who in his Trinitarian existence makes the possibility of a sheltering ingathering (*Einbergung*) of the finite and historical world into the infinite, eternal event of God appear credible to us, and in his 'Forty Days' [the time, Balthasar means, between Easter and Ascension] , and sending of the Spirit gives us some kind of foretaste of what the final salvation of man will be.[15]

And Balthasar draws attention to such traits of the life of the risen Christ as 'unknown freedom', 'unheard of vastness', 'incomprehensible lordship over his own bodiliness', and yet 'eucharistic distribution' of his substance so as to be tangible to the 'least of the brethren' (Matthew 25.40, 45; Acts 9.4). He concludes from these indices of the Paschal glad tidings that

> Of all that is so familiar to us on earth, nothing will be lost in God or excluded from him ... Once it has been transfigured, all that has been will remain present; now, for the first time, its full meaning will become clear.[16]

Man and nature exist *for* the Resurrection, which is therefore Christian doctrine's true centre.

The Ascension (itself an aspect of the gospel of Easter) confirms the theme of homecoming for which Balthasar uses another rich and translation-resistant German word, *Einbergung*, with its connotations of bringing to safe harbour (*bergen*), where all will be gathered in (*ein*). For the Christ ascends to 'prepare a place' for the disciples in that mansion of the Father's where there are 'many dwellings' (John 14.2) With the Ascension, earth arrives in heaven, a new dimension of the creation comes to be, 'in' not so much a place but (here Balthasar follows the thirteenth-century German Dominican Albert of Cologne) the Holy Trinity itself. At the Ascension, Heaven begins – so that all the visionary perceptions of a

15 *TD* V, p. 373. Translation author's.
16 *TD* V, p. 374.

heaven accessible to earth in, say the Old Testament, now possess the value only of metaphors. The 'Christ-event', is not, Balthasar stresses, simply 'personal' but 'archetypal-cosmological'. We are dealing here with a change come upon the world from the Trinity – from the dying Son, whose death contains the new world *in nucleo*, from the Father who raises him, and from the Holy Spirit who leaves upon the new-formed cosmos his own tell-tale sign of glory. And the change is – in, first of all, imagistic language – our *Einbergung* in the 'place' of Christ. There the victors will enjoy that transfigured existence which the Lord of the Apocalypse portrays in the Seven Letters to the Churches as a deluge of supernatural gifts. These, however, by no means lack relation to our earthly life for what

> the Son fulfils for himself and his own is always the creative work of the Father, who himself by giving and 'rewarding' co-works with the Son, and in this Father and Son (and with them the human beings on whom their gifts were showered) are flooded by the exuberance of *the* Gift, the Holy Spirit.[17]

The world of the resurrection will be a bodily world inasmuch as a medium is needed for the expression of our freedom in mutual communication; in the world to come that medium is utterly at the service of that freedom, as the resurrection narratives of the Gospels attest. Moreover, the new spatial dimension which Christ determines in his Resurrection is characterised by 'Eucharistic ubiquity' and so by endless sharing out and pouring forth, and of this condition, too, those who enjoy the new existence with Christ must be able – at least in some analogous sense – to partake. There, 'each is himself, in that he makes himself simultaneously "inhabitable" (*durchwohnbar*) for all others'.[18] Such eucharistic 'permeability' of all subjects for one another, and hence for that mortal life which is yet to enter the Kingdom is what fundamentally constitutes the communion of saints. It is not simply Christological but Trinitarian: for the Father does not wish to be seen as a separate subject but as the Love which shows itself in the Son's generation and his 'giving away' (*Verschenkung*) where the Holy Spirit too signals his being as the Logos incarnate flows forth into his mystical body in the world.

So far all this has been expressed in a heightened, imagistic language suggestive of biblical poetry. Can it be given more sober philosophical expression? How can there be a sheltering ingathering of the world of space and time into the Absolute without, on the one hand, pantheistic absorption and, on the other, the mere juxtaposition of these infinitely different realities?

One possible approach is that of Christian Platonism, which, on the one hand, posits the divine 'Idea' and, on the other, what stems from that Idea in the mind of God. For such Fathers as Augustine in the West and Maximus in the East, the archetypes of created things lie in the Creator Spirit himself such that, as St Thomas will put it in his commentary on the

17 *TD* V, p. 380–381. Translation author's.
18 *TD* V, p. 382. Translation author's.

Gospel of John, *creatura in Deo est creatrix essentia*: 'the creature in God *is* the creative Essence'.[19] Although the way of being of the created *thing* is 'truer' (*verius*) in the creature than in the divine Idea of it, the being of its divine archetype is 'truer and nobler' when considered sheerly *as* a mode of being, since what is then under discussion is nothing less than divine being itself. For Bonaventure, the likeness of the thing in the Word is *ipsa veritas expressiva*, 'expressive truth itself', and so expresses the creature better than the creature can. But our question is, Can the distance between the creature's existence and the divine idea of it be bridged? And Balthasar finds Bonaventure's attempt to bring out the Trinitarian dimension of the latter suggestive, for the line he wishes to follow is that when the God of Genesis acclaims the creation as 'very good', he does so in *foreknowledge of the incarnate Son*. Mysteriously eliminating the 'ever greater dissimilarity' that sunders the creature from its divine 'likeness' is a supernatural 'adequation' of the manifestation of God in the finite *through the Word made flesh*. The Incarnation does not, of course, abolish the difference between Creator and creature, but it *unifies the two in a common accord*. We are to move ever more towards the idea that God has of us, thus finding our measure at one and the same time both in God and in the creature that we are. As Ruysbroeck saw, our encounter with our own uncreated idea can only happen at that 'place' where 'the Father eternally generates both the Son and, simultaneously, that Idea of the world which is to be implemented in the Son'.[20] This generation takes place whenever God 'engenders' grace in the ground of any soul that is open to him – though to perceive this highest gracing deepest purity is needed. Our created being, for Ruysbroeck, so hangs on our eternal being in the Wisdom which is God himself that it can boast (in the German translation of Ruysbroeck's Middle Dutch text Balthasar used) an *Innebleiben ohne Unterschied*, a 'distinctionless indwelling', in God. But this must at once be qualified, with reference to the Son's eternal birth from the Father, by a statement of how our 'eternal' being issues in an *Andersheit mit Unterschied*, an 'otherness with a distinction', of a kind proper to an everlasting *image*. And this mystical metaphysics, founded on evangelical orthodoxy of a creationist and Trinitarian kind, is highly germane to Balthasar's purpose. In the words of *The Spiritual Marriage*:

> God wills that we shall go forth from ourselves in this Divine Light, and shall reunite ourselves in a supernatural way with this Image, which is our proper life, and shall possess it with him, in action and in fruition, in eternal bliss.[21]

It is not the relation between the eternal divine idea of the soul and God which interests Balthasar in all this, but what this 'ideal' holds out to me – its practical, or better, *dramatic*, potential. When the Logos becomes incarnate and begins his work of addressing individuals (not only in

19 Thomas Aquinas, *In Evangelium Johannis*, cap. I, lectio 2, iii.
20 *TD* V, p. 390.
21 C. A. Wynschenk (tr.), *John of Ruysbroeck, The Adornment of the Spiritual Marriage* (London 1916), Vol. 3, pp. 172–173, cited *TD* V, pp. 390–391.

speech but by his whole being), I am assured that the notion of access to the idea God has of me is no illusion. (Of course particular people may oppose the divine idea of them on earth but, consonant with his universalist hope, Balthasar supposes that Purgatory is the real *Umschmelzungsprozess des Ich*, the experience of the 'I''s re-moulding on the model of Christ's perfect self-abandonment to God.) If our creation in the Trinity is to come to term there must be a *Christological recreation* of all that we are.

And just as, for Balthasar, Trinitarian and Christological teaching are mutually conditioning, so too is it with Christology and ecclesiology. It follows from what Balthasar has said (following St Thomas) about the unity of Christ's eternal procession and his temporal mission on earth that the divine idea of us must be identical with the mission or charism we have received 'within the economy of Christ's universal body of redemption'. God's idea of us, as the Areopagite pointed out long ago, is his willing of us, and what can this willing be other than our destiny in Jesus Christ? All missions exist within that of the Son.

> If the mission is the real core of the personality, it opens up the latter – because it comes from eternity and is destined for eternity – far beyond the dimensions of which it is conscious in the world or which others allot to it. This is why a mission that is begun on earth, if it really originates in Christ's mission, does not cease with death but comes to perfection in eternal life. Little Thérèse had this certainty and showed it to be justified.[22]

---

22 *TD* V, pp. 393–394.

17

Homecoming

It remains for Balthasar to consider how a task that was never properly realised on earth can in heaven be valued as though it actually had been truly achieved – the nature, then, of the earth–heaven relationship. To this must be joined the question of how a temporal mission can be conceived within eternity – a matter of the reception of the world of becoming into the everlasting 'Event' which is the Holy Trinity.

Earth and heaven

Balthasar will not be discussing, in the remaining pages of *Theodramatik*, the way a world essentially 'outside' God might come to be 'in' him. He has already made it clear that the world is never 'outside God'. That is ruled out by:

1. the inner-divine 'livingness', precontaining, in super-essential fashion, all that is positive in creation;
2. the 'pilgrim condition' of the world, travelling as the latter is, via many deaths and resurrections, to a presently inconceivable condition of all-unifying definitiveness with God;
3. the creation's place within the Trinitarian relations where its finitude is at once accepted and overcome by the infinite difference of those Persons – Balthasar's version of creation 'in' the Son which has served, in the course of the dramatics, as his departure-point for a theology of salvation and transfiguration.

So what is at stake now is, rather, a change in the condition of a world which has always been near God, and immanent in him, and if we ask what that change may be, Balthasar can find no better words to sum up its character than those of St Anselm in the *Proslogion*:

> Lord, if you are not here, where am I to seek you being absent? But if you are everywhere, why do I not see you present?[1]

It is in that 'seeing the Lord present' that the final homecoming will consist – though Balthasar treats the term 'present' with a seriousness equal to

---

1 Anselm of Canterbury, *Proslogion*, 1, cited *TD* V, p. 395.

that he gives 'seeing': we shall have to do with 'a highest "presentness",
Gegenwärtigkeit, of that which lies beyond everything graspable'.
Conscious of the apophatic qualification of the language of the beatific
vision in classical Latin theology (for Aquinas, such 'seeing' is never
comprehension), of the objections of the Greeks to a face-to-face vision of
the divine *Essence*, and of the distinctive departures of his own thought in
the dramatics itself, he insists that the meeting with God cannot be
exhaustively evoked by any *visio*, since the Trinity is infinite freedom
whose 'spaces' are not so much to be gazed at as they are to be *traversed*.
And here Balthasar could summon to his side the witness of Gregory of
Nyssa (whose doctrine of *epektasis*, the continual, ever renewed, reaching
out into God of even the blessed, had inspired him since his student days
at Lyons), and of Ruysbroeck, that figure who (along with Adrienne von
Speyr, citations from whose work litter the footnotes) is never far away in
these closing sections of *Theo-Drama*.

Just as, in Balthasar's dramatic thinking, there is never any distance
between heaven and earth, for the supernatural goal of our life is set
within our real existence from the outset, but there *is* distance between
earth and heaven, since by definition 'earth' is our condition as *viatores*
(the problem is simply that we have not yet arrived), so the question of
the ingathering of our existence into the Blessed Trinity is insoluble from
our perspective because *we are not yet above*.

> The inconceivability of the welcoming ingathering of our existence
> in God turns on the fact that the modality of its happening from
> above is given from out of the supreme Trinitarian model itself,
> whereby our created modes (as copies and imitations) are not
> destroyed but raised above themselves and so arrive at their true
> destiny.[2]

What we can say, however, is that the promised new modality of our
being will do justice to the 'eternal surprise' of the triune vitality, to God's
'ever-greater' character, and to the way the 'supra-temporality' and
'supra-spatiality' which his infinite liberty and love require for their
deployment will transform our transience into a fresh form of abiding.
Something of that, Balthasar remarks, on a nod from Adrienne, is already
found in prayer.

And this is, not least, how *freedom* is fulfilled. The question of what will
happen *to* liberty as well as *by* liberty has been crucial to theo-drama from
the outset. Now we are in sight of journey's end, Balthasar can bring his
complex treatment to its resolution. Balthasar believed that his own
theodramatic theory, beginning as it did from the idea of the infinite
freedom of the Absolute, and its eternal novelty, as disclosed in its self-
revelation, has a better chance of doing justice to the *kind* of (perfected)
freedom which the blessed enjoy than do the earlier theologies of
Augustine and Thomas, characterised as (respectively) theologies of
'repose' and 'vision'. Earthly experience teaches that the most precious
thing about freedom is not the possibility of opting for the good, or

2 *TD* V, p. 400. Translation author's.

'creativity' in the sense of form-making, but expressive self-giving *vis-à-vis* another freedom like myself. Texts from Goethe which Balthasar adduces to support this contention may play down somewhat, he concedes, the contemplative aspect of the life to come. But by the same token, so Balthasar asks, do not the contemplation-centred eschatologies betray at times, by their emphasis on the delight of what is seen in heaven, an 'unconscious Epicureanism'? At any rate, when finite liberty discovers itself as 'caught up with' and 'overtaken by' infinite liberty it experiences, by that very fact, its own greatest possible fullness in act.

Not that Balthasar wishes to discard the entire problematic of the vision of God's Essence – affirmed by Pope Benedict XII in the West, denied by Gregory Palamas in the East. Indeed, he considers that his thesis of infinite freedom's fulfilment of the finite obliges him to enter this Catholic–Orthodox affray. However, Balthasar enters it, he believes, to bring peace. Just as the inexhaustible Freedom of God cannot be measured, so his Essence cannot be grasped. Yet that Freedom can be acknowledged for what it is; so, likewise, he can be seen. What ultimately unifies Byzantine Palamism with the Western magisterial tradition is the 'whylessness' of the Trinity, for the generation of the Son and spiration of the Spirit lie beyond both freedom and necessity, and the ultimate mystery of this 'love that no logic can assume' explains in the last analysis the interplay of vision and non-vision. Both sides have won and both shall receive prizes – though we can note that Balthasar does not accept the Essence/Energies distinction whereby Palamism gives expression to its own apophatic instinct – and in the theological logic he will make that refusal plain.

It follows from what Balthasar has said that he cannot accept the Scholastic *theologoumenon* that in the Kingdom hope will become comprehension, faith vision, since the virtues proper to 'travellers', *viatores*, remain for him pertinent in the endless adventure of heaven. And in any case Paul, in formulating the trio of the theological virtues in I Corinthians 13, does not say that only love will abide, but that all three shall perdure, the greatest of them being love. For Balthasar these virtues are essentially three ways of expressing the same underlying attitude of trusting self-surrender to the covenant God.[3] Life in God, Balthasar wants to say, will be no less dramatic for us than our earthly life now. If St Augustine, closing the *de civitate Dei* needed a quartet of verbs – *vacare, videre, amare, laudare* (not only seeing, loving and praising but perpetual holidaying) – to evoke what we shall be doing as the blessed, that testifies to the vitality of the life of unending discovery on which when we get there we shall be launched.

However, Balthasar's final emphasis will not be on *our* doing. While for him as for the Apocalypse of John – that book which has ever been at his elbow as *Theo-Drama* unrolls – earth and heaven are intimately inter-linked, with earthly events finding their constant echo in alleluia or lament in the world beyond, nonetheless, the new Jerusalem, the Bride of the Lamb, descends from heaven: it (or she) does not rise up from earth. Still, the divine aim is the perfect interchange of heaven and earth, and so in

---

3 This is what enabled his controversial ascription of faith to Christ himself in his essay '*Fides Christi*'. See above p. 202 n. 2.

that City, as John portrays it, the whole redeemed world is made present in multiple images of rivers and fruit trees, nations and kings. In good Chalcedonian style the two are united without ever being confused – though, as with the dogma of Chalcedon, the union is asymmetric: it is God who, at all times, holds the primacy.

In asking, as he now does, how nevertheless the new world constituted by the final action will still be *our* world, Balthasar tries to resolve that debate between incarnational humanists and eschatological theologians which has perplexed Catholic thought since the wide-ranging Franco-phone debate, 'Incarnation ou eschatologie?' of the later 1930s, 1940s and 1950s.[4] In his theology, everything lived out on earth, fragmentary and incomplete as it was, already had its deepest reality in heaven:

> In heaven we shall live the full and eternal content of what on earth was present only as a transcendent, unsatisfiable longing.[5]

Also in continuity with our heavenly life, for Balthasar, is our earthly mission, stemming as this does in its gracious, and ultimately Christo-logical, sense from God and constituting the heart of our theological personality. Our mission and the personal quality which, when seen theodramatically, it gives us can be filled out, certainly; it cannot be just cancelled. The 'Last Day', when the last of the elect has been gathered in, is not, for Balthasar, the termination of Christ's work in constructing the mystical body of the redeemed, but his inaugurating an incomparable fullness of activity – sending out 'new missions' to interrelate those who are his own in ever fresh ways. The 'great missions' of those outstanding saints who in enduring ways have moulded the Church in her history (Paul, Augustine, Ignatius and so forth) retain their form, so Balthasar believes, in heaven – that for him is the significance of the 'first resurrection' of Apocalypse 20 when the blessed rise as 'priests of God and of Christ and reign with him for a thousand years' (v. 6). The sign of that is the appearances of the Mother of God on earth, the Blessed Virgin, still carrying out that testimony she gave at the Annunciation, in the public ministry, by the Cross. Even more eloquently does the Holy Eucharist speak of heaven upon earth, for the Liturgy happened for the first time when the glorified Son, returning to the Father and pouring forth his Spirit on the Church, met the response of the Church's *fiat* to the heavenly completion of his sacrifice. Taking his cue from a study by the Abbé Jean Corbon,[6] later to be author of the treatise on prayer in the 1993 *Catechism of the Catholic Church*, Balthasar writes:

> The Son's return to the Father with his transfigured earthly body, which also pours forth and radiates eucharistically, causes his human nature to acquire trinitarian dimensions. In him 'the whole fullness dwells bodily' (Col. 1.19; 2.9), in him is manifested all the compassion, the 'torn love' of the Father (to whom, through the Son,

4 B. Besret, *Incarnation ou eschatologie? Contribution à l'histoire du vocabulaire religieux contemporain, 1935–1955* (Paris 1974).
5 *TD* V, p. 413.
6 J. Corbon, *Liturgie de source* (Paris 1980).

the liturgy is directed); in him the Spirit goes out into the world in union with the Church, in order to make present the sacrifice of the 'Lamb as it were slain' and thus to enable the Church to share – anew each time – in the Pasch of Christ, now that the Lamb's sacrifice has become heavenly and eternal.

In the Liturgy:

> heaven continues to have its effect on earth, but on the basis that what has been taken up into heaven has realized itself in time, that is, what has been taken up into heaven has been 'consummated' (John 19.30).[7]

The eschatological harvest must be *seeded* on earth, for the Kingdom is present as the 'entelechy' – the immanent purposive cause – of everything earthly that grows in a heavenward direction. The more the heavenly predominates (of which the final sign is for Balthasar the eliciting of *Hingabe*), the less there will be for the purging fire of God to do beyond earth.

It is not, then, Balthasar would stress, the most evolutionarily developed that is closest to heaven (think only of the parabolic rôle of the infant in the teaching of Jesus – subject of Balthasar's posthumous essay on the theology of childhood).[8] The undeveloped may have more 'latencies' than the highly developed in heaven's regard. After all, as he points out, the vision of heaven in the *New* Testament's final book is simply cluttered with furniture from the *Old*. Moreover, if what theo-dramatics has earlier established about the positiveness of the 'other' has any truth at all, then we can expect thwarted developments in the world's past to be in the Hegelian sense *aufgehoben*: not cast aside as obsolete but reclaimed for fuller reality. Though speculation on the future of the cosmos is hardly the New Testament's forte – as Balthasar points out, the heaven–earth relationship in any case surpasses anything that could be said in natural-scientific terms – Paul speaks nonetheless in a famous passage of Romans (8.19–21) of the groaning in expectation of the whole creation as it awaits liberation from corruption. Balthasar cannot accept the 'cruel judgment' of St Thomas that the renewed world of the Resurrection will include only humans (with their bodies) and the mineral realm.[9] Such a dismissal cannot easily be squared with the biblical conviction of the solidarity of the sub-human and human orders; with that experience of the *attrait* of the saints to animals which was charted in German by Joseph Bernhart as in English by Helen Waddell,[10] and, Balthasar would add, calling to his aid the poet-mystics of the Middle

---

7 *TD* V, p. 416.

8 *Wenn ihr nicht werdet wie dieses Kind* (Ostfildern 1989). See on this profoundly Balthasarian study by John Saward, *The Way of the Lamb: The Spirit of Childhood and the End of the Age* (Edinburgh 1999).

9 As Balthasar notes, this judgment of Aquinas was based in part on a thesis in 'scientific' cosmology: namely, that the cessation of the movement of the heavenly bodies would deprive the beasts of a necessary condition for their existence.

10 J. Bernhart, *Heilige und Tiere* (Munich 1937); H. Waddell, *Beasts and Saints* (London 1934).

Ages, with the rôle of *Tiergestalten*, zoomorphic forms, used ever since the Apocalypse to evoke the heavenly realm. When Mechthild of Hackeborn, for example, saw Christ dressed in a lordly mantle of fur, she took this to mean that, in the words of her 'revelations', 'all the hairs of man, animals and plants shimmer through the humanity of Christ in the Most Holy Trinity'.[11] Not only the pre-Christian human world but the pre-human cosmic world finds its place in the total *mise-en-scène* of the 'Last Act'. If for some exegetes – Balthasar has in mind a sharp attack by a German scholar on Teilhard's cosmologically conceived Christ – there can hardly be reconciliation in Christ (the New Testament's key eschatological idea) for what has never been non-reconciled since lacking the ability to sin,[12] Balthasar finds no contradiction in the thought that heaven may comprise both personal creatures now reconciled with God and non-personal creatures that never ceased to be: the Trinitarian 'diastasis' between Father and Son has space enough in its open amplitude for both.

Sharing in the Trinity

And this reminds Balthasar that he must gather up the threads of his account of the 'world in God' by speaking of the definitive participation of the redeemed cosmos in the (specifically) *Trinitarian* life. If the regenerate are (already) born in and from God and in possession of his Spirit, how could we not conceive human destiny under grace in such *participatory* terms? Balthasar rehearses beautifully the aboriginal New Testament expression of these themes – regeneration through the Son by filial adoption as the Father's own through the gift of the Spirit, prior to interrogating the history of theology for further enlightenment. He emphasises that it is not enough – with much of the better Neo-Scholastic divinity[13] – simply to affirm the indwelling of the Trinitarian persons in the souls of the just. More than this, we require, sheerly from fidelity to the New Testament witness, a doctrine of how believers become sharers *in those very relationships which the Trinitarian persons are.* Here he will turn (1) for an account of our 'co-spiration' of the Spirit to John of the Cross, (2) for a grasp of our 'birth in the Son' to the mystics of the Rhenish and Flemish schools issuing from Eckhart, rounding the latter off (3) by some texts from Hugo Rahner which lead into (4) his own most original theologising on the significance in this context of the communion of saints.

To describe the mystical anticipation of ultimate Glory John of the Cross used the image of the *lampares de fuego*, divine 'lamps of fire' which make the soul glow in such a way that it seems to be *within* their irradiation, and the soul itself a single flaming forth with the Holy Spirit. And this is true of souls on the threshold of eternal life even if, owing to the creaturely imperfection inevitable in everything on earth, the (Trinitarian) Wisdom, Beauty and Power appear in such graced human beings and their activities only in 'shadows' of heaven. As Balthasar rightly reports, St John identifies

---

11 Mechthild of Hackeborn, *Revelationes* IV. 3, cited *TD* V, p. 421, n. 18.
12 A. Vögtle, *Das Neue Testament und die Zukunft des Kosmos* (Düsseldorf 1970).
13 His chosen example of this approach – fine, *so far as it goes*, is the Jesuit Père Paul Galtier's *De SS. Trinitate in se et in nobis* (Rome 1953²).

this condition as a sharing in the personal relation which is the Holy Spirit. In David Lewis's translation:

> This is a certain faculty which God will there [in the beatific transformation] give the soul in the communication of the Holy Ghost, Who, like one breathing, raises the soul by His divine aspiration, informs it, strengthens it, so that it too may breathe in God with the same aspiration of love which the Father breathes with the Son, and the Son with the Father, which is the Holy Ghost Himself . . .[14]

By participation the saints do what the Son does by nature – breathe forth the Spirit.

Birth in the Son of God

By comparison with this relatively isolated but, Balthasar insists, scripturally well-founded notion, the idea of the *Sohnesgeburt* is attested in a host of late mediaeval mystics who drew out, on an experiential register, what is, once again, the deep conviction of the New Testament authors. Readers of Balthasar's *Herrlichkeit* will not be surprised that, though he honours Eckhart for giving this theme prominence, he does not favour drinking down the Meister neat: a cocktail of his disciples' mixing is more salutary. One hopes that Eckhart was employing hyperbole when he spoke of the soul's generation of the Son in herself as *one thing with* the intradivine filiation of the Word – but his lack of a doctrine of the analogy of being, and so any account of the receptive potency of the human disciple to the Lord (in Balthasar's preferred terminology, Eckhart's failure to grasp the *Marian principle* in the economy of grace) left him with little other option. And in any case, Eckhart's Neo-Platonising tendency to push back beyond the Trinitarian event (as if there *were* anything more primordial!) to absolute unicity[15] warns Balthasar off. Pulling down the curtain with anything less than a full-bloodedly Trinitarian interpretation of the biblical drama is quite unthinkable.

In Tauler, Suso and Ruysbroeck, the motif of *Gottesgeburt* (both birth *from* God and the birth *of* God) is handled in more orthodox fashion – which must surely mean, in the present context, more dramatically, because freed from confinement by a theology in perpetual danger of becoming a philosophy of identity of a sub-Trinitarian kind. For Tauler, there comes, as the summit of the three Masses of Christmas, after the eternal birth of the Logos and his temporal birth in Mary, his spiritual birth in ourselves – though this is impossible without a 'co-descending' and 'co-dying' with Christ. As Balthasar cites Tauler's sermons, *So viel der Entäusserung, so viel des Gottwerdens*, 'The measure of self-emptying is the

14 St John of the Cross, *A Spiritual Canticle of the Soul and the Bridegroom Christ*, translated by David Lewis, with Corrections and an Introduction by Benedict Zimmermann, OCD (London 1919), p. 292.

15 Here Balthasar appeals for corroboration to Louis Cognet, *Gottes Geburt in der Seele: Einführung in die deutsche Mystik* (Freiburg 1980) = *Introduction aux Mystiques rhéno-flamands* (Paris 1968).

16 J. Tauler, *Predigten* (Einsiedeln 1979²), p. 220, cited *TD* V, p. 451.

measure of divinization'.[16] With Suso too unification with the Trinity through the Word's birth in the soul is re-conceived in the practical terms ('useful', says divine Wisdom in Suso's *Büchlein der ewigen Weisheit*) of the imitation of Christ. Following the humble Christ of Eucharist and Cross leads to spiritual 'espousal' with the Wisdom of God, where the heart of God and the heart of man lie open one to the other. Ruysbroeck gives the picture more Trinitarian colouration. Correcting Eckhart, Ruysbroeck treats the Father as the *Urgrund*, the ultimate foundation of the divine unity, with the Spirit (the bond of unity in all Latin Christians who look for illumination to Augustine) as that unity's fulfilment. The unity of the divine Essence is not to be separated from the union of the Persons:

> The Son and the Spirit 'flow back' into the Father: this is both the self-transcendence of the Persons into the simple identity of essence and the highest bliss of love of the Persons, who are perfected as such in this very self-transcendence.[17]

And if a creature is to share in this Trinitarian 'event', that will only be through grace-enabled imitation of the Son.[18]

Everlasting nuptials

All this masculine language of our regeneration by the Logos in Jesus Christ must be completed, however, by the feminine language of our being carried in the womb of the Marian mother-Church. That theme of the mediating feminine principle is not only important for our grasp of the economy of salvation here and now (preserving us, for instance, from Eckhart's erroneous notion of the simultaneous generation of Son and world). It extends beyond our space and time into the everlasting nuptials – the *Hochzeit* ('wedding celebration', but the literal meaning of the German word, 'high time', is not without its relevance as well) of the Bride with the Lamb. Of course Mary and the Church share in the primordial fecundity of the Father through a creaturely reception thereof – but that is what their essential femininity (Balthasar refers back here to his theology of gender difference in, above all, volume III of *Theodramatik*) so superlatively enables them to do. The beautiful catena of patristic texts, both Eastern and Western, brought together by Hugo Rahner shows how too unilateral a stress on interiority, on inner devotion, among the Rhineland and Flemish mystics, can lead us to overlook the vital sense whereby the soul re-born in the Logos is always *anima ecclesiastica* – a soul

---

17 *TD* V, p. 459.
18 Balthasar has to admit that, really, the topic of 'birth in the Word' has little resonance in Ruysbroeck, and finds himself largely repeating the materials already set out in theologically aesthetic guise in his discussion of the Flemish spiritual theologian in *The Glory of the Lord*, V, *The Realm of Metaphysics in the Modern Age* (ET, Edinburgh and San Francisco 1991), pp. 68–76. Ruysbroeck's contribution to an account of 'life in the Trinity' is more pneumatological than Christological, and its distinctive value consists rather in its integration of contemplation and mission in the life of the truly 'catholic' man on earth.

that has the Church for its mother just as the head of the ecclesial body has the Virgin Mary for his.[19] Nor is it simply a question of the initiation of our supernatural life that is at stake here: the Church in Mary and Mary in the Church condition the entire development of that life in us until it reaches full term in heaven. As Balthasar explains, with hearty acknowledgements to Cyril of Alexandria, if it is the Holy Spirit who renders us participants in a process of divine formation, the model for our sanctification is always that imitation of Christ's birth from Mary which has its prolongation in his mystical body. Balthasar does not wish to exclude all 'generativity' from the 'Petrine' Church of office; but the apostolic 'virility' of the ministerial priesthood depends on the spiritual power given Christ by his Father: it lacks that immediacy to the Fatherly source which befits the 'Marian' Church that is its matrix.

And so, at last, after the entrance, and the exit from the stage, of so many theological figures and ideas, we come finally to the scene that will never end: the heavenly marriage feast. Of all the images for heaven in Scripture this twofold symbol – the banquet and the wedding – is, to Balthasar's judgment, the weightiest. Balthasar finds the parables of a Man who Gave a Great Banquet internally connected to those of the Marriage of a Bridegroom by such themes as surrender (*Hingabe*), nourishment, fruitfulness and joy, and would have it that the two motifs achieve their synthesis in the Wedding Banquet of the Lamb in Apocalypse 19. Since in both the Johannine discourse on the Bread of Life and Paul's Corinthian correspondence, the Lord's flesh is intimately commingled with that of the believer, and in a way which will last for ever, Balthasar feels justified in speaking of the everlasting celebration of a nuptial Eucharist in heaven, to which in the Church we already have anticipatory access on earth.

> The mystery of the marriage between heaven and earth that is celebrated in the Eucharist is both now and in eternity a mystery of body and spirit: the nuptial union depends both on the unitive power of Christ's flesh and blood, given up for us, and on the internalizing power of the Holy Spirit.[20]

We may object, But this is to materialise transcendence! It is to refuse to let go of the fleshly and sacramental domain! Balthasar's comeback is that both taking food and drink and marital congress include an element of transcendence, which goes beyond their normal earthly meaning, and belongs to the image of the Trinity in man. In this way, both can be the starting point of an ascending movement (an *anabasis*, as the Greek fathers would say) which can then encounter the descending movement (the *katabasis*) of the threefold God in its mediation through the humanity of Christ. The Spirit, who permits Father and Son to transcend each other in their common love, also allows man and wife to become fruitful in God-directed union. The taking of nourishment, too, need be no mere bodily

19 H. Rahner, SJ, 'Die Gottgeburt: Die Lehre der Kirchenväter von der Geburt Christi aus dem Herzen der Kirche und der Gläubigen', in idem., *Symbole der Kirche* (Salzburg 1964), pp. 11–87.
20 *TD* V, p. 472.

necessity, but an experience of nourishment by the divine Giver who enriches our substance by his generosity – hence the biblical deployment of the imagery of being fed and watered, wined and dined, by God.

Here Balthasar is assisted by the fact that the German language possesses two semantically distinct words for the body. The associations of *Körper*, the body of physiology and anatomy, may be often out of place in this eschatological finale to *Theodramatik*; but *Leib*, as the expression of spirit or of person does not suffer such inconveniences. Thus while Balthasar insists that the *dénouement* of theo-drama came about through the fruitful sacrifice of the only too material *Körper* of Jesus on the Cross (no Docetism there!), it is from his *Leib*, now in heaven, that there flow down those energies which can transfigure the image of the Trinity in human beings. 'Meal' and 'marriage' come together in the *Leib* which, marked by the experience, simultaneously spiritual and bodily, of the Passion, the Son placed unreservedly at the disposal of the Father in the consummation of his sacrifice, and which now the Holy Spirit renders eucharistically fruitful for the reconciled world. From the *Leib Christi*, as so understood, blood continues to flow, as Catherine of Siena saw, to feed and fertilise Church and world. Anyone who dismisses devotion to the Five Wounds of the Crucified and Risen Lord as mere 'late Gothic' devotion has missed, for Balthasar, the very 'centre of dogmatics'. And the Holy Eucharist, the gift of the Trinity (for in it, as in the Passion on which it depends, the 'remainderless surrender' of each divine hypostasis comes to expression) mediates the Trinitarian life while also fulfilling, in both image and reality, existence on earth. This is how Balthasar would understand Ignatius of Antioch's description of Communion as *pharmakon athanasias*, the 'medicine of immortality'.

Still, the duality of *Körper* and *Leib* must in no way lead to an Idealism: Balthasar insists on the 'mortal realism' of the physique (if so we may translate *Körper*) nailed to the Cross, without which the spiritual body of the risen Lord was impossible, just as without some share in its suffering of resistance to God our final transfiguration cannot proceed. Love is hard. Here the more wounded are in fact the more healthy, as a philosopher-poet, but also various saints, are made to testify.

Various saints: for the marriage banquet of heaven is enjoyed within the *communio sanctorum*. The self-giving circumincession of the divine persons now becomes the archetype for the human society. So great a share has the circling self-abandonment, one to another, of the redeemed in the mystery of the Trinity that concepts and words begin to elude us. But *Theo-Drama* has always taken as its *leitmotif* the *freedom* in which – not just, then, ethically but *dramatically* – the good shall be enjoyed. And so it is at the End. Since, as Balthasar argued in the second volume of the theological dramatics, the unique liberty of the divine nature is possessed by each hypostasis after its own fashion, such that the unity of the divine will is 'also the result of an integration of the intentions of the hypostases',[21] it is unthinkable that, in the communion of saints, the Trinitarian divine Freedom should simply absorb created freedoms.

21 *TD* V, p. 485.

Rather will it give itself to them with liberality, not merely leaving each but *enabling* each of the redeemed to acquire its own 'tone'. And if the Trinity thus respects (for it makes possible) the 'mysterious space of the individual creaturely spontaneities', can we expect that any of the redeemed themselves will be allowed to deprive their fellows of that mystery?

> In the community that comes into being through the Son's eternal *communio*, everyone is utterly open and available to each other, but this openness is not like the total perspicuity of states or situations; instead we have free persons freely available to each other on the basis of the unfathomable distinctness of each. What is offered to the other is thus always an unexpected and surprising gift.[22]

The final will of God is, as Balthasar puts it, not just 'analytic' – the formal basis of the condition of all the redeemed, the inner form of their own good willing. It is also 'synthetic': the sum total of all that they will. For this is the nature of the true God who has chosen, in accord with his own triune being, to preside over a heaven that is infinitely internally differentiated. His will is so 'liberal' that it embraces the plenitude of redeemed freedoms, that of the Son made man at their head. This is, Balthasar remarks, the true synthesis, achieved through the super-positive negation of the Cross, at which Hegel aimed, without knowing it, in his *Phenomenology of Spirit*. And without assent to that overarching freedom of God, protecting and integrating redeemed liberties, we should have to say that not Hegel but Nietzsche is the philosopher who was finally justified: the world would be ultimately chaotic, without sense or measure.

22 *TD* V, pp. 485–486.

18

Retrospective

Reaching the closing scene of the drama, Balthasar is suddenly afflicted with doubts – or, rather, becomes all at once aware of the variety of doubts that may afflict his readers. Is it not simplistic to make a single drama from the labyrinthine plots of the world? To tie all human action to a single key furnished by a nexus of past events – is not this historically suffocating? How plausible is it to describe as 'Love' the source of such a world as ours? And to see the offended divine Love as cosmically reconciled by one man's death? Are not the more ambitious Christologies of the New Testament hopelessly inflated accounts of the happenings they interpret? And in any case has the death of Jesus, understood as the world's atonement, actually changed the way the world goes? What is the evidence for claiming such? Are not the Church's dogmas castles in the air? And are not those who would channel into humanitarian causes the remaining energies of this ancient body realistic in implicitly recognising that fact? How spectral appears today a Church kitted out in the ragged robes of former triumphs!

The effect of these questions is to lead Balthasar back to that most basic of all enquiries into the Christian religion: what on earth *was die Sache Jesu*, the 'Cause' of Jesus? What was at stake in the 'Jesus affair'? In *Herrlichkeit*, Balthasar has shown how, in the unique form of Jesus' life, death and resurrection, aspects so prima facie contradictory defy integration from any one central point in the Jesus phenomenon. Here, 'phenomenon' draws us into the 'noumenon' of a further mystery. The New Testament, echoed by the German mystics, puts it by saying that, unless Jesus disappears, the Spirit cannot come to 'explain to you all things' (John 14.26). He could not be known as he was, so he must become absent in order to be truly present.[1] That reference to the inexplicability of Jesus except in terms of the pneumatological Other – the Holy Ghost – reminds Balthasar of the Gospel texts which have it that Jesus' behaviour is only intelligible in relation to the Father's 'sending', his visibility in relation to the invisibility of the paterological Other – the Father. Jesus' form, that of the 'central actor in Theo-Drama' – can be grasped only insofar as we enter with him into the ungraspable mystery of the Three-

---

1 *TD* V, p. 492.

in-One itself, while all the time insisting that what needs to be understood is not a 'piece of *maya*' (the ultimately illusory world-stuff of Hindu cosmology) but his flesh-and-blood.

But here Balthasar is not claiming merely that without the doctrines of Trinity and Incarnation we cannot make sense of the form Jesus' human agency takes. For the same 'transpsychological reciprocal indwelling' makes its appearance when we consider how in, say, the Letter to the Galatians, the New Testament understands the lives of Christians as well. Christ lives in Christ's faithful: his indwelling in us now is as much dependent on the essential 'being for' of the triune persons as was his vicariously substitutionary death on the Cross whereby the divine Triad originally showed its hand.[2] In other words: if the theodramatic appreciation of the Christ-event be rejected, out of the window flies at the same time any possibility of understanding the 'Christian thing' at all, as lived in everyday fashion in the workaday world.

The primacy of *Hingabe*, self-surrendering self-gift, is the tell-tale sign of the presence of the Trinity, and its prolongation through the Word incarnate in the Church, and not only in the Church – for can we deny all sign of *Hingabe* in the world? Yet when it comes to plotting the map of extra-ecclesial salvation 'here more than anywhere else must we let the mystery stand'. We must neither try to draw the sting from guilty man's 'alienation and enmity' *vis-à-vis* God, treating sin as ultimately a bagatelle (a Catholic and especially a Jesuitical temptation) nor so emphasise the power of God's substitutory atoning grace in Jesus Christ as not to require of sinners 'conversion and consent' (a Protestant and especially a Barthian-Evangelical temptation). It *is* tempting, says Balthasar, to think that the replacement of the attitudinally complex, alternatingly wrathful and merciful, God of the Old Testament by Jesus' 'loving Father' lays bare the mystery. Actually, it renders it more impenetrable, for this loving Father is the One who sent his Son to death and Hell. Balthasar is sufficiently impressed by Martin Luther's analysis of this literally dreadful dialectic to say that, at any rate, one must concede to the Reformer of Wittenberg that where God is best revealed there he is also most deeply concealed. A series of citations from Adrienne von Speyr, sparked off by remembering Paul's rebuke to the gnostic Christians at Corinth, makes the point that in this respect 'know-alls' prove they know nothing. Still – and here is where such epistemological reserve differs in Balthasar from what we might find in theological liberalism – such statements direct us not to limitations in human experience and thinking so much as to the *Trinitarian character of truth*: in saying which, Balthasar looks ahead to the theological logic which his trilogy must resume if it is ever to come to full term. For as the doctrine of the Trinity tells us, the true Logos (and so the key to the logic of the Absolute)

> can only *be* the Logos by *revealing* the Father's 'causeless' begetting and its unfathomably profound meaning and by causing himself to be interpreted by the Spirit of absolute love.[3]

2 *TD* V, p. 493.
3 *TD* V, p. 497.

People who do not get this message miss the aim of the drama of life, and those 'characters' who think they have the Absolute sewn up, by identification with their favourite good causes, in their own back pockets, likewise fail to find the truly unique One, Jesus Christ. He, unlike they, was content to be the interpreter of Another, the Father, and be interpreted by Yet Another, the Spirit, and in that way showed himself the adequate expression (the Letter to the Hebrews uses there the Greek word *charaktêr*, precisely) of the essence of truth.

Still struggling with the hard questions set against his entire project in *Theodramatik*, Balthasar now confronts the objection based on the sheer, outrageous volume of apparently meaningless suffering in this world, and, breathtakingly, he replies – in the deathbed accents of the German dramatist Karl Georg Büchner (1813–1837) and some lines of the Austrian poet Hugo von Hoffmansthal (1874–1929), our problem is that we suffer too little, not too much. While in the Letter to the Romans Paul weighed the suffering of this present age in a balance and considered it not to be compared with coming glory, in his Corinthian correspondence, by contrast, he found a causal nexus between the agony and the ecstasy: 'This slight momentary affliction is preparing for us an eternal weight of glory' (II Corinthians 4.17). The suffering of the creation, which Paul links to the mute 'sighing' of the Spirit for the world's final liberation, strikes us as excessive – but Balthasar links that excess to the transcendent goal for which the world is being made ready. Drawing on one of his favourite women mystics of the Middle Ages, Balthasar would link the pointless bloodshed of our television screens and hospital casualty wards to the Precious Blood by which the world was ransomed and lavered. May not – he asks with Mechthild of Hackeborn – the tears shed for our own griefs and those of others become fruitful for eternity? Jesus' Beatitudes would seem to imply so. Those renunciations which patients have thrust on them and agents accept for themselves are not declared 'blessed' by way of a sadomasochistic glorification of pain, but because what is at stake in them is a fundamental openness to the Kingdom.

> The suffering of the Crucified One can transform even worldly pain, unintelligible to itself, into a co-redemptive suffering.[4]

In the Saviour – and so in those whose sufferings are caught up into his – the Cross and the Glory were in one sense utterly contrasted but in another profoundly the same, for 'what on the Cross [he] experiences as total night is in God's sight the Son's ultimate obedience and hence his highest glory'.[5] Balthasar, meditating, doubtless with von Speyr's mystical effusions in mind, finds on the basis of this thought the 'ultimate Trinitarian mystery'. Taking further the speculations on the inner-Trinitarian freedom of the Son he has already offered in *Theo-Drama*'s course, he exclaims:

> The Son is eternally begotten by the Father: within the infinite divine nature, in other words, one Person is 'let be' in absolute

4 *TD* V, p. 501.
5 Ibid.

Otherness; what deep abysses are here! God has *always* plumbed them, but once a finite world of creatures has been opened up, these depths must be traversed stepwise as forms of alienation. Nonetheless these steps can only be taken as part of a journey already (and always) accomplished in the infinite Trinity. And when the particular mystery of the Son's Incarnation takes place, he traverses – as man and together with all sufferers and on their behalf – the realms of forsakenness that, as God, he has already (and has always) traversed.[6]

But, quite apart from the pain of the world, what the Scholastics called 'physical evil', there is also the question of 'moral evil', the sort which has its origin in the free rejection of God and his will. This is one area of experience where Balthasar is certainly *not* willing to postulate some kind of condition of possibility in the Trinitarian processions. Yet even here, we can at least say that

> evil, in spite of the baffling freedom it has, has only enough power to manifest the far more baffling mercy of God, which causes the fountain of salvation to spring forth from the very wounds that evil has inflicted.[7]

In all other respects evil is, Balthasar concludes, essentially banal: if word-painters like Dostoevsky and Bernanos have been able to conjure up its fearsomeness and powers of seduction, the more lasting discovery is of its narrowness and delusion. For this reason, Balthasar does not credit the claims of that long tradition of Christian thought, sometimes termed 'aesthetic theodicy', for which the contrast of good with evil is indispensable in any appreciation of the divine richness of the world. 'It is not evil that makes the world more interesting but multiplicity of the good, freely brought into being'.[8] The only 'night' which heavenly day needs for its appreciation is that of the experienced inexhaustibility of the liberty of God.

And if the good that endures ills and the evil that inflicts them are, respectively, triumphant and depotentiated in the Kingdom, a final word needs saying about that ambiguous 'inbetween realm' of eros, which, in the dramatic context, Balthasar links above all to the plays of Schiller. The Swedish Lutheran Anders Nygren in his celebrated study *Eros och Agape* went too far in counter-posing the two,[9] yet Balthasar accepts there is an element in eros so irredeemably fused with the conditions of finitude here below that it cannot – even by purification and transfiguration – have its home in the world to come. Marriage, for instance, must shed its sexual finality – and yet its features of nuptial closeness and fruitfulness *can* be fulfilled there. How else could the order of divinisation be the completion of the order of original creation at all?

6 *TD* V, p. 502.
7 *TD* V, p. 503.
8 *TD* V, pp. 503–504.
9 A. Nygren, *Den kristna kärlekstanken genom tiderna: Eros och agape* (Stockholm 1947, I³, II²); ET, *Agape and Eros* (London 1957, 2 vols).

Though we cannot speak of the world of creation and redemption as supplementing God's plenitude, which is already overflowing fullness, Balthasar does feel able to put the question, What does the entire work of creation and redemption *mean* for God? – while confessing that such a query may well seem unanswerable. Joining the theological dramatics in their ending to the theological aesthetics, Balthasar insists that any answer must have something to do with God's *glory*. In contrast to the general line of an average Scholasticism, however, Balthasar does not speak of God's glorifying himself in the blessed considered as the final destinees of his world-making work, but of the divine persons so collaborating one with another in that work that each of the three augments the glory of the other two. The sharing of creatures in the inner-divine life thus becomes a gift of each person to the rest – and thus is avoided, as Balthasar points out, any false implication that the divine pursuit of glory in the world is somehow solipsistic. It is in this perspective that one might be forced to speak of 'tragedy in God' if indeed there are those who are finally reprobate: in them the Trinitarian glorification has failed to reach its end. (Balthasar does not refuse to contemplate this as a real possibility, since he refrains from recommending active hope for the final destiny of the fallen angels.)

Balthasar is not enamoured of the (seemingly) quantitative connotations of the language of 'augmenting' glory. And he wonders whether the mathematical equation 'God plus the world equals God' can really be called helpful, since it fails to take into account the freedom of God to be for what is not God that which he has always been – sheer 'whyless' love – in his own inner-Trinitarian life. '[I]nfinite richness is rich in freedom and can enrich others (and hence itself) in ways that are ever new',[10] and if that is true of the *theologia*, of the immanent or absolute Trinity, God in himself, why should it cease to be true – Balthasar asks – of the *oikonomia*, the economic self-manifestation of the Trinity, which, after all, is always 'embedded' (*eingebettet*) in the 'theology'.

And what is involved in that? The answer recapitulates the theological dramatics as a whole. Balthasar lays out its course in three brief but dense synopses.

1. The inner-Trinitarian 'dialogue' is the basis of the possibility of including within God's loving life a world in itself non-divine. For finite freedom to take its sense from infinite freedom there was needed the Incarnation of the Son which brings first Church then world within the Son's own relations to Father and Spirit. More than this, there was needed the Cross of the Incarnate One, which (citing Adrienne) 'grounds the world more deeply in God than sin could ever estrange it from him'.[11] The overcoming of the world's alienation from God by the blood of the Cross is for ever 'comprehended' in the divine 'conversation' – prior to all other provision for human salvation. The Son offered his sacrifice to the Father right from the start, just as the Father, who made a 'pre-sacrifice' of his

---

10 *TD* V, p. 509.
11 A. von Speyr, *Das Wort und die Mystik*. II. *Objektive Mystik* (Einsiedeln 1980), p. 92.

own in generating the Son in the first place, draws out of this 'renunciation', given the eventuality of sin, the abandonment of the Son on the Cross. The meaning of the Cross is complete only *in* God, and it is into this eternal meaning that temporal reality enters with the Parousia of the Lord at the end of time. Lest meanwhile we forget that Calvary can never be *passé*, we have the sacrament of this sacrifice, Holy Mass, to be celebrated 'in his memory' until he comes again. What we are to 'remember' is not just a historical happening but what the event in history (on Balthasar's view) reveals – the fact that 'sacrifice, suffering, Cross and death ... are nothing other than phenomenal forms of what constitutes heaven: the love of God that goes to the very end'.[12]

2. The eternal life of God is his eternal livingness, an uninterrupted vitality which implies a continual novelty – without, however, the shade of a suspicion that his (consequent) 'becoming' is other than his abiding being. No 'process theology' for Balthasar. Nonetheless, it is this divine attribute, on the view of the founder of theological dramatics, that makes our life an echo, however distant, of God's, and allows us to speak of a vital relation between heaven and earth. When the Son takes flesh, accordingly, the time he lives out as man between Incarnation and Ascension is not separated from the divine eternity, for he is 'eternity thrown open, come into world and time'.[13] Here Balthasar agrees with von Speyr that those theologians who have posited a kenosis in which the properties of the Son's divine nature mutate to allow their manifestation on earth failed to recognise this salient fact. The Son's heavenly life and his earthly life are altogether compatible: the total *disponibilité* by which he stands ready to do the Father's will on earth is simply the economic expression of what in the inner-Trinitarian life the Son is always like. And yet we should not for all that deny to the glorious Crucified One his 'enriching of heaven', his 'adornment of the Father's Kingdom', phrases taken, once again, from Adrienne.[14] In love's overcoming justice on the Cross Balthasar does not hesitate to say that something became other in the intimate intra-divine life – yet qualifies this assertion with the thought that this only confirms the unchangingness of the divine being in that permanent note of surprise which the Trinitarian relationships ever strike.

3. And so finally, everything that seemed negative in the divine Economy finds its explanation in the utter positivity of the Theology, God in his own blessed life. The Son took on the form of a servant in order to show more love; he assumed a human nature, something which thus became proper to himself for neither the Father nor the Spirit did so, in order to have more to give away. His

---

12 Idem., *Die Bergpredigt: Betrachtungen über Matthäus 5–7* (Einsiedeln 1971), p. 229.
13 Idem., *Die Katholische Briefe*. II (Einsiedeln 1961), p. 66.
14 Idem., *Johannes*. IV. *Geburt der Kirche: Betrachtungen über das Johannesevangelium, Kapitel 18–21* (Einsiedeln 1949), p. 163.

'Having' a human nature, which is given away without reserve in the Eucharist is therefore nothing other than the earthly representation of the Trinitarian poverty, in which everything is always already given away.[15]

Such poverty is, evidently, God's endless richness. One can speak in this connexion of the poverty of the Father in 'renouncing' the Son for our sake, so long as we remember that this 'poverty' is inseparable from the riches of his generative love for the Son: the Father's sending the Son is simultaneously his consent to the Son's will to bring home the world to the Father. Similarly, the Son's poverty in his apparent passivity in the conception as man, is seen once again from the standpoint of the 'Theology', no different from his continually permitting himself to be generated by the Father, for in both by 'his perfect divine freedom he regards the execution of the Father's will as the best expression of his filial love'.[16] This is how the 'supreme creaturely negativity' of the abandonment on the Cross is in fact the epiphany of the 'supreme positivity of the Trinitarian love' – a motif Balthasar singles out as 'one of the most important themes of this volume'.[17] And if that should serve to silence those who accuse Balthasar's staurology of putting at risk the unity of the divine nature, his remarks serve, in the context of the dramatics and its close, less for an apologia and more for a prelude to a statement of what good the Cross serves. The good it serves is 'to complete the world's incorporation (*Hineinnahme*) into the triune life'.[18] The Son may return to heaven, but heaven's gates do not close behind him: rather does the Ascension mystery declare how now they stand open for evermore. If we are risen with Christ we are co-sharers at his heavenly table. The Christian lives – as (so Balthasar must surely at this point be recalling) Adrienne von Speyr's extraordinary testimony bears witness – as much in heaven as on earth. In the Son the Father has torn the barriers down. But this means that his abiding with the Father will be henceforth a perpetual coming to ourselves: what else do the closing words of St Matthew's Gospel mean? For the carrying out of his Great Commission he is 'with us all days, even to the end of the world' (Matthew 28.20).

The time – or rather the meta-time – will arrive, however, when all commissions come to an end, the moment of the plenary victory of the Son. Then as Paul assures the Corinthian church (I Corinthians 15.28):

When all things are subjected to him, then the Son himself will also be subjected to him who put all things under him, that God may be everything to everyone.

15 *TD* V, p. 516.
16 *TD* V, p. 517.
17 Ibid.
18 *TD* V, p. 518.

And that means, Balthasar concludes, that the world is a gift, a gift presented by the Father to the Son, and by the Son to the Father, and by the Spirit to them both. It is a gift, to the Trinity because, as *Theo-Drama* has shown, each of the divine Persons, in the way that is their own, has enabled the world to have some part in the wondrous exchange of the inner-divine life. So what those Three give each other in the gift of the world is not simply the effect of the divine creative action. It is more. They give each other with the world the divine play in which creation is amazingly involved. Theatregoers who have attended to Balthasar's theologically dramatic *mise-en-scène* should see this for themselves.

Select Bibliography

A. General studies of Balthasar

J. GODENIR, *Jésus, l'Unique: Introduction à la théologie de Hans Urs von Balthasar* (Paris-Namur 1984).

E. GUERRIERO, *Hans Urs von Balthasar* (Milan 1991).

M. KEHL and W. LÖSER (eds), *The von Balthasar Reader* (ET, New York 1982).

B. McGREGOR, OP, and T. NORRIS (eds), *The Beauty of Christ: An Introduction to the Theology of Hans Urs von Balthasar* (Edinburgh 1994).

A. MODA, *Hans Urs von Balthasar: Un' espozione critica del suo pensiero* (Bari 1976).

E. T. OAKES, *The Pattern of Redemption: The Theology of Hans Urs von Balthasar* (New York 1994).

J. O'DONNELL, SJ, *Hans Urs von Balthasar* (London 1992).

J. SAWARD, *The Mysteries of March: Hans Urs von Balthasar on the Incarnation and Easter* (London 1990).

D. L. SCHINDLER (ed.), *Hans Urs von Balthasar: His Life and Work* (San Francisco 1991).

A. SCOLA, *Hans Urs von Balthasar: Uno stile teologico* (Milan 1991); ET, *Hans Urs von Balthasar: A Theological Style* (Edinburgh 1995).

B. Studies of Balthasar's dramatics and related themes

E. BISER, 'Theologische Kategorienwechsel: Zum Eingangsband von Hans Urs von Balthasars *Theodramatik*', *Theologische Revue* 72 (1976), pp. 441–450.

T. G. DALZELL, S.M., *The Dramatic Encounter of Divine and Human Freedom in the Theology of Hans Urs von Balthasar* (Frankfurt 1997).

P. ESCOBAR, 'Das *Universale Concretum* Jesus Christi und die eschatologische Reduktion bei Hans Urs von Balthasar', *Zeitschrift für katholische Theologie* 100 (1978), pp. 560–595.

H.-P. HEINZ, *Der Gott des Je-Mehr: Der christologische Ansatz Hans Urs von Balthasars* (Berne-Frankfurt 1975).

M. Jöhri, *Descensus Dei: Teologia della croce nell'opera di Hans Urs von Balthasar*, Corona Lateranensis, 30 (Roma 1981).

T. R. Krenski, *Passio caritatis: Trinitarische Passiologie im Werk Hans Urs von Balthasars* (Einsiedeln 1990).

W. van Laak, *Allversöhnung: Die Lehre von der Apokatastasis. Ihre Grundlegung durch Origenes und ihre Bewertung in der gegenwärtigen Theologie bei Karl Barth und Hans Urs von Balthasar* (Sinzig 1990).

B. Leahy, *The Marian Principle in the Church according to Hans Urs von Balthasar* (Frankfurt 1996).

M. Lochbrunner, *Analogia caritatis: Darstellung und Deutung der Theologie Hans Urs von Balthasars* (Freiburg 1981).

K. O. Meuffels, *Einbergung des Menschen in das Mysterium der dreieinigen Liebe: eine trinitarische Anthropologie nach H. U. von Balthasar* (Würzburg 1991).

J. Naduvilekut, *Christus der Heilsweg: Soteria als Theodrama im Werk Hans Urs von Balthasars* (St Ottilien 1987).

M. Ouellet, *L'Existence comme mission: L'anthropologie théologique de Hans Urs von Balthasar* (Rome 1983).

A. Peelman, *Hans Urs von Balthasar et la théologie de l'histoire* (Berne-Frankfurt-Las Vegas 1978) .

L. Sabbioni, *Giudizio e salvezza nella escatologia di Hans Urs von Balthasar* (Milan 1990).

D. L. Schindler, *Heart of the World, Center of the Church* (Edinburgh and Grand Rapids 1996).

G. de Schrijver, *Le merveilleux accord de l'homme et Dieu: Etude de l'analogie de l'être chez Hans Urs von Balthasar* (Louvain 1983).

R. Schwäger, SJ, 'Der Sohn Gottes und die Weltsünde: Zur Erlösungslehre von Hans Urs von Balthasar', *Zeitschrift für katholische Theologie* 108 (1986), pp. 5–44.

K. J. Wallner, OCist, *Gott als Eschaton: Trinitarische Dramatik als Voraussetzung göttlicher Universalität bei Hans Urs von Balthasar* (Heiligenkreuz and Vienna 1992).

Index of Subjects

Index of Names